ALGORITHMS OF OPPRESSION

Algorithms of Oppression

How Search Engines Reinforce Racism

Safiya Umoja Noble

NEW YORK UNIVERSITY PRESS

New York

NEW YORK UNIVERSITY PRESS
New York
www.nyupress.org

References to Internet websites (URLs) were accurate at the time of writing. Neither the author nor New York University Press is responsible for URLs that may have expired or changed since the manuscript was prepared.

Library of Congress Cataloging-in-Publication Data
Names: Noble, Safiya Umoja, author.
Title: Algorithms of oppression : how search engines reinforce racism / Safiya Umoja Noble.
Description: New York : New York University Press, [2018] |
Includes bibliographical references and index.
Identifiers: LCCN 2017014187| ISBN 9781479849949 (cl : alk. paper) |
ISBN 9781479837243 (pb : alk. paper)
Subjects: LCSH: Search engines—Sociological aspects. | Discrimination. | Google.
Classification: LCC ZA4230 .N63 2018 | DDC 025.04252—dc23
LC record available at https://lccn.loc.gov/2017014187

New York University Press books are printed on acid-free paper, and their binding materials are chosen for strength and durability. We strive to use environmentally responsible suppliers and materials to the greatest extent possible in publishing our books.

Manufactured in the United States of America

10 9

Also available as an ebook

For Nico and Jylian

CONTENTS

ACKNOWLEDGMENTS

I want to acknowledge the support of the many people and organizations that made this research possible. First, my husband and life partner, Otis Noble III, is truly my most ardent and loving advocate and has borne the brunt of what it took for me to write this book and go around the country sharing it prior to its publication. I am eternally grateful for his support. For many years, he knew that I wanted to leave corporate America to pursue a Ph.D. and fulfill a lifelong dream of becoming a professor. When I met Otis, this was only a concept and something so far-fetched, so ridiculously impossible, that he set a course to make it happen despite my inability to believe it could come true. I am sure that this is the essence of love: the ability to see the best in others, to see the most profound, exceptional version of them when they cannot see it for themselves. This is what he did for me through the writing of this book, and somehow, given all the stress it has put us under, he has continued to love me each day as I've worked on this goal. I am equally indebted to my son, who gives me unwavering, unconditional love and incredible joy, despite my flaws as a parent and the time I've directed away from playing or going to the pool to write this book. I am also grateful to have watched my bonus-daughter grow into her own lovely womanhood through the many years I've spent becoming a scholar. I hope that you realize all of your dreams too.

My life, and the ability to pursue work as a scholar, is influenced by the experiences of moving to the Midwest and living and loving in a blended family, with all its joys and complexities. This research would not be nearly as meaningful, or even possible, without the women and girls, as well as the men, who have become my family through marriage. The Nobles have become the epicenter of my family life, and I appreciate our good times together. My many families, biological, by marriage, and by choice, have left their fingerprints on me for the better. My sister has become a great support to me that I deeply treasure; and my "favorite brother," who will likely have the most to say about this research, keeps me sharp because we so rarely see eye to eye on politics, and we love each other anyway. I appreciate you both, and your families, for being happy for me even when you don't understand me. I am also grateful to George Green and Otis Noble, Jr., for being kind and loving. You were, and are, good fathers to me.

My chosen sisters, Tranine, Tamara, Veda, Louise, Nadine, Imani, Lori, Tiy, Molly, and Ryan, continually build me up and are intellectual and political sounding boards. I also could not have completed this book without support from my closest friends scattered across the United States, many of whom may not want to be named, but you know who you are, including Louise, Bill and Lauren Godfrey, Gia, Amy, Jenny, Christy, Tamsin, and Sandra. These lifelong friends (and some of their parents and children) from high school, college, corporate America, and graduate school, are incredibly special to me, and I hope they know how deeply appreciated they are, despite the quality time I have diverted away from them and their families to write this book.

The passion in this research was ignited in a research group led by Dr. Lisa Nakamura at Illinois, without whose valuable conversations I could not have taken this work to fruition. My most trustworthy sister-scholars, Sarah T. Roberts and Miriam Sweeney, kept a critical eye on this research and pushed me, consoled me, made me laugh, and inspired me when the reality of how Black women and girls were represented in commercial search would deplete me. Sarah, in particular, has been a powerful intellectual ally through this process, and I am grateful for our many research collaborations over the years and all those to come. Our writing partnerships are in service of addressing the many affordances and consequences of digital technologies and are one of the most energizing and enjoyable parts of this career as a scholar.

There are several colleagues who have been helpful right up to the final stages of this work. They were subjected to countless hours of reading my work, critiquing it, and sharing articles, books, websites, and resources with me. The best thinking and ideas in this work stem from tapping into the collective intelligence that is fostered by surrounding oneself with brilliant minds and subject-matter experts. I am in awe of the number of people it takes to support the writing of a book, and these are the many people and organizations that had a hand in providing key support while I completed this research. Undoubtedly, some may not be explicitly named, but I hope they know their encouragement has contributed to this book.

I am grateful to my editors, Ilene Kalish and Caelyn Cobb at New York University Press, for bringing this book to fruition. I want to thank the editors at *Bitch* magazine for giving me my first public-press start, and I appreciate the many journalists who have acknowledged the value of my work for the public, including *USA Today* and the *Chronicle of Higher Education*.

Professors Sharon Tettegah, Rayvon Fouché, Lisa Nakamura, and Leigh Estabrook were instrumental in green-lighting this research in one form or another, at various stages of its development. Important guidance and support along the way came from my early adviser, Caroline Haythornthwaite, and from the former dean of the Information School at Illinois, John Unsworth.

Dr. Linda C. Smith at the University of Illinois at Urbana-Champaign continues to be an ardent supporter, and her quiet but mighty championing of critical information scholars has transformed the field and supported me and my family in ways I will never be able to fully repay. This research would not have happened without her leadership, compassion, humor, and incredible intelligence, for which I am so thankful. I suffer in trying to find ways to repay her because what may have been small gestures on her part were enormous to me. She is an incredible human being. I want to thank her for launching me into my career and for believing my work is a valuable and original contribution, despite the obstacles I faced or moments I felt unsupported by those whose validation I thought I needed. Her stamp of approval is something I hold in very high regard, and I appreciate her so very much.

Dr. Sharon Tettegah taught me how to be a scholar, and I would not have had the career I've had so far without her mentorship. I respect her national leadership in making African American women's contributions to STEM fields a priority and her relentless commitment to doing good work that makes a difference. She has made a tremendous difference in my life.

I am indebted to several Black feminists who provided a mirror for me to see myself as a scholar and contributor and consistently inspire my love for the study of race, gender, and society: Sharon Elise, Angela

Y. Davis, Jemima Pierre, Vilna Bashi Treitler, Imani Bazzell, Helen Neville, Cheryl Harris, Karen Flynn, Alondra Nelson, Kimberlé Crenshaw, Mireille Miller-Young, bell hooks, Brittney Cooper, Catherine Squires, Barbara Smith, and Janell Hobson, some of whom I have never met in person but whose intellectual work has made a profound difference for me for many years. I deeply appreciate the work and influence of Isabel Molina, Sandra Harding, Sharon Traweek, Jean Kilbourne, Naomi Wolfe, and Naomi Klein too. Herbert Schiller's and Vijay Prashad's work has also been important to me.

I was especially intellectually sustained by a number of friends whose work I respect so much, who kept a critical eye on my research or career, and who inspired me when the reality of how women and girls are represented in commercial search would deplete me (in alphabetical order): André Brock, Ergin Bulut, Michelle Caswell, Sundiata Cha-Jua, Kate Crawford, Jessie Daniels, Christian Fuchs, Jonathan Furner, Anne Gilliland, Tanya Golash-Boza, Alex Halavais, Christa Hardy, Peter Hudson, John I. Jennings, Gregory Leazer, David Leonard, Cameron McCarthy, Charlton McIlwain, Malika McKee-Culpepper, Molly Niesen, Teri Senft, Tonia Sutherland, Brendesha Tynes, Siva Vaidhyanathan, Zuelma Valdez, Angharad Valdivia, Melissa Villa-Nicolas, and Myra Washington. I offer my deepest gratitude to these brilliant scholars, both those named here and those unnamed but cited throughout this book.

My colleague Sunah Suh from Illinois and Jessica Jaiyeola at UCLA helped me with data collection, for which I remain grateful. Drs. Linde Brocato and Sarah T. Roberts were extraordinary coaches, editors, and lifelines. Myrna Morales, Meadow Jones, and Jazmin Dantzler gave me many laughs and moments of tremendous support. Deep thanks to Patricia Ciccone and Dr. Diana Ascher, who contributed greatly to my ability to finish this book and launch new ventures along the way.

I could not have completed this research without financial support from the Graduate School of Education & Information Studies at UCLA, the College of Media at Illinois, the Information School at Illinois, and the Information in Society fellowship funded by the Institute of Museum and Library Services and led by Drs. Linda C. Smith and Dan Schiller. Support also came from the Community Informatics Initiative at Illinois. I am deeply appreciative to the Institute for Computing in the Humanities, Arts and Social Sciences (I-CHASS) and the leadership and friendship of Dr. Kevin Franklin at Illinois and key members of the HASTAC community for supporting me at the start of this research. Illinois and UCLA sent fantastic students my way to learn and grow with as a teacher. More recently, I was sustained and supported by colleagues in the Departments of Information Studies, African American Studies, and Gender Studies at the University of California, Los Angeles (UCLA), who have been generous advocates of my work up through the publication of this book. Thank you to my colleagues in these world-class universities who were tremendously supportive, including my new friends at the Annenberg School of Communication at the University of Southern California under the leadership of the amazing Dr. Sarah Banet-Weiser, whose support means so much to me.

Many people work hard every day to make environments where I could soar, and as such, I could not have thrived through this process without the office staff at Illinois and UCLA who put out fires, solved problems, made travel arrangements, scheduled meetings and spaces, and offered kind words of encouragement on a regular basis.

Support comes in many different forms, and my friends at tech companies Pixo in Urbana and Pathbrite in San Francisco—both founded by brilliant women CEOs—have been a great source of knowledge that have sharpened my skills. I appreciate the collaborations with the City of Champaign, the City of Urbana, and the Center for Digital Inclusion at Illinois. The Joint Center for Political and Economic Studies in Washington, D.C., gave me great opportunities to learn and contribute as well, as did the students at the School for Designing a Society and the Independent Media Center in Urbana, Illinois.

Thank you to the brilliant #critlib librarians and information professionals of Twitter, which has been a powerful community of financial and emotional support for my work. I am immensely grateful to all of you.

Lastly, I want to thank those on whose shoulders I stand, including my mother. It is she who charted the course, who cut a path to a life unimaginable for me. When she passed, fifteen years ago, most of my reasons for living died with her. Every accomplishment in my life was to make her proud, and I had many dreams that we had cooked up together still to be fulfilled with her by my side. Her part in this work is at the core: she raised me as a Black girl, despite her not being a Black woman herself. Raising a Black girl was not without a host of challenges and opportunities, and she took the job of making me a strong, confident person very seriously. She was quite aware that racism and sexism were big obstacles that would confront me, and she educated me to embrace and celebrate my identity by surrounding me with a community, in addition to a fantastically diverse family and friendship circle. Much of my life was framed by music, dolls, books, art, television, and experiences that celebrated Black culture, an intentional act of love on her part to ensure that I would not be confused or misunderstood by trying to somehow leverage her identity as my own. She taught me to respect everybody, as best I could, but to understand that neither prejudice at a personal level nor oppression at a systematic level is ever acceptable. She taught me how to critique racism, quite vocally, and it was grounded in our own experiences together as a family. I am grateful that she had the foresight to know that I would need to feel good about who I am in the world, because I would be bombarded by images and stories and stereotypes about Black people, and Black women, that could tear me down and harm me. She wanted me to be a successful, relevant, funny woman—and she never saw anything wrong with me adding "Black" to that identity. She saw the recognition of the contributions and celebrations of Black people as a form of resistance to bigotry. She was never colorblind, and she had a critique of that before anyone I knew. She knew "not seeing color" was a dangerous idea, because color was not the point; culture was. She saw a negation or denial of Black culture as a form of racism, and she never wanted me to deny that part of me, the part she thought made me beautiful and different and special in our family. She was my first educator about race, gender, and class. She always spoke of the brilliance of women and surrounded me with strong, smart, sassy women like my grandmother Marie Thayer and her best friend, my aunt Darris, who modeled hard work, compassion, beauty, and success. In the spirit of these strong women, this work has been bolstered by the love and support of my mother-in-law, Alice Noble, who consistently tells me she's proud of me and offers me the mother-love I still need in my life.

My mentors, Drs. James Rogers, Adewole Umoja, Sharon Elise, Wendy Ng, Francine Oputa, Malik Simba, and professor Thomas Witt-

Ellis from the world-class California State University system, paved the way for my research career to unfold these many years later in life.

Anything I have accomplished has been from the legacies of those who came before me. Any omissions or errors are my own. I hope to leave something helpful for my students and the public that will provoke thinking about the impact of automated decision-making technologies, and why we should care about them, through this book and my public lectures about it.

Introduction $\mathbb{Q}$

The Power of Algorithms

This book is about the power of algorithms in the age of neoliberalism and the ways those digital decisions reinforce oppressive social relationships and enact new modes of racial profiling, which I have termed *technological redlining*. By making visible the ways that capital, race, and gender are factors in creating unequal conditions, I am bringing light to various forms of technological redlining that are on the rise. The near-ubiquitous use of algorithmically driven software, both visible and invisible to everyday people, demands a closer inspection of what values are prioritized in such automated decision-making systems. Typically, the practice of redlining has been most often used in real estate and banking circles, creating and deepening inequalities by race, such that, for example, people of color are more likely to pay higher interest rates or premiums just because they are Black or Latino, especially if they live in low-income neighborhoods. On the Internet and in our everyday uses of technology, discrimination is also embedded in computer code and, increasingly, in artificial intelligence technologies that we are reliant on, by choice or not. I believe that artificial intelligence will become a major human rights issue in the twenty-first century. We are only beginning to understand the long-term consequences of these decision-making tools in both masking and deepening social inequality. This book is just the start of trying to make these consequences visible. There will be many more, by myself and others, who will try to make sense of the consequences of automated decision making through algorithms in society.

Part of the challenge of understanding algorithmic oppression is to understand that mathematical formulations to drive automated decisions are made by human beings. While we often think of terms such as "big data" and "algorithms" as being benign, neutral, or objective, they are anything but. The people who make these decisions hold all types of values, many of which openly promote racism, sexism, and false notions of meritocracy, which is well documented in studies of Silicon Valley and other tech corridors.

For example, in the midst of a federal investigation of Google's alleged persistent wage gap, where women are systematically paid less than men in the company's workforce, an "antidiversity" manifesto authored by James Damore went viral in August 2017,[1] supported by many Google employees, arguing that women are psychologically inferior and incapable of being as good at software engineering as men, among other patently false and sexist assertions. As this book was moving into press, many Google executives and employees were actively rebuking the assertions of this engineer, who reportedly works on Google search infrastructure. Legal cases have been filed, boycotts of Google from the political far right in the United States have been invoked, and calls for greater expressed commitments to gender and racial equity at Google and in Silicon Valley writ large are under way. What this antidiversity screed has underscored for me as I write this book is that some of the very people who are developing search algorithms and architecture are willing to promote sexist and racist attitudes openly at work and beyond, while we are supposed to believe that these same employees are developing "neutral" or "objective" decision-making tools. Human beings are developing the digital platforms we use, and as I present evidence of the recklessness and lack of regard that is often shown to women and people of color in some of the output of these systems, it will become increasingly difficult for technology companies to separate their systematic and inequitable employment practices, and the far-right ideological bents of some of their employees, from the products they make for the public.

My goal in this book is to further an exploration into some of these digital sense-making processes and how they have come to be so fundamental to the classification and organization of information and at what cost. As a result, this book is largely concerned with examining the commercial co-optation of Black identities, experiences, and communities in the largest and most powerful technology companies to date, namely, Google. I closely read a few distinct cases of algorithmic oppression for the depth of their social meaning to raise a public discussion of the broader implications of how privately managed, black-boxed information-sorting tools have become essential to many data-driven decisions. I want us to have broader public conversations about the implications of the artificial intelligentsia for people who are already systematically marginalized and oppressed. I will also provide evidence and argue, ultimately, that large technology monopolies such as Google need to be broken up and regulated, because their consolidated power and cultural influence make competition largely impossible. This monopoly in the information sector is a threat to democracy, as is currently coming to the fore as we make sense of information flows through digital media such as Google and Facebook in the wake of the 2016 United States presidential election.

I situate my work against the backdrop of a twelve-year professional career in multicultural marketing and advertising, where I was invested in building corporate brands and selling products to African Americans and Latinos (before I became a university professor). Back then, I believed, like many urban marketing professionals, that companies must pay attention to the needs of people of color and demonstrate respect for consumers by offering services to communities of color, just as is done for most everyone else. After all, to be responsive and responsible to marginalized consumers was to create more market opportunity. I spent an equal amount of time doing risk management and public relations to insulate companies from any adverse risk to sales that they might experience from inadvertent or deliberate snubs to consumers of color who might perceive a brand as racist or insensitive. Protecting my former clients from enacting racial and gender insensitivity and helping them bolster their brands by creating deep emotional and psychological attachments to their products among communities of color was my professional concern for many years, which made an experience I had in fall 2010 deeply impactful. In just a few minutes while searching on the web, I experienced the perfect storm of insult and injury that I could not turn away from. While Googling things on the Internet that might be interesting to my stepdaughter and nieces, I was overtaken by the results. My search on the keywords "black girls" yielded HotBlackPussy. com as the first hit.

Hit indeed.

Since that time, I have spent innumerable hours teaching and researching all the ways in which it could be that Google could completely fail when it came to providing reliable or credible information about

> ► Sugary Black Pussy .com-**Black girls** in a hardcore action galeries
> sugaryblackpussy.com/
> (black pussy and hairy black pussy,black sex,black booty,black ass,black teen pussy,big
> black ass,black porn star,hot **black girl**) ...

Figure I.1. First search result on keywords "black girls," September 2011.

women and people of color yet experience seemingly no repercussions whatsoever. Two years after this incident, I collected searches again, only to find similar results, as documented in figure I.1.

In 2012, I wrote an article for *Bitch* magazine about how women and feminism are marginalized in search results. By August 2012, Panda (an update to Google's search algorithm) had been released, and pornography was no longer the first series of results for "black girls"; but other girls and women of color, such as Latinas and Asians, were still pornified. By August of that year, the algorithm changed, and porn was suppressed in the case of a search on "black girls." I often wonder what kind of pressures account for the changing of search results over time. It is impossible to know when and what influences proprietary algorithmic design, other than that human beings are designing them and that they are not up for public discussion, except as we engage in critique and protest.

This book was born to highlight cases of such algorithmically driven data failures that are specific to people of color and women and to underscore the structural ways that racism and sexism are fundamental to what I have coined *algorithmic oppression*. I am writing in the spirit of other critical women of color, such as Latoya Peterson, cofounder of the blog *Racialicious*, who has opined that racism is the fundamental application program interface (API) of the Internet. Peterson has argued that anti-Blackness is the foundation on which all racism toward other groups is predicated. Racism is a standard protocol for organizing behavior on the web. As she has said, so perfectly, "The idea of a n*gger API makes me think of a racism API, which is one of our core arguments all along—oppression operates in the same formats, runs the same scripts over and over. It is tweaked to be context specific, but it's all the same source code. And the key to its undoing is recognizing how many of us are ensnared in these same basic patterns and modifying our own actions."[2] Peterson's allegation is consistent with what many people feel about the hostility of the web toward people of color, particularly in its anti-Blackness, which any perusal of YouTube comments or other message boards will serve up. On one level, the everyday racism and commentary on the web is an abhorrent thing in itself, which has been detailed by others; but it is entirely different with the corporate platform vis-à-vis an algorithmically crafted web search that offers up racism and sexism as the first results. This process reflects a corporate logic of either willful neglect or a profit imperative that makes money from racism and sexism. This inquiry is the basis of this book.

In the following pages, I discuss how "hot," "sugary," or any other kind of "black pussy" can surface as the primary representation of Black girls and women on the first page of a Google search, and I suggest that something other than the best, most credible, or most reliable information output is driving Google. Of course, Google Search is an advertising company, not a reliable information company. At the very least, we must ask when we find these kinds of results, Is this the best information? For whom? We must ask ourselves who the intended audience is for a variety of things we find, and question the legitimacy of being in a "filter bubble,"[3] when we do not want racism and sexism, yet they still find their way to us. The implications of algorithmic decision making of this sort extend to other types of queries in Google and other digital media platforms, and they are the beginning of a much-needed reassessment of information as a public good. We need a full-on reevaluation of the implications of our information resources being governed by corporate-controlled advertising companies. I am adding my voice to a number of scholars such as Helen Nissenbaum and Lucas Introna, Siva Vaidhyanathan, Alex Halavais, Christian Fuchs, Frank Pasquale, Kate Crawford, Tarleton Gillespie, Sarah T. Roberts, Jaron Lanier, and Elad Segev, to name a few, who are raising critiques of Google and other forms of corporate information control (including artificial intelligence) in hopes that more people will consider alternatives.

Over the years, I have concentrated my research on unveiling the many ways that African American people have been contained and constrained in classification systems, from Google's commercial search engine to library databases. The development of this concentration was born of my research training in library and information science. I think of these issues through the lenses of critical information studies and critical race and gender studies. As marketing and advertising have directly shaped the ways that marginalized people have come to be represented by digital records such as search results or social network activities, I have studied why it is that digital media platforms are resoundingly characterized as "neutral technologies" in the public domain and often, unfortunately, in academia. Stories of "glitches" found in systems do not suggest that the organizing logics of the web could be broken but, rather, that these are occasional one-off moments when something goes terribly wrong with near-perfect systems. With the exception of the many scholars whom I reference throughout this work and the journalists, bloggers, and whistleblowers whom I will be remiss in not naming, very few people are taking notice. We need all the voices to come to the fore and impact public policy on the most unregulated social experiment of our times: the Internet.

These data aberrations have come to light in various forms. In 2015, *U.S. News and World Report* reported that a "glitch" in Google's algorithm led to a number of problems through auto-tagging and facial-recognition software that was apparently intended to help people search through images more successfully. The first problem for Google was that its photo application had automatically tagged African Americans as "apes" and "animals."[4] The second major issue reported by the *Post* was that Google Maps searches on the word "N*gger"[5] led to a map of the White House during Obama's presidency, a story that went viral on the Internet after the social media personality Deray McKesson tweeted it.

These incidents were consistent with the reports of Photoshopped images of a monkey's face on the image of First Lady Michelle Obama that were circulating through Google Images search in 2009. In 2015, you could still find digital traces of the Google autosuggestions that associated Michelle Obama with apes. Protests from the White House led to Google forcing the image down the image stack, from the first page, so that it was not as visible.[6] In each case, Google's position is that it is not responsible for its algorithm and that problems with the results would be quickly resolved. In the *Washington Post* article about "N*gger House," the response was consistent with other apologies by the company: "'Some inappropriate results are surfacing in Google Maps that should not be, and we apologize for any offense this may have caused,'

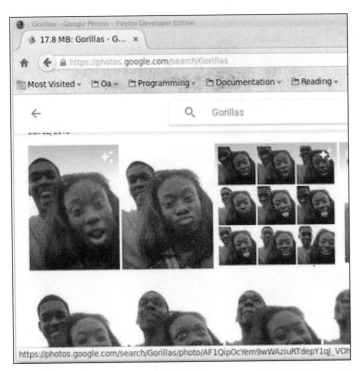

Figure I.2. Google Images results for the keyword "gorillas," April 7, 2016.

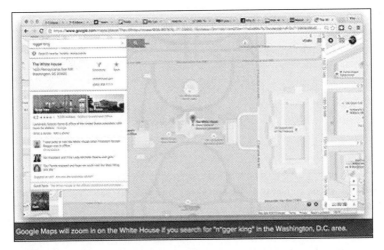

Figure I.3. Google Maps search on "N*gga House" leads to the White House, April 7, 2016.

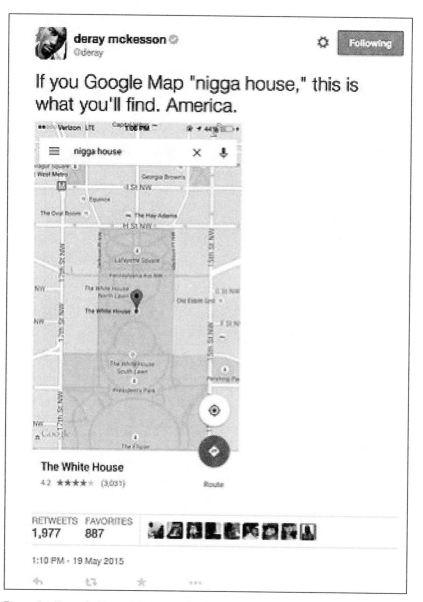

Figure I.4. Tweet by Deray McKesson about Google Maps search and the White House, 2015.

Figure I.5. Standard Google's "related" searches associates "Michelle Obama" with the term "ape."

a Google spokesperson told U.S. News in an email late Tuesday. 'Our teams are working to fix this issue quickly.'"[7]

* * *

These human and machine errors are not without consequence, and there are several cases that demonstrate how racism and sexism are part of the architecture and language of technology, an issue that needs attention and remediation. In many ways, these cases that I present are specific to the lives and experiences of Black women and girls, people largely understudied by scholars, who remain ever precarious, despite our living in the age of Oprah and Beyoncé in Shondaland. The implications of such marginalization are profound. The insights about sexist or racist biases that I convey here are important because information organizations, from libraries to schools and universities to governmental agencies, are increasingly reliant on or being displaced by a variety of web-based "tools" as if there are no political, social, or economic consequences of doing so. We need to imagine new possibilities in the area of information access and knowledge generation, particularly as headlines about "racist algorithms" continue to surface in the media with limited discussion and analysis beyond the superficial.

Inevitably, a book written about algorithms or Google in the twenty-first century is out of date immediately upon printing. Technology is changing rapidly, as are technology company configurations via mergers, acquisitions, and dissolutions. Scholars working in the fields of information, communication, and technology struggle to write about specific moments in time, in an effort to crystallize a process or a phenomenon that may shift or morph into something else soon thereafter. As a scholar of information and power, I am most interested in communicating a series of processes that have happened, which provide evidence of a constellation of concerns that the public might take up as meaningful and important, particularly as technology impacts social relations and creates unintended consequences that deserve greater attention. I have been writing this book for several years, and over time, Google's algorithms have admittedly changed, such that a search for "black girls" does not yield nearly as many pornographic results now as it did in 2011. Nonetheless, new instances of racism and sexism keep appearing in news and social media, and so I use a variety of these cases to make the point that algorithmic oppression is not just a glitch in the system but, rather, is fundamental to the operating system of the web. It has direct impact on users and on our lives beyond using Internet applications. While I have spent considerable time researching Google, this book tackles a few cases of other algorithmically driven platforms to illustrate how algorithms are serving up deleterious information about people, creating and normalizing structural and systemic isolation, or practicing digital redlining, all of which reinforce oppressive social and economic relations.

While organizing this book, I have wanted to emphasize one main point: there is a missing social and human context in some types of algorithmically driven decision making, and this matters for everyone engaging with these types of technologies in everyday life. It is of particular concern for marginalized groups, those who are problematically represented in erroneous, stereotypical, or even pornographic ways in search engines and who have also struggled for nonstereotypical or nonracist and nonsexist depictions in the media and in libraries. There is a deep body of extant research on the harmful effects of stereotyping of women and people of color in the media, and I encourage readers of this book who do not understand why the perpetuation of racist and sexist images in society is problematic to consider a deeper dive into such scholarship.

This book is organized into six chapters. In chapter 1, I explore the important theme of corporate control over public information, and I show several key Google searches. I look to see what kinds of results Google's search engine provides about various concepts, and I offer a cautionary discussion of the implications of what these results mean in historical and social contexts. I also show what Google Images offers on basic concepts such as "beauty" and various professional identities and why we should care.

In chapter 2, I discuss how Google Search reinforces stereotypes, illustrated by searches on a variety of identities that include "black girls," "Latinas," and "Asian girls." Previously, in my work published in the *Black Scholar*,[8] I looked at the postmortem Google autosuggest searches following the death of Trayvon Martin, an African American teenager whose murder ignited the #BlackLivesMatter movement on Twitter and brought attention to the hundreds of African American children, women, and men killed by police or extrajudicial law enforcement. To add a fuller discussion to that research, I elucidate the processes involved in Google's PageRank search protocols, which range from leveraging digital footprints from people[9] to the way advertising and marketing interests influence search results to how beneficial this is to the interests of Google as it profits from racism and sexism, particularly at the height of a media spectacle.

In chapter 3, I examine the importance of noncommercial search engines and information portals, specifically looking at the case of how a mass shooter and avowed White supremacist, Dylann Roof, allegedly used Google Search in the development of his racial attitudes, attitudes that led to his murder of nine African American AME Church members while they worshiped in their South Carolina church in the summer of 2015. The provision of false information that purports to be credible news, and the devastating consequences that can come from this kind of algorithmically driven information, is an example of why we cannot afford to outsource and privatize uncurated information on the increasingly neoliberal, privatized web. I show how important records are to the public and explore the social importance of both remembering and forgetting, as digital media platforms thrive on never or rarely forgetting. I discuss how information online functions as a type of record, and I argue that much of this information and its harmful effects should be regulated or subject to legal protections. Furthermore, at a time when "right to be forgotten" legislation is gaining steam in the European Union, efforts to regulate the ways that technology companies hold a monopoly on public information about individuals and groups need further attention in the United States. Chapter 3 is about the future of information culture, and it underscores the ways that information is not neutral and how we can reimagine information culture in the service of eradicating social inequality.

Chapter 4 is dedicated to critiquing the field of information studies and foregrounds how these issues of public information through classification projects on the web, such as commercial search, are old problems that we must solve as a scholarly field of researchers and practitioners. I offer a brief survey of how library classification projects undergird the invention of search engines such as Google and how our field is implicated in the algorithmic process of sorting and classifying information and records. In chapter 5, I discuss the future of knowledge in the public and reference the work of library and information professionals, in particular, as important to the development and cultivation of equitable classification systems, since these are the precursors to commercial search engines. This chapter is essential history for library and information professionals, who are less likely to be trained on the politics of cataloguing and classification bias in their professional training. Chapter 6 explores public policy and why we need regulation in our information environments, particularly as they are increasingly controlled by corporations.

To conclude, I move the discussion beyond Google, to help readers think about the impact of algorithms on how people are represented in other seemingly benign business transactions. I look at the "color-blind" organizing logic of Yelp and how business owners are revolting due to loss of control over how they are represented and the impact of how the public finds them. Here, I share an interview with Kandis from New York,[10] whose livelihood has been dramatically affected by public-policy changes such as the dismantling of affirmative action on college campuses, which have hurt her local Black-hair-care business in a prestigious college town. Her story brings to light the power that algorithms have on her everyday life and leaves us with more to think about in the ecosystem of algorithmic power. The book closes with a call to recognize the importance of how algorithms are shifting social relations in many ways—more ways than this book can cover—and should be regulated with more impactful public policy in the United States than we currently have. My hope is that this book will directly impact the many kinds of algorithmic decisions that can have devastating consequences for people who are already marginalized by institutional racism and sexism, including the 99% who own so little wealth in the United States that the alarming trend of social inequality is not likely to reverse without our active resistance and intervention. Electoral politics and financial markets are just two of many of these institutional wealth-consolidation projects that are heavily influenced by algorithms and artificial intelligence. We need to cause a shift in what we take for granted in our everyday use of digital media platforms.

I consider my work a practical project, the goal of which is to eliminate social injustice and change the ways in which people are oppressed with the aid of allegedly neutral technologies. My intention in looking at these cases serves two purposes. First, we need interdisciplinary research and scholarship in information studies and library and information science that intersects with gender and women's studies, Black/African American studies, media studies, and communications to better describe and understand how algorithmically driven platforms are situated in intersectional sociohistorical contexts and embedded within social relations. My hope is that this work will add to the voices of my many colleagues across several fields who are raising questions about the legitimacy and social consequences of algorithms and artificial intelligence. Second, now, more than ever, we need experts in the social sciences and digital humanities to engage in dialogue with activists and organizers, engineers, designers, information technologists, and public-policy makers before blunt artificial-intelligence decision making trumps nuanced human decision making. This means that we must look at how the outsourcing of information practices from the public sector facilitates privatization of what we previously thought of as the public domain[11] and how corporate-controlled governments and companies subvert our ability to intervene in these practices.

We have to ask what is lost, who is harmed, and what should be forgotten with the embrace of artificial intelligence in decision making. It is of no collective social benefit to organize information resources on the web through processes that solidify inequality and marginalization—on that point I am hopeful many people will agree.

1

A Society, Searching $\mathcal{Q}$

On October 21, 2013, the United Nations launched a campaign directed by the advertising agency Memac Ogilvy & Mather Dubai using "genuine Google searches" to bring attention to the sexist and discriminatory ways in which women are regarded and denied human rights. Christopher Hunt, art director of the campaign, said, "When we came across these searches, we were shocked by how negative they were and decided we had to do something with them." Kareem Shuhaibar, a copywriter for the campaign, described on the United Nations website what the campaign was determined to show: "The ads are shocking because they show just how far we still have to go to achieve gender equality. They are a wake up call, and we hope that the message will travel far."[1] Over the mouths of various women of color were the autosuggestions that reflected the most popular searches that take place on Google Search. The Google Search autosuggestions featured a range of sexist ideas such as the following:

- Women cannot: drive, be bishops, be trusted, speak in church
- Women should not: have rights, vote, work, box
- Women should: stay at home, be slaves, be in the kitchen, not speak in church
- Women need to: be put in their places, know their place, be controlled, be disciplined

While the campaign employed Google Search results to make a larger point about the status of public opinion toward women, it also served, perhaps unwittingly, to underscore the incredibly powerful nature of search engine results. The campaign suggests that search is a mirror of users' beliefs and that society still holds a variety of sexist ideas about women. What I find troubling is that the campaign also reinforces the idea that it is not the search engine that is the problem but, rather, the users of search engines who are. It suggests that what is most popular is simply what rises

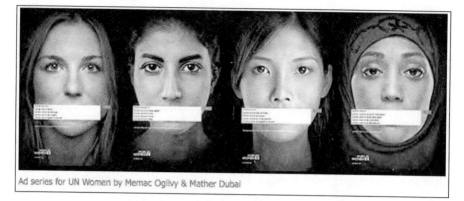

Ad series for UN Women by Memac Ogilvy & Mather Dubai

Figure 1.1. Memac Ogilvy & Mather Dubai advertising campaign for the United Nations.

to the top of the search pile. While serving as an important and disturbing critique of sexist attitudes, the campaign fails to implicate the algorithms or search engines that drive certain results to the top. This chapter moves the lens onto the search architecture itself in order to shed light on the many factors that keep sexist and racist ideas on the first page.

One limitation of looking at the implications of search is that it is constantly evolving and shifting over time. This chapter captures aspects of commercial search at a particular moment—from 2009 to 2015—but surely by the time readers engage with it, it will be a historical rather than contemporary study. Nevertheless, the goal of such an exploration of why we get troublesome search results is to help us think about whether it truly makes sense to outsource all of our knowledge needs to commercial search engines, particularly at a time when the public is increasingly reliant on search engines in lieu of libraries, librarians, teachers, researchers, and other knowledge keepers and resources.

What is even more crucial is an exploration of how people living as minority groups under the influence of a majority culture, such as people of color and sexual minorities in the United States, are often subject to the whims of the majority and other commercial influences such as advertising when trying to affect the kinds of results that search engines offer about them and their identities. If the majority rules in search engine results, then how might those who are in the minority ever be able to influence or control the way they are represented in a search engine? The same might be true of how men's desires and usage of search is able to influence the values that surround women's identities in search engines, as the Ogilvy campaign might suggest. For these reasons, a deeper exploration into the historical and social conditions that give rise to problematic search results is in order, since rarely are they questioned and most Internet users have no idea how these ideas come to dominate search results on the first page of results in the first place.

Google Search: Racism and Sexism at the Forefront

My first encounter with racism in search came to me through an experience that pushed me, as a researcher, to explore the mechanisms—both technological and social—that could render the pornification of Black women a top search result, naturalizing Black women as sexual objects so effortlessly. This encounter was in 2009 when I was talking to a friend, André Brock at the University of Michigan, who causally mentioned one day, "You should see what happens when you Google 'black girls.'" I did and was stunned. I assumed it to be an aberration that could potentially shift over time. I kept thinking about it. The second time came one spring morning in 2011, when I searched for activities to entertain my preteen stepdaughter and her cousins of similar age, all of whom had made a weekend visit to my home, ready for a day of hanging out that would inevitably include time on our laptops. In order to break them away from mindless TV watching and cellphone gazing, I wanted to engage them in conversations about what was important to them and on their mind, from their perspective as young women growing up in downstate Illinois, a predominantly conservative part of Middle America. I felt that there had to be some great resources for young people of color their age, if only I could locate them. I quickly turned to the computer I used for my research (I was pursuing doctoral studies at the time), but I did not let the group of girls gather around me just yet. I opened up Google to enter in search terms that would reflect their interests, demographics, and information needs, but I liked to prescreen and anticipate what could be found on the web, in order to prepare for what might be in store. What came back from that simple, seemingly innocuous search was again nothing short of shocking: with the girls just a few feet away giggling and snorting at their own jokes, I again retrieved a Google Search results page filled with porn when I looked for "black girls." By then, I thought that my own search history and engagement with a lot of Black feminist texts, videos, and books on my laptop would have shifted the kinds of results I would get. It had not. In intending to help the girls search for information about themselves, I had almost inadvertently exposed them to one of the most graphic and overt illustrations of what the advertisers already thought about them: Black girls were still the fodder of porn sites, dehumanizing them as commodities, as products and as objects of sexual gratification. I closed the laptop and redirected our attention to fun things we might do, such as see a movie down the street. This best information, as listed by rank in the search results, was certainly not the best information for me or for the children I love. For whom, then, was this the best information, and who decides? What were the profit and other motives driving this information to the top of the results? How had the notion of neutrality in information ranking and retrieval gone so sideways as to be perhaps one of the worst examples of racist and sexist classification of Black women in the digital age yet remain so unexamined and without public critique? That moment, I began in earnest a series of research inquiries that are central to this book.

Of course, upon reflection, I realized that I had been using the web and search tools long before the encounters I experienced just out of view of my young family members. It was just as troubling to realize that I had undoubtedly been confronted with the same type of results before but had learned, or been trained, to somehow become inured to it, to take it as a given that any search I might perform using keywords connected to my physical self and identity could return pornographic and otherwise disturbing results. Why was this the bargain into which I had tacitly entered with digital information tools? And who among us did not have to bargain in this way? As a Black woman growing up in the late twentieth century, I also knew that the presentation of Black women and girls that I discovered in my search results was not a new development of the digital age. I could see the connection between search results and tropes of African Americans that are as old and endemic to the United States as the history of the country itself. My background as a student and scholar of Black studies and Black history, combined with my doctoral studies in the political economy of digital information, aligned with my righteous indignation for Black girls everywhere. I searched on.

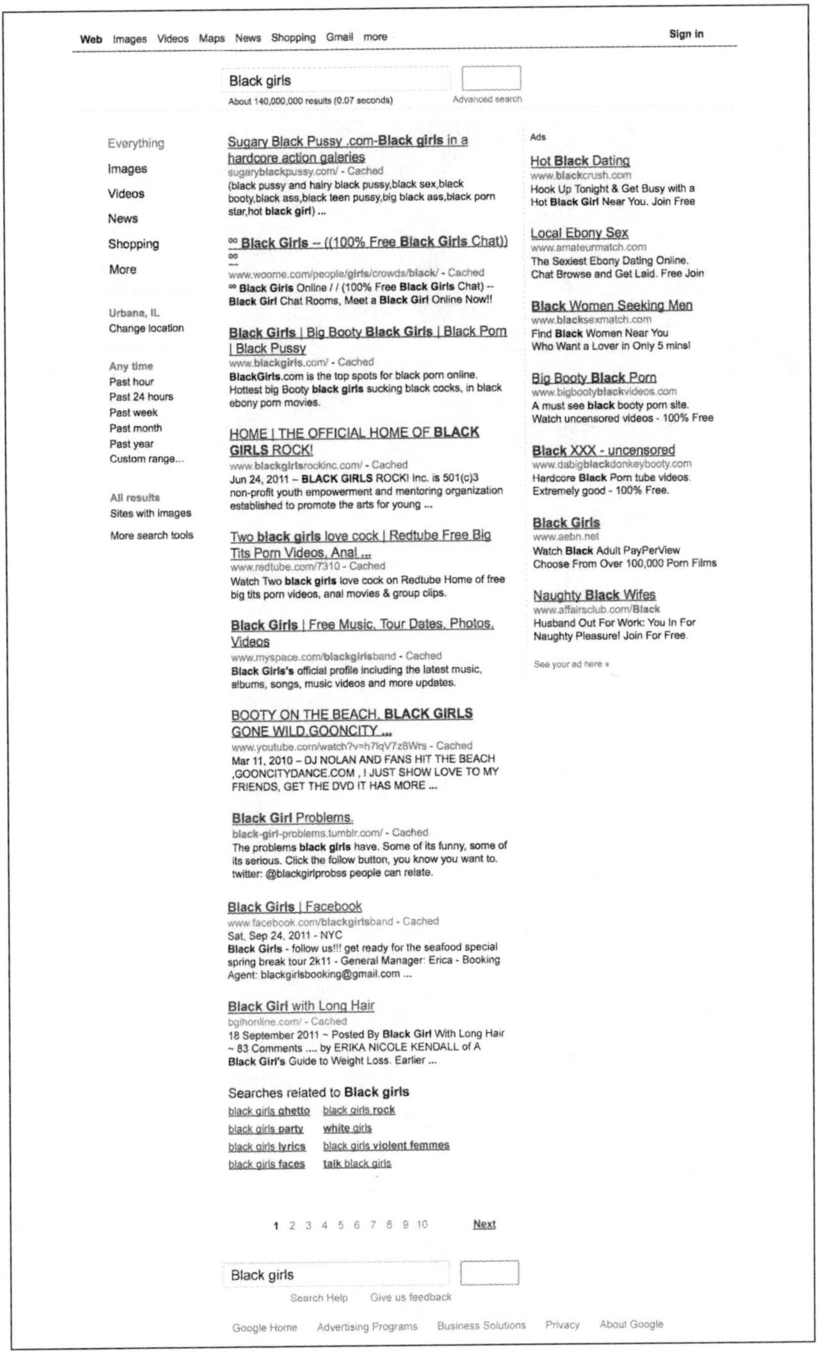

Figure 1.2. First page of search results on keywords "black girls," September 18, 2011.

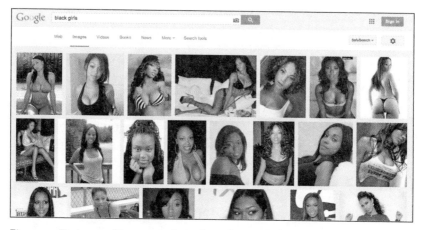

Figure 1.3. First page of image search results on keywords "black girls," April 3, 2014.

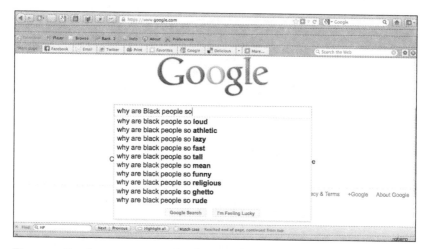

Figure 1.4. Google autosuggest results when searching the phrase "why are black people so," January 25, 2013.

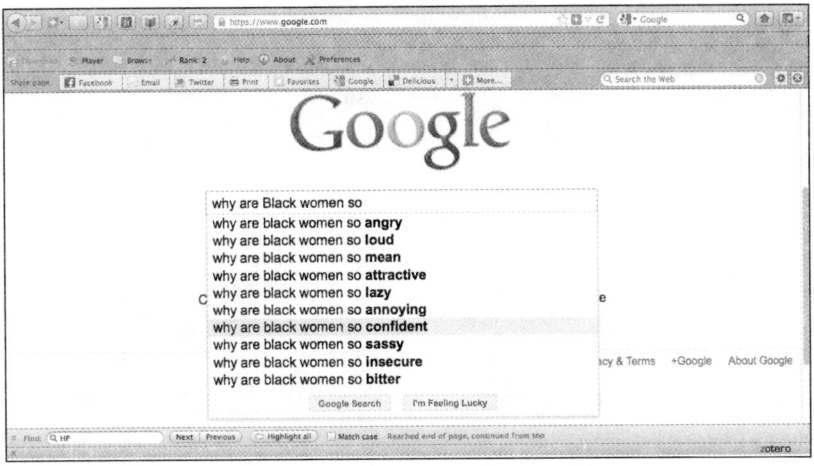

Figure 1.5. Google autosuggest results when searching the phrase "why are black women so," January 25, 2013.

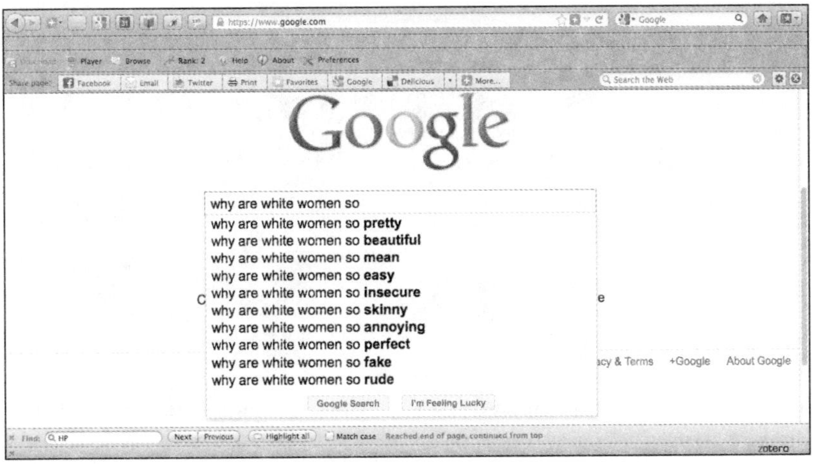

Figure 1.6. Google autosuggest results when searching the phrase "why are white women so," January 25, 2013.

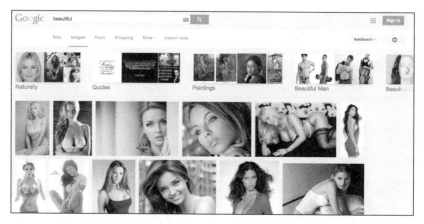

Figure 1.7. Google Images results when searching the concept "beautiful" (did not include the word "women"), December 4, 2014.

Figure 1.8. Google Images results when searching the concept "ugly" (did not include the word "women"), January 5, 2013.

Figure 1.9. Google Images results when searching the phrase "professor style" while logged in as myself, September 15, 2015.

What each of these searches represents are Google's algorithmic conceptualizations of a variety of people and ideas. Whether looking for autosuggestions or answers to various questions or looking for notions about what is beautiful or what a professor may look like (which does not account for people who look like me who are part of the professoriate—so much for "personalization"), Google's dominant narratives reflect the kinds of hegemonic frameworks and notions that are often resisted by women and people of color. Interrogating what advertising companies serve up as credible information must happen, rather than have a public instantly gratified with stereotypes in three-hundredths of a second or less.

In reality, information monopolies such as Google have the ability to prioritize web search results on the basis of a variety of topics, such as promoting their own business interests over those of competitors or smaller companies that are less profitable advertising clients than larger multinational corporations are.[2] In this case, the clicks of users, coupled with the commercial processes that allow paid advertising to be prioritized in search results, mean that representations of women are ranked on a search engine page in ways that underscore women's historical and contemporary lack of status in society—a direct mapping of old media traditions into new media architecture. Problematic representations and biases in classifications are not new. Critical library and information science scholars have well documented the ways in which some groups are more vulnerable than others to misrepresentation and misclassification.[3] They have conducted extensive and important critiques of library cataloging systems and information organization patterns that demonstrate how women, Black people, Asian Americans, Jewish people, or the Roma, as "the other," have all suffered from the insults of misrepresentation and derision in the Library of Congress Subject Headings (LCSH) or through the Dewey Decimal System. At the same time, other scholars underscore the myriad ways that social values around race and gender are directly reflected in technology design.[4] Their contributions have made it possible for me to think about the ways that race and gender are embedded in Google's search engine and to have the courage to raise critiques of one of the most beloved and revered contemporary brands.

Search happens in a highly commercial environment, and a variety of processes shape what can be found; these results are then normalized as believable and often presented as factual. The associate professor of sociology at Arizona State University and former president of the Association of Internet Researchers Alex Halavais points to the way that heavily used technological artifacts such as the search engine have become such a normative part of our experience with digital technology and computers that they socialize us into believing that these artifacts must therefore also provide access to credible, accurate information that is depoliticized and neutral:

> Those assumptions are dangerously flawed; . . . unpacking the black box of the search engine is something of interest not only to technologists and marketers, but to anyone who wants to understand how we make sense of a newly networked world. Search engines have come to play a central role in corralling and controlling the ever-growing sea of information that is available to us, and yet they are trusted more readily than they ought to be. They freely provide, it seems, a sorting of the wheat from the chaff, and answer our most profound and most trivial questions. They have become an object of faith.[5]

Unlike the human-labor curation processes of the early Internet that led to the creation of online directories such as Lycos and Yahoo!, in the current Internet environment, information access has been left to the complex algorithms of machines to make selections and prioritize results for users. I agree with Halavais, and his is an important critique of search engines as a window into our own desires, which can have an impact on the values of society. Search is a symbiotic process that both informs and is informed in part by users. Halavais suggests that every user of a search engine should know how the system works, how information is collected, aggregated, and accessed. To achieve this vision, the public would have to have a high degree of computer programming literacy to engage deeply in the design and output of search.

Alternatively, I draw an analogy that one need not know the mechanism of radio transmission or television spectrum or how to build a cathode ray tube in order to critique racist or sexist depictions in song lyrics played on the radio or shown in a film or television show. Without a doubt, the public is unaware and must have significantly more algorithmic literacy. Since all of the platforms I interrogate in this book are proprietary, even if we had algorithmic literacy, we still could not intervene in these private, corporate platforms.

To be specific, knowledge of the technical aspects of search and retrieval, in terms of critiquing the computer programming code that underlies the systems, is absolutely necessary to have a profound impact on these systems. Interventions such as Black Girls Code, an organization focused on teaching young, African American girls to program, is the kind of intervention we see building in response to the ways Black women have been locked out of Silicon Valley venture capital and broader participation. Simultaneously, it is important for the public, particularly people who are marginalized—such as women and girls and people of color—to be critical of the results that purport to represent them in the first ten to twenty results in a commercial search engine. They do not have the economic, political, and social capital to withstand the consequences of misrepresentation. If one holds a lot of power, one can withstand or buffer misrepresentation at a group level and often at the individual level. Marginalized and oppressed people are linked to the status of their group and are less likely to be afforded individual status and insulation from the experiences of the groups with which they are identified. The political nature of search demonstrates how algorithms are a fundamental invention of computer scientists who are human beings—and code is a language full of meaning and applied in varying ways to different types of information. Certainly, women and people of color could benefit tremendously from becoming programmers and building alternative search engines that are less disturbing and that reflect and prioritize a wider range of informational needs and perspectives.

There is an important and growing movement of scholars raising concerns. Helen Nissenbaum, a professor of media, culture, and communication and computer science at New York University, has written with Lucas Introna, a professor of organization, technology, and ethics at the Lancaster University Management School, about how search engines bias information toward the most powerful online. Their work was corroborated by Alejandro Diaz, who wrote his dissertation at Stanford on sociopolitical bias in Google's products. Kate Crawford and Tarleton Gillespie, two researchers at Microsoft Research New England, have written extensively about algorithmic bias, and Crawford recently coorganized a summit with the White House and New York University for academics, industry, and activists concerned with the social impact of artificial intelligence in society. At that meeting, I participated in a working group on artificial-intelligence social inequality, where tremendous concern was raised about deep-machine-learning projects and software applications, including concern about furthering social injustice and structural racism. In attendance was the journalist Julia Angwin, one of the investigators of the breaking story about courtroom sentencing software Northpointe, used for risk assessment by judges to determine the alleged future criminality of defendants.[6] She and her colleagues determined that this type of artificial intelligence miserably mispredicted future criminal activity and led to the overincarceration of Black defendants. Conversely, the reporters found it was much more likely to predict that White criminals would not offend again, despite the data showing that this was not at all accurate. Sitting next to me was Cathy O'Neil, a data scientist and the author of the book *Weapons of Math Destruction*, who has an insider's view of the way that math and big data are directly implicated in the financial and housing crisis of 2008 (which, incidentally, destroyed more African American wealth than any other event in the United States, save for not compensating African Americans for three hundred years of forced enslavement). Her view from Wall Street was telling:

> The math-powered applications powering the data economy were based on choices made by fallible human beings. Some of these choices were no doubt made with the best intentions. Nevertheless, many of these models encoded human prejudice, misunderstanding, and bias into the software systems that increasingly managed our lives. Like gods, these mathematical models were opaque, their workings invisible to all but the highest priests in their domain: mathematicians and computer scientists. Their verdicts, even when wrong or harmful, were beyond dispute or appeal. And they tended to punish the poor and the oppressed in our society, while making the rich richer.[7]

Our work, each of us, in our respective way, is about interrogating the many ways that data and computing have become so profoundly their own "truth" that even in the face of evidence, the public still struggles to hold tech companies accountable for the products and errors of their ways. These errors increasingly lead to racial and gender profiling, misrepresentation, and even economic redlining.

At the core of my argument is the way in which Google biases search to its own economic interests—for its profitability and to bolster its market dominance at any expense. Many scholars are working to illuminate the ways in which users trade their privacy, personal information, and immaterial labor for "free" tools and services offered by Google (e.g., search engine, Gmail, Google Scholar, YouTube) while the company profits from data mining its users. Recent research on Google by Siva Vaidhyanathan, professor of media studies at the University of Virginia, who has written one of the most important books on Google to date, demonstrates its dominance over the information landscape and forms the basis of a central theme in this research. Frank Pasquale, a professor of law at the University of Maryland, has also forewarned of the increasing levels of control that algorithms have over the many decisions made about us, from credit to dating options, and how difficult it is to intervene in their discriminatory effects. The political economic critique of Google by Elad Segev, a senior lecturer of media and communication in the Department of Communication at Tel Aviv University, charges that we can no longer ignore the global dominance of Google and the implications of its power in furthering digital inequality, particularly as it serves as a site of fostering global economic divides.

However, what is missing from the extant work on Google is an intersectional power analysis that accounts for the ways in which marginalized people are exponentially harmed by Google. Since I began writing this book, Google's parent company, Alphabet, has expanded its power into drone technology,[8] military-grade robotics, fiber networks, and behavioral surveillance technologies such as Nest and Google Glass.[9] These are just several of many entry points to thinking about the implications of artificial intelligence as a human rights issue. We need to be concerned about not only how ideas and people are represented but also the ethics of whether robots and other forms of automated decision making can end a life, as in the case of drones and automated weapons. To whom do we appeal? What bodies govern artificial intelligence, and where does the public raise issues or lodge complaints with national and international courts? These questions have yet to be fully answered.

In the midst of Google's expansion, Google Search is one of the most underexamined areas of consumer protection policy,[10] and regulation has been far less successful in the United States than in the European Union. A key aspect of generating policy that protects the public is the accumulation of research about the impact of what an unregulated commercial information space does to vulnerable populations. I do this by taking a deep look at a snapshot of the web, at a specific moment in time, and interpreting the results against the history of race and gender in the U.S. This is only one of many angles that could be taken up, but I find it to be one of the most compelling ways to show how data is biased and perpetuates racism and sexism. The problems of big data go deeper than misrepresentation, for sure. They include decision-making protocols that favor corporate elites and the powerful, and they are implicated in global economic and social inequality. Deep machine learning, which is using algorithms to replicate human thinking, is predicated on specific values from specific kinds of people— namely, the most powerful institutions in society and those who control them. Diana Ascher,[11] in her dissertation on yellow journalism and cultural time orientation in the Department of Information Studies at UCLA, found there was a stark difference between headlines generated by social media managers from the *LA Times* and those provided by automated, algorithmically driven software, which generated severe backlash on Twitter. In this case, Ascher found that automated tweets in news media were more likely to be racist and misrepresentative, as in the case of police shooting victim Keith Lamont Scott of Charlotte, North Carolina, whose murder triggered nationwide protests of police brutality and excessive force.

There are many such examples. In the ensuing chapters, I continue to probe the results that are generated by Google on a variety of keyword combinations relating to racial and gender identity as a way of engaging a commonsense understanding of how power works, with the goal of changing these processes of control. By seeing and discussing these intersectional power relations, we have a significant opportunity to transform the consciousness embedded in artificial intelligence, since it is in fact, in part, a product of our own collective creation.

Figure 1.10. Automated headline generated by software and tweeted about Keith Lamont Scott, killed by police in North Carolina on September 20, 2016, as reported by the *Los Angeles Times*.

Theorizing Search: A Black Feminist Project

The impetus for my work comes from theorizing Internet search results from a Black feminist perspective; that is, I ask questions about the structure and results of web searches from the standpoint of a Black woman—a standpoint that drives me to ask different questions than have been previously posed about how Google Search works. This study builds on previous research that looks at the ways in which racialization is a salient factor in various engagements with digital technology represented in video games,[12] websites,[13] virtual worlds,[14] and digital media platforms.[15] A Black feminist perspective offers an opportunity to ask questions about the quality and content of racial hierarchies and stereotyping that appear in results from commercial search engines such as Google's; it contextualizes them by decentering the dominant lenses through which results about Black women and girls are interpreted. By doing this, I am purposefully theorizing from a feminist perspective, while addressing often-overlooked aspects of race in feminist theories of technology. The professor emeritus of science and technology at UCLA Sandra Harding suggests that there is value in identifying a feminist method and epistemology:

> Feminist challenges reveal that the questions that are asked—and, even more significantly, those that are not asked—are at least as determinative of the adequacy of our total picture as are any answers that we can discover. Defining what is in need of scientific explanation only from the perspective of bourgeois, white men's experiences leads to partial and even perverse understandings of social life. One distinctive feature of feminist research is that it generates problematics from the perspective of women's experiences.[16]

Rather than assert that problematic or racist results are impossible to correct, in the ways that the Google disclaimer suggests,[17] I believe a feminist lens, coupled with racial awareness about the intersectional aspects of identity, offers new ground and interpretations for understanding the implications of such problematic positions about the benign instrumentality of technologies. Black feminist ways of knowing, for example, can look at searches on terms such as "black girls" and bring into the foreground evidence about the historical tendencies to misrepresent Black women in the media. Of course, these misrepresentations and the use of big data to maintain and exacerbate social relationships serve a powerful role in maintaining racial and gender subjugation. It is the persistent normalization of Black people as aberrant and undeserving of human rights and dignity under the banners of public safety, technological innovation, and the emerging creative economy that I am directly challenging by showing the egregious ways that dehumanization is rendered a legitimate free-market technology project.

I am building on the work of previous scholars of commercial search engines such as Google but am asking new questions that are informed by a Black feminist lens concerned with social justice for people who are systemically oppressed. I keep my eye on complicating the notion that information assumed to be "fact" (by virtue of its legitimation at the top of the information pile) exists because racism and sexism are profitable under our system of racialized capitalism. The ranking hierarchy that the public embraces reflects our social values that place a premium on being number one, and search-result rankings live in this de facto system of authority. Where other scholars have problematized Google Search in terms of its lack of neutrality and prioritization of its own commercial interests, my critiques aim to explicitly address racist and sexist bias in search, fueled by neoliberal technology policy over the past thirty years.

Black Feminism as Theoretical and Methodological Approach

The commodified online status of Black women's and girls' bodies deserves scholarly attention because, in this case, their bodies are defined by a technological system that does not take into account the broader social, political, and historical significance of racist and sexist representations. The very presence of Black women and girls in search results is misunderstood and clouded by dominant narratives of the authenticity and lack of bias of search engines. In essence, the social context or meaning of derogatory or problematic Black women's representations in Google's ranking is normalized by virtue of their placement, making it easier for some people to believe that what exists on the page is strictly the result of the fact that more people are looking for Black women in pornography than anything else. This is because the public believes that what rises to the top in search is either the most popular or the most credible or both.

Yet this does not explain why the word "porn" does not have to be included in keyword searches on "black girls" and other girls and women of color to bring it to the surface as the primary data point about girls and women. The political and social meaning of such output is stripped away when Black girls are explicitly sexualized in search rankings without any explanation, particularly without the addition of the words "porn" or "sex" to the keywords. This phenomenon, I argue, is replicated from offline social relations and deeply embedded in the materiality of technological output; in other words, traditional misrepresentations in old media are made real once again online and situated in an authoritative mechanism that is trusted by the public: Google. The study of Google searches as an Internet artifact is telling. Black feminist scholars have already articulated the harm of such media misrepresentations:[18]

gender, class, power, sexuality, and other socially constructed categories interact with one another in a matrix of social relations that create conditions of inequality or oppression.

Black feminist thought offers a useful and antiessentializing lens for understanding how both race and gender are socially constructed and mutually constituted through historical, social, political, and economic processes,[19] creating interesting research questions and new analytical possibilities. As a theoretical approach, it challenges the dominant research on race and gender, which tends to universalize problems assigned to race or Blackness as "male" (or the problems of men) and organizes gender as primarily conceived through the lenses and experiences of White women, leaving Black women in a precarious and understudied position. Popular culture provides countless examples of Black female appropriation and exploitation of negative stereotypes either to assert control over the representation or at least to reap the benefits of it. The Black feminist scholar bell hooks has written extensively on the ways that neoliberal capitalism is explicitly implicated in misrepresentations and hypersexualization of Black women. hooks's work is a mandate for Black women interested in theorizing in the new media landscape, and I use it as both inspiration and a call to action for other Black women interested in engaging in critical information studies. In total, this research is informed by a host of scholars who have helped me make sense of the ways that technology ecosystems—from traditional classification systems such as library databases to new media technologies such as commercial search engines—are structuring narratives about Black women and girls. In the cases I present, I demonstrate how commercial search engines such as Google not only mediate but are mediated by a series of profit-driven imperatives that are supported by information and economic policies that underwrite the commodification of women's identities. Ultimately, this book is designed to "make it plain," as we say in the Black community, just exactly how it can be that Black women and girls continue to have their image and representations assaulted in the new media environments that are not so unfamiliar or dissimilar to old, traditional media depictions. I intend to meaningfully articulate the ways that commercialization is the source of power that drives the consumption of Black women's and girls' representative identity on the web.

While primarily offering reflection on the effects of search-engine-prioritized content, this research is at the same time intended to bring about a deeper inquiry and a series of strategies that can inform public-policy initiatives focused on connecting Black people to the Internet, in spite of the research that shows that cultural barriers, norms, and power relations alienate Black people from the web.[20] After just over a decade of focus on closing the digital divide,[21] the research questions raised here are meant to provoke a discussion about "what then?" What does it mean to have every Black woman, girl, man, and boy in the United States connected to the web if the majority of them are using a search engine such as Google to access content—whether about themselves or other things—only to find results like those with which I began this introduction? The race to digitize cultural heritage and knowledge is important, but it is often mediated by a search engine for the user who does not know precisely how to find it, much the way a library patron is reliant on deep knowledge and skills of the reference librarian to navigate the vast volumes of information in the library stacks.

The Importance of Google

Google has become a ubiquitous entity that is synonymous for many everyday users with "the Internet" itself. From serving as a browser of the Internet to handling personal email or establishing Wi-Fi networks and broadband projects in municipalities across the United States, Google, unlike traditional telecommunications companies, has unprecedented access to the collection and provision of data across a variety of platforms in a highly unregulated marketplace and policy environment. We must continue to study the implications of engagement with commercial entities such as Google and what makes them so desirable to consumers, as their use is not without consequences of increased surveillance and privacy invasions and participation in hidden labor practices. Each of these enhances the business model of Google's parent company, Alphabet, and reinforces its market dominance across a host of vertical and horizontal markets.[22] In 2011, the Federal Trade Commission started looking into Google's near-monopoly status and market dominance and the harm this could cause consumers. By March 16, 2012, Google was trading on NASDAQ at $625.04 a share, with a market capitalization of just over $203 billion. At the time of the hearings, Google's latest income statement, for December 2011, showed gross profit at $24.7 billion. It had $43.3 billion cash on hand and just $6.21 billion in debt. Google held 66.2% of the search engine market industry in 2012. Google Search's profits have only continued to grow, and its holdings have become so significant that the larger company has renamed itself Alphabet, with Google Search as but one of many holdings. By the final writing of this book in August 2017, Alphabet was trading at $936.38 on NASDAQ, with a market capitalization of $649.49 billion.

The public is aware of the role of search in everyday life, and people's opinions on search are alarming. Recent data from tracking surveys and consumer-behavior trends by the comScore Media Metrix consumer panel conducted by the Pew Internet and American Life Project show that search engines are as important to Internet users as email is. Over sixty million Americans engage in search, and for the most part, people report that they are satisfied with the results they find in search engines. The 2005 and 2012 Pew reports on "search engine use" reveal that 73% of all Americans have used a search engine, and 59% report using a search engine every day.[23] In 2012, 83% of search engine users used Google. But Google Search prioritizes its own interests, and this is something far less visible to the public. Most people surveyed could not tell the difference between paid advertising and "genuine" results.

If search is so trusted, then why is a study such as this one needed? The exploration beyond that first simple search is the substance of this book. Throughout the discussion of these and other results, I want to emphasize the main point: there is a missing social context in commercial digital media platforms, and it matters, particularly for marginalized groups that are problematically represented in stereotypical or pornographic ways, for those who are bullied, and for those who are consistently targeted. I use only a handful of illustrative searches to underscore the point and to raise awareness—and hopefully intervention—of how important what we find on the web through commercial search engines is to society.

Search Results as Power

Search results reflect the values and norms of the search company's commercial partners and advertisers and often reflect our lowest and most demeaning beliefs, because these ideas circulate so freely and so often that they are normalized and extremely profitable. Search results are more than simply what is popular. The dominant notion of search results as being both "objective" and "popular" makes it seem as if misogynist or racist search results are a simple mirror of the collective. Not only do problematic search results seem "normal," but they seem completely unavoidable as well, even though these ideas have been thoroughly debunked by scholars. Unfortunately, users of Google give consent to the algorithms' results through their continued use of the product, which is largely unavoidable as schools, universities, and libraries integrate Google products into our educational experiences.[24]

Google's monopoly status,[25] coupled with its algorithmic practices of biasing information toward the interests of the neoliberal capital and social elites in the United States, has resulted in a provision of information that purports to be credible but is actually a reflection of advertising interests. Stated another way, it can be argued that Google functions in the interests of its most influential paid advertisers or through an intersection of popular and commercial interests. Yet Google's users think of it as a public resource, generally free from commercial interest. Further complicating the ability to contextualize Google's results is the power of its social hegemony.[26] Google benefits directly and materially from what can be called the "labortainment"[27] of users, when users consent to freely give away their labor and personal data for the use of Google and its products, resulting in incredible profit for the company.

There are many cases that could be made to show how overreliance on commercial search by the public, including librarians, information professionals, and knowledge managers—all of whom are susceptible to overuse of or even replacement by search engines—is something that we must pay closer attention to right now. Under the current algorithmic constraints or limitations, commercial search does not provide appropriate social, historical, and contextual meaning to already overracialized and hypersexualized people who materially suffer along multiple axes. In the research presented in this study, the reader will find a more meaningful understanding of the kind of harm that such limitations can cause for users reliant on the web as an artifact of both formal and informal culture.[28] In sum, search results play a powerful role in providing fact and authority to those who see them, and as such, they must be examined carefully. Google has become a central object of study for digital media scholars,[29] due to recognition on these scholars' parts of the power and impact wielded by the necessity to begin most engagements with social media via a search process and the near universality with which Google has been adopted and embedded into all aspects of the digital media landscape to respond to that need. This work is addressing a gap in scholarship on how search works and what it biases, public trust in search, the relationship of search to information studies, and the ways in which African Americans, among others, are mediated and commodified in Google.

To start revealing some of the processes involved, it is important to think about how results appear. Although one might believe that a query to a search engine will produce the most relevant and therefore useful information, it is actually predicated on a matrix of ways in which pages are hyperlinked and indexed on the web.[30] Rendering web content (pages) findable via search engines is an expressly social, economic, and human project, which several scholars have detailed. These renderings are delivered to users through a set of steps (algorithms) implemented by programming code and then naturalized as "objective." One of the reasons this is seen as a neutral process is because algorithmic, scientific, and mathematical solutions are evaluated through procedural and mechanistic practices, which in this case includes tracing hyperlinks among pages. This process is defined by Google's founders, Sergey Brin and Larry Page, as "voting," which is the term they use to describe how search results move up or down in a ranked list of websites. For the most part, many of these processes have been automated, or they happen through graphical user interfaces (GUIs) that allow people who are not programmers (i.e., not working at the level of code) to engage in sharing links to and from websites.[31]

Research shows that users typically use very few search terms when seeking information in a search engine and rarely use advanced search queries, as most queries are different from traditional offline information-seeking behavior.[32] This front-end behavior of users appears to be simplistic; however, the information retrieval systems are complex, and the formulation of users' queries involves cognitive and emotional processes that are not necessarily reflected in the system design.[33] In essence, while users use the simplest queries they can in a search box because of the way interfaces are designed, this does not always reflect how search terms are mapped against more complex thought patterns and concepts that users have about a topic. This disjunction between, on the one hand, users' queries and their real questions and, on the other, information retrieval systems makes understanding the complex linkages between the content of the results that appear in a search and their import as expressions of power and social relations of critical importance.

The public generally trusts information found in search engines. Yet much of the content surfaced in a web search in a commercial search engine is linked to paid advertising, which in part helps drive it to the top of the page rank, and searchers are not typically clear about the distinctions between "real" information and advertising. Given that advertising is a fundamental part of commercial search, using content analysis to make sense of what *actually* is served up in search is appropriate and consistent with the articulation of feminist critiques of the images of women in print advertising.[34] These scholars have shown the problematic ways that women have been represented—as sex objects, incompetent, dependent on men, or underrepresented in the workforce[35]—and the content and representation of women and girls in search engines is consistent with the kinds of problematic and biased ideas that live in other advertising channels. Of course, this makes sense, because Google Search is in fact an advertising platform, not intended to solely serve as a public information resource in the way that, say, a library might. Google creates advertising algorithms, not information algorithms.

To understand search in the context of this book, it is important to look at the description of the development of Google outlined by the former Stanford computer science graduate students and cofounders of the company, Sergey Brin and Larry Page, in "The Anatomy of a Large-Scale Hypertextual Web Search Engine." Their paper, written in graduate school, serves as the architectural framework for Google's PageRank. In addition, it is crucial to also look at the way that citation analysis, the foundational notion behind Brin and Page's idea, works as a bibliometric project that has been extensively developed by library and information science scholars. Both of these dynamics are often misunderstood because they do not account for the complexities of human intervention involved in vetting of information, nor do they pay attention

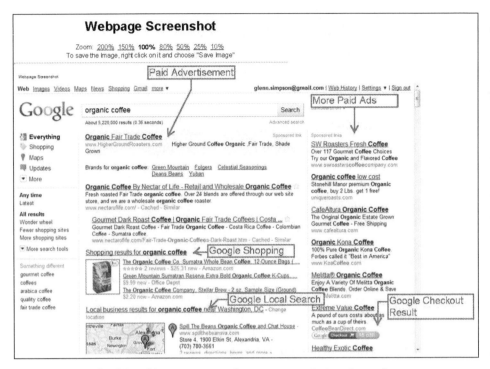

Figure 1.11. Example of Google's prioritization of its own properties in web search. Source: Inside Google (2010).

to the relative weight or importance of certain types of information.[36] For example, in the process of citing work in a publication, all citations are given equal weight in the bibliography, although their relative importance to the development of thought may not be equal at all. Additionally, no relative weight is given to whether a reference is validated, rejected, employed, or engaged—complicating the ability to know what a citation actually *means* in a document. Authors who have become so mainstream as not to be cited, such as not attributing modern discussions of class or power dynamics to Karl Marx or the notion of "the individual" to the scholar of the Italian Renaissance Jacob Burckhardt, mean that these intellectual contributions may undergird the framework of an argument but move through works without being cited any longer. Concepts that may be widely understood and accepted ways of knowing are rarely cited in mainstream scholarship, an important dynamic that

Linda Smith, former president of the Association for Information Science and Technology (ASIS&T) and associate dean of the Information School at the University of Illinois at Urbana-Champaign, argues is part of the flawed system of citation analysis that deserves greater attention if bibliometrics are to serve as a legitimating force for valuing knowledge production.

Brin and Page saw the value in using works that others cite as a model for thinking about determining what is legitimate on the web, or at least to indicate what is popular based on many people acknowledging particular types of content. In terms of outright co-optation of the citation, vis-à-vis the hyperlink, Brin and Page were aware of some of the challenges I have described. They were clearly aware from the beginning of the potential for "gaming" the system by advertising companies or commercial interests, a legitimated process now known as "search engine optimization," to drive ads or sites to the top of a results list for a query, since clicks on web links can be profitable, as are purchases gained by being vetted as "the best" by virtue of placement on the first page of PageRank. This is a process used for web results, not paid advertising, which is often highlighted in yellow (see figure 1.6). Results that appear not to be advertising are in fact influenced by the advertising algorithm. In contrast to scientific or scholarly citations, which once in print are persistent and static, hyperlinking is a dynamic process that can change from moment to moment.[37] As a result, the stability of results in Google ranking shifts and is prone to being affected by a number of processes that I will cover, primarily search engine optimization and advertising. This means that results shift over time. The results of what is most hyperlinked using Google's algorithm today will be different at a later date or from the time that Google's web-indexing crawlers move through the web until the next cycle.[38]

Citation importance is a foundational concept for determining scholarly relevance in certain disciplines, and citation analysis has largely been considered a mechanism for determining whether a given article or scholarly work is important to the scholarly community. I want to revisit this concept because it also has implications for thinking about the legitimation of information, not just citability or popularity. It is also a function of human beings who are engaged in a curation practice, not entirely left to automation. Simply put, if scholars choose to cite a study or document, they have signaled its relevance; thus, human beings (scholars) are involved in making decisions about a document's relevance, although all citations in a bibliography do not share the same level of meaningfulness. Building on this concept of credibility through citation, PageRank is what Brin and Page call the greater likelihood that a document is relevant "if there are many pages that point to it" versus "the probability that the random surfer visits a page."[39] In their research, which led to the development of Google Search, Brin and Page discuss the possibility of monopolizing and manipulating keywords through commercialization of the web search process. Their information-retrieval goal was to deliver the most relevant or very best ten or so documents out of the possible number of documents that could be returned from the web. The resulting development of their search architecture is PageRank—a system that is based on "the objective measure of its citation importance that corresponds well with people's subjective idea of importance."[40]

One of the most profound parts of Brin and Page's work is in appendix A, in which they acknowledge the ways that commercial interests can compromise the quality of search result retrieval. They state, citing Ben Bagdikian, "It is clear that a search engine which was taking money for showing cellular phone ads would have difficulty justifying the page that our system returned to its paying advertisers. For this type of reason and historical experience with other media, we expect that advertising funded search engines will be inherently biased towards the advertisers and away from the needs of the consumers."[41] Brin and Page outline a clear roadmap for how bias would work in advertising-oriented search and the effects this would have, and they directly suggest that it is in the consumer's interest not to have search compromised by advertising and commercialism. To some degree, PageRank was intended to be a measure of relevance based on popularity—including what both web surfers and web designers link to from their sites. As with academic citations, Brin and Page decided that citation analysis could be used as a model for determining whether web links could be ranked according to their importance by measuring how much they were back-linked or hyperlinked to or from. Thus, the model for web indexing pages was born. However, in the case of citation analysis, a scholarly author goes through several stages of vetting and credibility testing, such as the peer-review process, before work can be published and cited. In the case of the web, such credibility checking is not a factor in determining what will be hyperlinked. This was made explicitly clear in the many news reports covering the 2016 U.S. presidential election, where clickbait and manufactured "news" from all over the world clouded accurate reporting of facts on the presidential candidates.

Another example of the shortcomings of removing this human curation or decision making from the first page of results at the top of PageRank, in addition to the results that I found for "black girls," can be found in the more public dispute over the results that were returned on searches for the word "Jew," which included a significant number of anti-Semitic pages. As can be seen by Google's response to the results of a keyword search for "Jew," Google takes little responsibility toward the ways that it provides information on racial and gendered identities, which are curated in more meaningful ways in scholarly databases. Siva Vaidhyanathan's 2011 book *The Googlization of Everything (And Why We Should Worry)* chronicles recent attempts by the Jewish community and Anti-Defamation League to challenge Google's priority ranking to the first page of anti-Semitic, Holocaust-denial websites. So troublesome were these search results that in 2011, Google issued a statement about its search process, encouraging people to use "Jews" and "Jewish people" in their searches, rather than the seemingly pejorative term "Jew"— claiming that the company can do nothing about the word's co-optation by White supremacist groups (see figure 1.12).

Google, according to its own disclaimer, will only remove pages that are considered unlawful, as is the case in France and Germany, where selling or distributing neo-Nazi materials is prohibited. Without such limits on derogatory, racist, sexist, or homophobic materials, Google allows its algorithm—which is, as we can see, laden with what Diaz calls "sociopolitics"—to stand without debate while protesting its inability to remove pages. As recently as June 27, 2012, Google settled a claim by the French antiracism organization the International League Against Racism over Google's use of ethnic identity—"Jew"—in association with popular searches.[42] Under French law, racial identity markers cannot be stored in databases, and the auto-complete techniques used in the Google search box link names of people to the word "Jew" on the basis of past user searches. What this recent case points to is another effort to

Google

An explanation of our search results

If you recently used Google to search for the word "Jew," you may have seen results that were very disturbing. We assure you that the views expressed by the sites in your results are not in any way endorsed by Google. We'd like to explain why you're seeing these results when you conduct this search.

A site's ranking in Google's search results relies heavily on computer algorithms using thousands of factors to calculate a page's relevance to a given query. Sometimes subtleties of language cause anomalies to appear that cannot be predicted. A search for "Jew" brings up one such unexpected result.

If you use Google to search for "Judaism," "Jewish" or "Jewish people," the results are informative and relevant. So why is a search for "Jew" different? One reason is that the word "Jew" is often used in an anti-Semitic context. Jewish organizations are more likely to use the word "Jewish" when talking about members of their faith. The word has become somewhat charged linguistically, as noted on websites devoted to Jewish topics such as these:

- http://www.jewishworldreview.com/cols/jonah081500.asp

Someone searching for information on Jewish people would be more likely to enter terms like "Judaism," "Jewish people," or "Jews" than the single word "Jew" In fact, prior to this incident, the word "Jew" only appeared about once in every 10 million search queries. Now it's likely that the great majority of searches on Google for "Jew" are by people who have heard about this issue and want to see the results for themselves.

The beliefs and preferences of those who work at Google, as well as the opinions of the general public, do not determine or impact our search results. Individual citizens and public interest groups do periodically urge us to remove particular links or otherwise adjust search results. Although Google reserves the right to address such requests individually, Google views the comprehensiveness of our search results as an extremely important priority. Accordingly, we do not remove a page from our search results simply because its content is unpopular or because we receive complaints concerning it. We will, however, remove pages from our results if we believe the page (or its site) violates our Webmaster Guidelines, if we believe we are required to do so by law, or at the request of the webmaster who is responsible for the page.

We apologize for the upsetting nature of the experience you had using Google and appreciate your taking the time to inform us about it.

Sincerely,
The Google Team

P.S. You may be interested in some additional information the Anti-Defamation League has posted about this issue at http://www.adl.org/rumors/google_search_rumors.asp. In addition, we call your attention to Google's search results on this topic.

©2011 Google

Figure 1.12. Explanation of results by Google. Source: www.google.com/explanation. html (originally available in 2005).

redefine distorted images of people in new media. These cases of distortion, however, continue to accumulate.

The public's as well as the Jewish community's interest in accurate information about Jewish culture and the Holocaust should be enough motivation to provoke a national discussion about consumer harm, to which my research shows we can add other cultural and gender-based identities that are misrepresented in search engines. However, Google's assertion that its search results, though problematic, were computer generated (and thus not the company's fault) was apparently a good-enough answer for the Anti-Defamation League (ADL), which declared, "We are extremely pleased that Google has heard our concerns and those of its users about the offensive nature of some search results and the unusually high ranking of peddlers of bigotry and anti-Semitism."[43] The ADL does acknowledge on its website its gratitude to Sergey Brin, cofounder of Google and son of Russian Jewish immigrants, for his personal letter to the organization and his mea culpa for the "Jew" search-term debacle. The ADL generously stated in its press release about the incident that Google, as a resource to the public, should be forgiven because "until the technical modifications are implemented, Google has placed text on its site that gives users a clear explanation of how search results are obtained. Google searches are automatically determined using computer algorithms that take into account thousands of factors to calculate a page's relevance."[44]

If there is a technical fix, then what are the constraints that Google is facing such that eight years later, the issue has yet to be resolved? A search for the word "Jew" in 2012 produces a beige box at the bottom of the results page from Google linking to its lengthy disclaimer about the results—which remain a mix of both anti-Semitic and informative sites (see figure 1.13). That Google places the responsibility for bad results back on the shoulders of information searchers is a problem, since most of the results that the public gets on broad or open-ended racial and gendered searches are out of their control and entirely within the control of Google Search.

It is important to note that Google has conceded the fact that anti-Semitism as the primary information result about Jewish people is a problem, despite its disclaimer that tries to put the onus for bad results on the searcher. In Germany and France, for example, it is illegal to sell

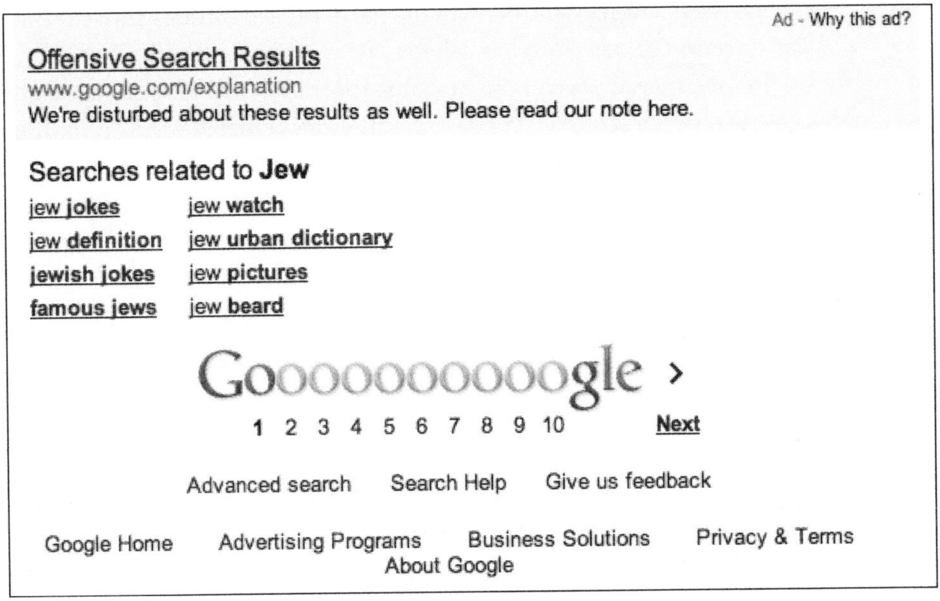

Figure 1.13. Google's bottom-of-the-page beige box regarding offensive results, which previously took users to "An Explanation of Our Search Results." Source: www.google.com/explanation (no longer available).

Nazi memorabilia, and Google has had to put in place filters that ensure online retailers of such are not visible in search results. In 2002, Benjamin Edelman and Jonathan Zittrain at Harvard University's Berkman Center for Internet and Society concluded that Google was filtering its search results in accordance with local law and precluding neo-Nazi organizations and content from being displayed.[45] While this indicates that Google can in fact remove objectionable hits, it is equally troubling, because the company provided search results without informing searchers that information was being deleted. That is to say that the results were presented as factual and complete without mention of omission. Yahoo!, another leading U.S. search engine, was forced into a protracted legal battle in France for allowing pro-Nazi memorabilia to be sold through its search engine, in violation of French law. What these cases point to is that search results are deeply contextual and easily manipulated, rather than objective, consistent, and transparent, and that they can be legitimated only in social, political, and historical context.

The issue of unlawfulness over the harm caused by derogatory results is a question of considerable debate. For example, in the United States, where free speech protections are afforded to all kinds of speech, including hate speech and racist or sexist depictions of people and communities, there is a higher standard of proof required to show harm toward disenfranchised or oppressed people. We need legal protections now more than ever, as automated decision-making systems wield greater power in society.

Gaming the System: Optimizing and Co-opting Results in Search Engines

Google's advertising tool or optimization product is AdWords. AdWords allows anyone to advertise on Google's search pages and is highly customizable. With this tool, an advertiser can set a maximum amount of money that it wants to spend on a daily basis for advertising. The model for AdWords is that Google will display ads on search pages that it believes are relevant to the kind of search query that is taking place by a user. If a user clicks on an ad, then the advertiser pays. And Google incentivizes advertisers by suggesting that their ads will show up in searches and display, but the advertiser (or Google customer) pays for the ad only when a user (Google consumer) clicks on the advertisement, which is the cost per click (CPC). The advertiser selects a series of "keywords" that it believes closely align with its product or service that it is advertising, and a customer can use a Keyword Estimator tool in order to see how much the keywords they choose to associate with their site might cost. This advertising mechanism is an essential part of how PageRank prioritizes ads on a page, and the association of certain keywords with particular industries, products, and services derives from this process, which works in tandem with PageRank.

In order to make sense of the specific results in keyword searches, it is important to know how Google's PageRank works, what commercial processes are involved in PageRank, how search engine optimization (SEO) companies have been developed to influence the process of moving up results,[46] and how Google bombing[47] occurs on occasion. Google bombing is the practice of excessively hyperlinking to a website (repeatedly coding HTML to link a page to a term or phrase) to cause it to rise to the top of PageRank, but it is also seen as a type of "hit and run" activity that can deliberately co-opt terms and identities on the web for political, ideological, and satirical purposes. Judit Bar-Ilan, a professor of information science at Bar-Ilan University, has studied this practice to see if the effect of forcing results to the top of PageRank has a lasting effect on the result's persistence, which can happen in well-orchestrated campaigns. In essence, Google bombing is the process of co-opting content or a term and redirecting it to unrelated content. Internet lore attributes the creation of the term "Google bombing" to Adam Mathes, who associated the term "talentless hack" with a friend's website in 2001. Practices such as Google bombing (also known as Google washing) are impacting both SEO companies and Google alike. While Google is invested in maintaining the quality of search results in PageRank and policing companies that attempt to "game the system," as Brin and Page foreshadowed, SEO companies do not want to lose ground in pushing their clients or their brands up in PageRank.[48] SEO is the process of "using a range of techniques, including augmenting HTML code, web page copy editing, site navigation, linking campaigns and more, in order to improve how well a site or page gets listed in search engines for particular search topics,"[49] in contrast to "paid search," in which the company pays Google for its ads to be displayed when specific terms are searched. A media spectacle of this nature is the case of Senator Rick Santorum, Republican of Pennsylvania, whose website and name were associated with insults in order to drive objectionable content to the top of PageRank.[50] Others who have experienced this kind of co-optation of identity or less-than-desirable association of their name with an insult include former president George W. Bush and the pop singer Justin Bieber.

All of these practices of search engine optimization and Google bombing can take place independently of and in concert with the process of crawling and indexing the web. In fact, being found gives meaning to a website and creates the conditions in which a ranking can happen. Search engine optimization is a major factor in findability on the web. What is important to note is that search engine optimization is a multibillion-dollar industry that impacts the value of specific keywords; that is, marketers are invested in using particular keywords, and keyword combinations, to optimize their rankings.

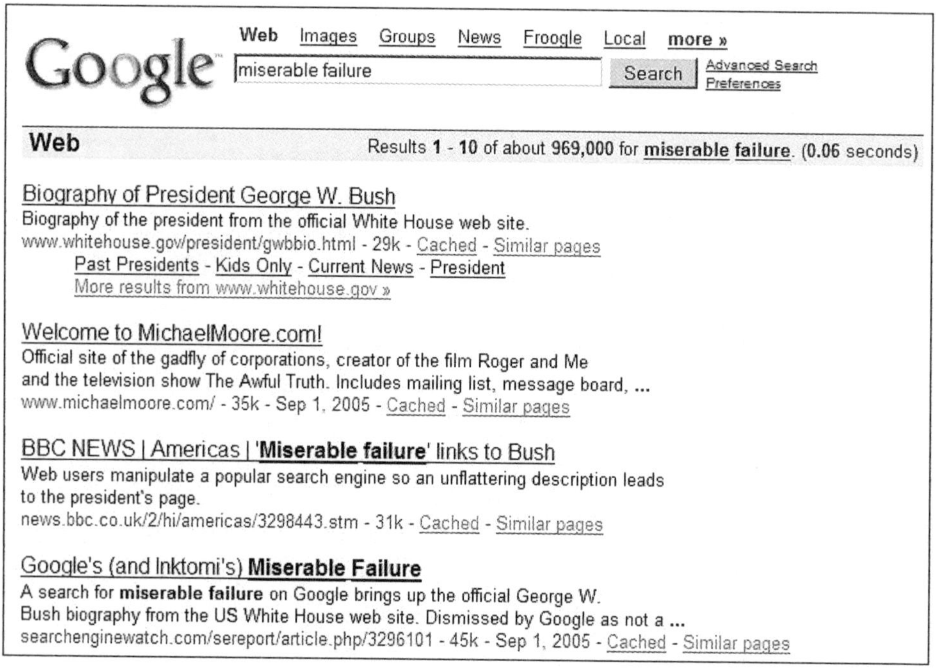

Figure 1.14. Example of a Google bomb on George W. Bush and the search terms "miserable failure," 2005.

Despite the widespread beliefs in the Internet as a democratic space where people have the power to dynamically participate as equals, the Internet is in fact organized to the benefit of powerful elites,[51] including corporations that can afford to purchase and redirect searches to their own sites. What is most popular on the Internet is not wholly a matter of what users click on and how websites are hyperlinked—there are a variety of processes at play. Max Holloway of *Search Engine Watch* notes, "Similarly, with Google, when you click on a result—or, for that matter, don't click on a result—that behavior impacts future results. One consequence of this complexity is difficulty in explaining system behavior. We primarily rely on performance metrics to quantify the success or failure of retrieval results, or to tell us which variations of a system work better than others. Such metrics allow the system to be continuously improved upon."[52] The goal of combining search terms, then, in the context of the landscape of the search engine optimization logic, is only the beginning.

Much research has now been done to dispel the notion that users of the Internet have the ability to "vote" with their clicks and express interest in individual content and information, resulting in democratic practices online.[53] Research shows the ways that political news and information in the blogosphere are mediated and directed such that major news outlets surface to the top of the information pile over less well-known websites and alternative news sites in the blogosphere, to the benefit of elites.[54] In the case of political information seeking, research has shown how Google directs web traffic to mainstream corporate news conglomerates, which increases their ability to shape the political discourse. Google too is a mediating platform that, at least at one moment in time, in September 2011, allowed the porn industry to take precedence in the representations of Black women and girls over other possibilities among at least eleven and a half billion documents that could have been indexed.[55] That moment in 2011 is, however, emblematic of Google's ongoing dynamic. It has since produced many more problematic results.

As the Federal Communications Commission declares broadband "the new common medium,"[56] the role of search engines is taking on even greater importance to "the widest possible dissemination of information from diverse and antagonistic sources . . . essential to the welfare of the public."[57] This political economy of search engines and traditional advertisers includes search engine optimization companies that operate in a secondary or gray market (often in opposition to Google). Ultimately, the results we get are about the financial interest that Google or SEOs have in helping their own clients optimize their rankings. In fact, Google is in the business of selling optimization. Extensive critiques of Google have been written on the political economy of search[58] and the way that consolidations in the search engine industry market contribute to the erosion of public resources, in much the way that the media scholars Robert McChesney, former host of nationally syndicated radio show *Media Matters*, and John Nichols, a writer for the *Nation*, critique the consolidation of the mass-media news markets. Others have spoken to the inherent democratizing effect of search engines, such that search is adding to the diversity of political organization and discourse because the public is able to access more information in the marketplace of ideas.[59] Mounting evidence shows that automated decision-making systems are disproportionately harmful to the most vulnerable and the least powerful, who have little ability to intervene in them—from mis-representation to prison sentencing to accessing credit and other life-impacting formulas.

This landscape of search engines is important to consider in under-standing the meaning of search for the public, and it serves as a basis for examining why information quality online is significant. We must trouble the notion of Google as a public resource, particularly as institutions be-come more reliant on Google when looking for high-quality, contextual-ized, and credible information. This shift from public institutions such as libraries and schools as brokers of information to the private sector, in projects such as Google Books, for example, is placing previously public assets in the hands of a multinational corporation for private exploita-tion. Information is a new commodity, and search engines can function as private information enclosures.[60] We need to make more visible the commercial interests that overdetermine what we can find online.

The Enclosure of the Public Domain through Search Engines

At the same time that search engines have become the dominant portal for information seeking by U.S. Internet users, the rise of commercial media-tion of information in those same search engines is further enclosing the public domain. Decreases in funding for public information institutions such as libraries and educational institutions and shifts of responsibil-ity to individuals and the private sector have reframed the ways that the public conceives of what can and should be in the public domain. Yet Google Search is conceived of as a public resource, even though it is a multinational advertising company. These shifts of resources that were once considered public have been impacted by increased intellectual property rights, licensing, and publishing agreements for companies and private individuals in the domain of copyrights, patents, and other legal protections. The move of community-based assets and culture to pri-vate hands is arguably a crisis that has rolled back the common good, but there are still possible strategies that can be explored for maintain-ing what can remain in the public domain. Commercial control over the Internet, often considered a "commons," has moved it further away from the public through a series of national and international regulations and intellectual and commercial borders that exist in the management of the network.[61] Beyond the Internet and the control of the network, public information—whether delivered over the web or not—continues to be outsourced to the private sphere, eroding the public information commons that has been a basic tenet of U.S. democracy.

The critical media scholar Herbert Schiller, whose work foreshadowed many of the current challenges in the information and communications landscape, provides a detailed examination of the impact of outsourcing and deregulation in the spheres of communication and public information. His words are still timely: "The practice of selling government (or any) information serves the corporate user well. Ordinarily individual users go to the end of the dissemination queue. Profoundly antidemocratic in its effect, privatizing and/or selling information, which at one time was considered public property, has become a standard practice in recent years."[62] What this critique shows is that the privatization and commercial nature of information has become so normalized that it not only becomes obscured from view but, as a result, is increasingly difficult to critique within the public domain. The Pew Internet and American Life Project corroborates that the public trusts multinational corporations that provide information over the Internet and that there is a low degree of distrust of the privatization of information.[63] Part of this process of acquiescence to the increased corporatization of public life can be explained by the economic landscape, which is shaped by military-industrial projects such as the Internet that have emerged in the United States,[64] increasing the challenge of scholars who are researching the impact of such shifts in resources and accountability. Molly Niesen at the University of Illinois has written extensively on the loss of public accountability by federal agencies such as the Federal Trade Commission (FTC), which is a major contribution to our understanding of where the public can focus attention on policy interventions.[65] We should leverage her research to think about the FTC as the key agency to manage and intervene in how corporations control the information landscape.

The Cultural Power of Algorithms

The public is minimally aware of these shifts in the cultural power and import of algorithms. In a 2015 study by the Pew Research Center,

Figure 1.15. *Forbes*'s online reporting (and critique) of the Epstein and Robertson study.

"American's Privacy Strategies Post-Snowden," only 34% of respondents who were aware of the surveillance that happens automatically online through media platforms, such as search behavior, email use, and social media, reported that they were shifting their online behavior because of concerns of government surveillance and the potential implications or harm that could come to them.[66] Little of the American public knows that online behavior has more importance than ever. Indeed, Internet-based activities are dramatically affecting our notions of how democracy and freedom work, particularly in the realm of the free flow of information and communication. Our ability to engage with the information landscape subtly and pervasively impacts our understanding of the world and each other.

An example of how information flow and bias in the realm of politics have recently come to the fore can be found in an important new study about how information bias can radically alter election outcomes. The former editor of *Psychology Today* and professor Robert Epstein and Ronald Robertson, the associate director of the American Institute for Behavioral Research and Technology, found in their 2013 study that democracy was at risk because manipulating search rankings could shift voters' preferences, substantially and without their awareness. In their study, they note that the tenor of stories about a candidate in search engine results, whether favorable or unfavorable, dramatically affected the way that people voted. Seventy-five percent of participants were not aware that the search results had been manipulated. The researchers concluded, "The outcomes of real elections—especially tight races—can conceivably be determined by the strategic manipulation of search engine rankings and . . . that the manipulation can be accomplished without people being aware of it. We speculate that unregulated search engines could pose a serious threat to the democratic system of government."[67]

In March 2012, the Pew Internet and American Life Project issued an update to its 2005 "Search Engine Users" study. The 2005 and 2012 surveys tracking consumer-behavior trends from the comScore Media Metrix consumer panel show that search engines are as important to Internet users as email is. In fact, the *Search Engine Use 2012* report suggests that the public is "more satisfied than ever with the quality of search results."[68] Further findings include the following:

- 73% of all Americans have used a search engine, and 59% report using a search engine every day.
- 83% of search engine users use Google.

Especially alarming is the way that search engines are increasingly positioned as a trusted public resource returning reliable and credible information. According to Pew, users report generally good outcomes and relatively high confidence in the capabilities of search engines:

- 73% of search engine users say that most or all the information they find as they use search engines is accurate and trustworthy.

Yet, at the same time that search engine users report high degrees of confidence in their skills and trust in the information they retrieve from engines, they have also reported that they are naïve about how search engines work:

- 62% of search engine users are not aware of the difference between paid and unpaid results; that is, only 38% are aware, and only 8% of search engine users say that they can always tell which results are paid or sponsored and which are not.

- In 2005, 70% of search engine users were fine with the concept of paid or sponsored results, but in 2012, users reported that they are not okay with targeted advertising because they do not like having their online behavior tracked and analyzed.
- In 2005, 45% of search engine users said they would stop using search engines if they thought the engines were not being clear about offering some results for pay.
- In 2005, 64% of those who used engines at least daily said search engines are a fair and unbiased source of information; the percentage increased to 66% in 2012.

Users in the 2012 Pew study also expressed concern about personalization:

- 73% reported that they would *not be okay* with a search engine keeping track of searches and using that information to personalize future search results. Participants reported that they feel this to be an invasion of privacy.

In the context of these concerns, a 2011 study by the researchers Martin Feuz and Matthew Fuller from the Centre for Cultural Studies at the University of London and Felix Stalder from the Zurich University of the Arts found that personalization is not simply a service to users but rather a mechanism for better matching consumers with advertisers and that Google's personalization or aggregation is about actively matching people to groups, that is, categorizing individuals.[69] In many cases, different users are seeing similar content to each other, but users have little ability to see how the platform is attempting to use prior search history and demographic information to shape their results. Personalization is, to some degree, giving people the results they want on the basis of what Google knows about its users, but it is also generating results for viewers to see what Google Search thinks might be good for advertisers by means of compromises to the basic algorithm. This new wave of interactivity, without a doubt, is on the minds of both users and search engine optimizing companies and agencies. Google applications such as Gmail or Google Docs and social media sites such as Facebook track identity and previous searches in order to surface targeted ads for users by analyzing users' web traces. So not only do search engines increasingly remember the digital traces of where we have been and what links we have clicked in order to provide more custom content (a practice that has begun to gather more public attention after Google announced it would use past search practices and link them to users in its privacy policy change in 2012),[70] but search results will also vary depending on whether filters to screen out porn are enabled on computers.[71]

It is certain that information that surfaces to the top of the search pile is not exactly the same for every user in every location, and a variety of commercial advertising, political, social, and economic decisions are linked to the way search results are coded and displayed. At the same time, results are generally quite similar, and complete search personalization—customized to very specific identities, wants, and desires—has yet to be developed. For now, this level of personal-identity personalization has less impact on the variation in results than is generally believed by the public.

Losing Control of Our Images and Ourselves in Search

It is well known that traditional media have been rife with negative or stereotypical images of African American / Black people,[72] and the web as the locus of new media is a place where traditional media interests are replicated. Those who have been inappropriately and unfairly represented in racist and sexist ways in old media have been able to cogently critique those representations and demand expanded representations, protest stereotypes, and call for greater participation in the production of alternative, nonstereotypical or oppressive representations. This is part of the social charge of civil rights organizations such as the Urban League[73] and the National Association for the Advancement of Colored People, which monitor and report on minority misrepresentations, as well as celebrate positive portrayals of African Americans in the media.[74] At a policy level, some civil rights organizations and researchers such as Darnell Hunt, dean of the division of social science and department chair of sociology at UCLA,[75] have been concerned with media representations of African Americans, and mainstream organizations such as Free Press have been active in providing resources about the impact of the lack of diversity, stereotyping, and hate speech in the media. Indeed, some of these resources have been directed toward net-neutrality issues and closing the digital divide.[76] Media advocacy groups that focus on the pornification of women or the stereotyping of people of color might turn their attention toward the Internet as another consolidated media resource, particularly given the evidence showing Google's information and advertising monopoly status on the web.

Bias in Search

"Traffic Report: How Google Is Squeezing Out Competitors and Muscling Into New Markets," by ConsumerWatchdog.org's Inside Google (June 2010), details how Google effectively blocks sites that it competes with and prioritizes its own properties to the top of the search pile (YouTube over other video sites, Google Maps over MapQuest, and Google Images over Photobucket and Flickr). The report highlights the process by which Universal Search is not a neutral and therefore universal process but rather a commercial one that moves sites that buy paid advertising to the top of the pile. Amid these practices, the media, buttressed by an FTC investigation,[77] have suggested that algorithms are not at all unethical or harmful because they are free services and Google has the right to run its business in any way it sees fit. Arguably, this is true, so true that the public should be thoroughly informed about the ways that Google biases information—toward largely stereotypic and decontextualized results, at least when it comes to certain groups of people. Commercial platforms such as Facebook and YouTube go to great lengths to monitor uploaded user content by hiring web content screeners, who at their own peril screen illicit content that can potentially harm the public.[78] The expectation of such filtering suggests that such sites vet content on the Internet on the basis of some objective criteria that indicate that some content is in fact quite harmful to the public. New research conducted by Sarah T. Roberts in the Department of Information Studies at UCLA shows the ways that, in fact, commercial content moderation (CCM, a term she coined) is a very active part of determining what is allowed to surface on Google, Yahoo!, and other commercial text, video, image, and audio engines.[79] Her work on video content moderation elucidates the ways that commercial digital media platforms currently outsource or insource image and video content filtering to comply with their terms of use agreements. What is alarming about Roberts's work is that it reveals the processes by which content is already being screened and assessed according to a continuum of values that largely reflect U.S.-based social norms, and these norms reflect a number of racist and stereotypical ideas that make screening racism and sexism and the abuse of humans in racialized ways "in" and perfectly acceptable, while other ideas such as the abuse of animals (which is also unacceptable) are "out" and screened or blocked from view. She details an interview with one of the commercial content moderators (CCMs) this way:

> We have very, very specific itemized internal policies . . . the internal policies are not made public because then it becomes very easy to skirt them to essentially the point of breaking them. So yeah, we had very specific internal policies that we were constantly, we would meet once a week with SecPol to discuss, there was one, blackface is not technically considered hate speech by default. Which always rubbed me the wrong way, so I had probably ten meltdowns about that. When we were having these meetings discussing policy and to be fair to them, they always listened to me, they never shut me up. They didn't agree, and they never changed the policy but they always let me have my say, which was surprising. (Max Breen, MegaTech CCM Worker).

The MegaTech example is an illustration of the fact that social media companies and platforms make active decisions about what kinds of racist, sexist, and hateful imagery and content they will host and to what extent they will host it. These decisions may revolve around issues of "free speech" and "free expression" for the user base, but on commercial social media sites and platforms, these principles are always counterbalanced by a profit motive; if a platform were to become notorious for being too restrictive in the eyes of the majority of its users, it would run the risk of losing participants to offer to its advertisers. So MegaTech erred on the side of allowing more, rather than less, racist content, in spite of the fact that one of its own CCM team members argued vociferously against it and, by his own description, experienced emotional distress ("meltdowns") around it.[80]

This research by Roberts, particularly in the wake of leaked reports from Facebook workers who perform content moderation, suggests that people and policies are put in place to navigate and moderate content on the web. Egregious and racist content, content that is highly profitable, proliferates because many tech platforms are interested in attracting the interests and attention of the majority in the United States, not of racialized minorities.

Challenging Race- and Gender-Neutral Narratives

These explorations of web results on the first page of a Google search also reveal the default identities that are protected on the Internet or are less susceptible to marginalization, pornification, and commodification. The research of Don Heider, the dean of Loyola University Chicago's School of Communication, and Dustin Harp, an assistant professor in the Department of Communication at the University of Texas, Arlington, shows that even though women constitute just slightly over half of Internet users, women's voices and perspectives are not as loud and do not have as much impact online as those of men. Their work demonstrates how some users of the Internet have more agency and can dominate the web, despite the utopian and optimistic view of the web as a socially equalizing and democratic force.[81] Recent research on the male gaze and pornography on the web argue that the Internet is a communications environment that privileges the male, pornographic gaze and marginalizes women as objects.[82] As with other forms of pornographic representations, pornography both structures and reinforces the domination of women, and the images of women in advertising and art are often "constructed for viewing by a male subject,"[83] reminiscent of the journalist and producer John Berger's canonical work *Ways of Seeing*, which describes this objectification in this way: "Women are depicted in a quite different way from men—not because the feminine is different from the masculine—but because the 'ideal' spectator is always assumed to be male and the image of the woman is designed to flatter him."[84]

The previous articulations of the male gaze continue to apply to other forms of advertising and media—particularly on the Internet—and the pornification of women on the web is an expression of racist and sexist hierarchies. When these images are present, White women are the norm, and Black women are overrepresented, while Latinas are under-represented.[85] Tracey A. Gardner characterizes the problematic characterizations of African American women in pornographic media by suggesting that "pornography capitalizes on the underlying historical myths surrounding and oppressing people of color in this country which makes it racist."[86] These characterizations translate from old media representations to new media forms. Structural inequalities of society are being reproduced on the Internet, and the quest for a race-, gender-, and class-less cyberspace could only "perpetuate and reinforce current systems of domination."[87]

More than fifteen years later, the present research corroborates these concerns. Women, particularly of color, are represented in search queries against the backdrop of a White male gaze that functions as the dominant paradigm on the Internet in the United States. The Black studies and critical Whiteness scholar George Lipsitz, of the University of California, Santa Barbara, highlights the "possessive investment in Whiteness" and the ways that the American construction of Whiteness is more "nonracial" or null. Whiteness is more than a legal abstraction formulated to conceptualize and codify notions of the "Negro," "Black Codes," or the racialization of diverse groups of African peoples under the brutality of slavery—it is an imagined and constructed community uniting ethnically diverse European Americans. Through cultural agreements about who subtly and explicitly constitutes "the other" in traditional media and entertainment such as minstrel shows, racist films and television shows produced in Hollywood, and Wild West narratives, Whiteness consolidated itself "through inscribed appeals to the solidarity of White supremacy."[88] The cultural practices of our society—which I argue include representations on the Internet—are part of the ways in which race-neutral narratives have increased investments in Whiteness. Lipsitz argues it this way:

> As long as we define social life as the sum total of conscious and deliberate individual activities, then only *individual* manifestations of personal prejudice and hostility will be seen as racist. Systemic, collective, and co-ordinated behavior disappears from sight. Collective exercises of group power relentlessly channeling rewards, resources, and opportunities from one group to another will not appear to be "racist" from this perspective

because they rarely announce their intention to discriminate against individuals. But they work to construct racial identities by giving people of different races vastly different life chances.[89]

Consistent with trying to make sense of the ways that racial order is built, maintained, and made difficult to parse, Charles Mills, in his canonical work, *The Racial Contract*, put it this way:

> One could say then, as a general rule, that *white misunderstanding, misrepresentation, evasion, and self-deception on matters related to race* are among the most pervasive mental phenomena of the past few hundred years, a cognitive and moral economy psychically required for conquest, colonization and enslavement. And these phenomena are in no way *accidental*, but *prescribed* by the Racial Contract, which requires a certain schedule of structured blindness and opacities in order to establish and maintain the white polity.[90]

This, then, is a challenge, because in the face of rampant denial in Silicon Valley about the impact of its technologies on racialized people, it becomes difficult to foster an understanding and appropriate intervention into its practices. Group identity as invoked by keyword searches reveals this profound power differential that is reflected in contemporary U.S. social, political, and economic life. It underscores how much engineers have control over the mechanics of sense making on the web about complex phenomena. It begs the question that if the Internet is a tool for progress and advancement, as has been argued by many media scholars, then cui bono—to whose benefit is it, and who holds the power to shape it? Tracing these historical constructions of race and gender offline provides more information about the context in which technological objects such as commercial search engines function as an expression of a series of social, political, and economic relations— relations often obscured and normalized in technological practices, which most of Silicon Valley's leadership is unwilling to engage with or take up.[91]

Studying Google keyword searches on identity, and their results, helps further thinking about what this means in relationship to marginalized groups in the United States. I take up the communications scholar Norman Fairclough's rationale for doing this kind of critique of the discourses that contribute to the meaning-making process as a form of "critical social science."[92] To contextualize my method and its appropriateness to my theoretical approach, I note here that scholars who work in critical race theory and Black feminism often use a qualitative method such as close reading, which provides more than numbers to explain results and which focuses instead on the material conditions on which these results are predicated.

Challenging Cybertopias

All of this leads to more discussion about ideologies that serve to stabilize and normalize the notion of commercial search, including the still-popular and ever-persistent dominant narratives about the neutrality and objectivity of the Internet itself—beyond Google and beyond utopian visions of computer software and hardware. The early cybertarian John Perry Barlow's infamous "A Declaration of the Independence of Cyberspace" argued in part, "We are creating a world that all may enter without privilege or prejudice accorded by race, economic power, military force, or station of birth. We are creating a world where anyone, anywhere may express his or her beliefs, no matter how singular, without fear of being coerced into silence or conformity."[93] Yet the web is not only an intangible space; it is also a physical space made of brick, mortar, metal trailers, electronics containing magnetic and optical media, and fiber infrastructure. It is wholly material in all of its qualities, and our experiences with it are as real as any other aspect of life. Access to it is predicated on telecommunications companies, broadband providers, and Internet service providers (ISPs). Its users live on Earth in myriad human conditions that make them anything but immune from privilege and prejudice, and human participation in the web is mediated by a host of social, political, and economic access points—both locally in the United States and globally.[94]

Since Barlow's declaration, many scholars have challenged the utopian ideals associated with the rise of the Internet and its ability to free us, such as those espoused by Barlow, linking them to neoliberal notions of individualism, personal freedom, and individual control. These linkages are important markers of the shift from public- or state-sponsored institutions, including information institutions, as the arbiters of social freedoms to the idea that free markets, corporations, and individualized pursuits should serve as the locus of social organization. These ideas are historically rooted in notions of the universal human being, unmarked by difference, that serve as the framework for a specific tradition of thinking about *individual* pursuits of equality. Nancy Leys Stepan of Cornell University aptly describes an enduring feature of the past 270 years of liberal individualism, reinvoked by Enlightenment thinkers during the rising period of modern capitalism:

> Starting in the seventeenth century, and culminating in the writings of the new social contract philosophers of the eighteenth century, a new concept of the political individual was formulated—an abstract and innovative concept, an apparent oxymoron—the imagined *universal individual* who was the bearer of equal political rights. The genius of this concept, which opened the door to the modern polis, was that it defined at least theoretically, an individual being who could be imagined so stripped of individual substantiation and specification (his unique self), that he could stand for every man. Unmarked by the myriad specificities (e.g., of wealth, rank, education, age, sex) that make each person unique, one could imagine an abstract, non-specific individual who expressed a common psyche and political humanity.[95]

Of course, these notions have been consistently challenged, yet they still serve as the basis for beliefs in an ideal of an unmarked humanity— nonracialized, nongendered, and without class distinction—as the final goal of human transcendence. This teleology of the abstracted individual is challenged by the inevitability of such markers and the ways that the individual particularities they signal afford differential realities and struggles, as well as privileges and possibilities. Those who become "marked" by race, gender, or sexuality as other are deviations from the universal human—they are often lauded for "transcending" their markers—while others attempt to "not see color" in a failing quest for colorblindness. The pretext of universal humanity is never challenged, and the default and idealized human condition is unencumbered by racial and gender distinction. This subtext is an important part of the narrative that somehow personal liberties can be realized through technology because of its ability to supposedly strip us of our specifics and make us equal. We know, of course, that nothing could be further from the truth. Just ask the women of #Gamergate[96] and observe the ways that racist, sexist, and homophobic comments and trolling occur every minute of every hour of every day on the web.

As I have suggested, there are many myths about the Internet, including the notion that what rises to the top of the information pile is *strictly* what is most popular as indicated by hyperlinking. Were that even true, what is most popular is not necessarily what is *most true*. It is on this basis that I contend there is work to be done to contextualize and reveal the many ways that Black women are embedded within the most popular commercial search engine—Google Search—and that this embeddedness warrants an exploration into the complexities of whether the content surfaced is a result of popularity, credibility, commerciality, or even a combination thereof. Using the flawed logic of democracy in web rankings, the outcome of the searches I conducted would suggest that both sexism and pornography are the most "popular" values on the Internet when it comes to women, especially women and girls of color. In reality, there is more to result ranking than just how we "vote" with our clicks, and various expressions of sexism and racism are related.

2

Searching for Black Girls Q

On June 28, 2016, Black feminist and mainstream social media erupted with the announcement that Black Girls Code, an organization dedicated to teaching and mentoring African American girls interested in computer programming, would be moving into Google's New York offices. The partnership was part of Google's effort to spend $150 million on diversity programs that could create a pipeline of talent into Silicon Valley and the tech industries. But just two years before, searching on "black girls" surfaced "Black Booty on the Beach" and "Sugary Black Pussy" to the first page of Google results, out of the trillions of web-indexed pages that Google Search crawls. In part, the intervention of teaching computer code to African American girls through projects such as Black Girls Code is designed to ensure fuller participation in the design of software and to remedy persistent exclusion. The logic of new pipeline investments in youth was touted as an opportunity to foster an empowered vision for Black women's participation in Silicon Valley industries. Discourses of creativity, cultural context, and freedom are fundamental narratives that drive the coding gap, or the new coding divide, of the twenty-first century.

Part of the ethos of engaging African American women and girls in this initiative is about moving the narrative from African Americans as digitally divided to digitally *undivided*. In this framing, Black women are the targets of a variety of neoliberal science, technology, and digital innovation programs. Neoliberalism has emerged and served as a framework for developing social and economic policy in the interest of elites, while simultaneously crafting a new worldview: an ideology of individual freedoms that foreground personal creativity, contribution, and participation, as if these engagements are not interconnected to broader labor practices of systemic and structural exclusion. In the case of Google's history of racist bias in search, no linkages are made between Black Girls Code and remedies to the company's current employment

practices and product designs. Indeed, the notion that lack of participation by African Americans in Silicon Valley is framed as a "pipeline
issue" posits the lack of hiring Black people as a matter of people unpre-
pared to participate, despite evidence to the contrary. Google, Facebook,
and other technology giants have been called to task for this failed logic.
Laura Weidman Powers of CODE2040 stated in an interview by Jessica
Guynn at *USA Today*, "This narrative that nothing can be done today
and so we must invest in the youth of tomorrow ignores the talents and
achievements of the thousands of people in tech from underrepresented
backgrounds and renders them invisible."[1] Blacks and Latinos are underemployed despite the increasing numbers graduating from college
with degrees in computer science.

Filling the pipeline and holding "future" Black women programmers
responsible for solving the problems of racist exclusion and misrepresentation in Silicon Valley or in biased product development is not the
answer. Commercial search prioritizes results predicated on a variety
of factors that are anything but objective or value-free. Indeed, there
are infinite possibilities for other ways of designing access to knowledge and information, but the lack of attention to the kind of White
and Asian male dominance that Guynn reported sidesteps those who
are responsible for these companies' current technology designers and
their troublesome products. Few voices of African American women
innovators and tech-company leaders in Silicon Valley have emerged to
reframe the "diversity problems" that keep African American women at
bay. One essay that grabbed the attention of many people, written for
Recode by Heather Hiles, the former CEO of an educational technology e-portfolio company, Pathbrite, spoke directly to the limits for Black
women in Silicon Valley:

> I'm writing this post from the Austin airport, headed home to Oakland
> from SXSW. Before pulling out my laptop to compose this, I read a post
> on Medium that named me as one of three black women known to have
> raised millions in venture capital. The article began with the startling
> fact that less than .1 percent of venture capital in the United States is
> invested in black women founders. I'm not sure what sub-percentage of
> these are women in tech, but it doesn't really matter when the overall
> numbers are so abysmal. The problem isn't a lack of compelling women

of color to invest in; it's a system in Silicon Valley that isn't set up to develop, encourage and create pathways for blacks, Latinos or women. Don't just take my word for it—listen to industry leaders interviewed for a USA Today story on the Valley's lack of commitment to diversity. Jessica Guynn reports that "venture capitalists tell [Mitch Kapor] all the time that they are 'color blind' when funding companies. He's not sure they are ready to let go of a deeply rooted sense that Silicon Valley is a meritocracy."[2]

Hiles goes on to discuss the exclusionary practices of Silicon Valley, challenging the notion that merit and opportunity go to the smartest people prepared to innovate. Despite her being the only openly gay Black women to raise $12 million in venture capital for her company, she still faces tremendous obstacles that her non-Black counterparts do not. By rendering people of color as nontechnical, the domain of technology "belongs" to Whites and reinforces problematic conceptions of African Americans.[3] This is only exacerbated by framing the problems as "pipeline" issues instead of as an issue of racism and sexism, which extends from employment practices to product design. "Black girls need to learn how to code" is an excuse for not addressing the persistent marginalization of Black women in Silicon Valley.

Who Is Responsible for the Results?

As a result of the lack of African Americans and people with deeper knowledge of the sordid history of racism and sexism working in Silicon Valley, products are designed with a lack of careful analysis about their potential impact on a diverse array of people. If Google software engineers are not responsible for the design of their algorithms, then who is? These are the details of what a search for "black girls" would yield for many years, despite that the words "porn," "pornography," or "sex" were not included in the search box. In the text for the first page of results, for example, the word "pussy," as a noun, is used four times to describe Black girls. Other words in the lines of text on the first page include "sugary" (two times), "hairy" (one), "sex" (one), "booty/ass" (two), "teen" (one), "big" (one), "porn star" (one), "hot" (one), "hardcore" (one), "action" (one), "galeries [sic]" (one).

Black girls

About 140,000,000 results (0.07 seconds)   Advanced search

Everything

Images

Videos

News

Shopping

More

Urbana, IL
Change location

Any time
Past hour
Past 24 hours
Past week
Past month
Past year
Custom range...

All results
Sites with images

More search tools

Sugary Black Pussy .corn-Black girls in a
hardcore action galeries
sugaryblackpussy.com/ - Cached
(black pussy and hairy black pussy,black sex,black
booty,black ass,black teen pussy,big black ass,black porn
star,hot black girl) ...

∞ Black Girls -- ((100% Free Black Girls Chat))
∞
www.wooma.com/people/girls/crowds/black/ - Cached
∞ Black Girls Online / / (100% Free Black Girls Chat) --
Black Girl Chat Rooms, Meet a Black Girl Online Now!!

Black Girls | Big Booty Black Girls | Black Porn
| Black Pussy
www.blackgirls.com/ - Cached
BlackGirls.com is the top spots for black porn online.
Hottest big Booty black girls sucking black cocks, in black
ebony porn movies.

HOME | THE OFFICIAL HOME OF BLACK
GIRLS ROCK!
www.blackgirlsrockinc.com/ - Cached
Jun 24, 2011 – BLACK GIRLS ROCK! Inc. is 501(c)3
non-profit youth empowerment and mentoring organization
established to promote the arts for young ...

Two black girls love cock | Redtube Free Big
Tits Porn Videos, Anal ...
www.redtube.com/7310 - Cached
Watch Two black girls love cock on Redtube Home of free
big tits porn videos, anal movies & group clips.

Black Girls | Free Music, Tour Dates, Photos,
Videos
www.myspace.com/blackgirlsband - Cached
Black Girls's official profile including the latest music,
albums, songs, music videos and more updates.

BOOTY ON THE BEACH, BLACK GIRLS
GONE WILD,GOONCITY ...
www.youtube.com/watch?v=h7iqV7z8Wrs - Cached
Mar 11, 2010 – DJ NOLAN AND FANS HIT THE BEACH
,GOONCITYDANCE.COM , I JUST SHOW LOVE TO MY
FRIENDS, GET THE DVD IT HAS MORE ...

Black Girl Problems.
black-girl-problems.tumblr.com/ - Cached
The problems black girls have. Some of its funny, some of
its serious. Click the follow button, you know you want to.
twitter: @blackgirlprobss people can relate.

Black Girls | Facebook
www.facebook.com/blackgirlsband - Cached
Sat, Sep 24, 2011 - NYC
Black Girls - follow us!!! get ready for the seafood special
spring break tour 2k11 - General Manager: Erica - Booking
Agent: blackgirlsbooking@gmail.com ...

Black Girl with Long Hair
bglhonline.com/ - Cached
18 September 2011 ~ Posted By Black Girl With Long Hair
~ 83 Comments .... by ERIKA NICOLE KENDALL of A
Black Girl's Guide to Weight Loss. Earlier ...

Searches related to **Black girls**
black girls ghetto   black girls rock
black girls party   white girls
black girls lyrics   black girls violent femmes
black girls faces   talk black girls

1 2 3 4 5 6 7 8 9 10   Next

Black girls

Search Help   Give us feedback

Figure 2.1. First page of search results on keywords "black girls," September 18, 2011.

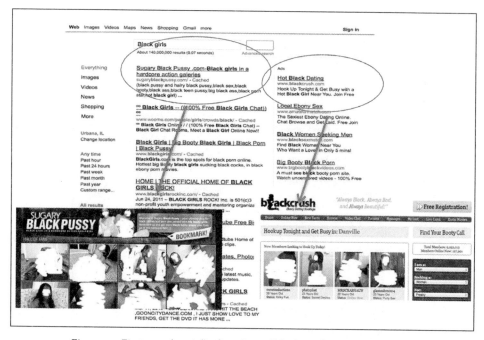

Figure 2.2. First page (partial) of results on "black girls" in a Google search with the first result's detail and advertising.

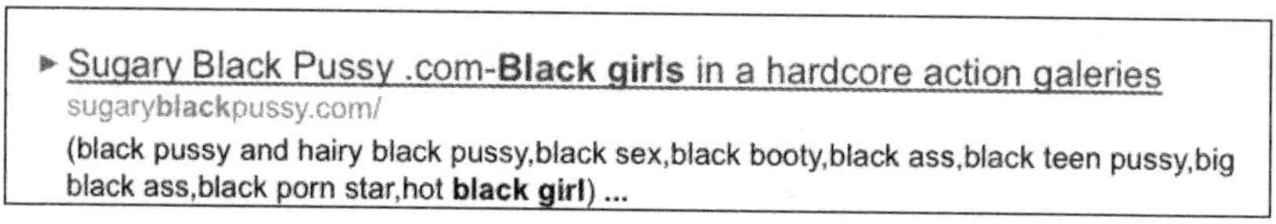

▶ Sugary Black Pussy .com-**Black girls** in a hardcore action galeries
sugary**black**pussy.com/
(black pussy and hairy black pussy,black sex,black booty,black ass,black teen pussy,big black ass,black porn star,hot **black girl**) ...

Figure 2.3. First results on the first page of a keyword search for "black girls" in a Google search.

In the case of the first page of results on "black girls," I clicked on the link for both the top search result (unpaid) and the first paid result, which is reflected in the right-hand sidebar, where advertisers that are willing and able to spend money through Google AdWords[4] have their content appear in relationship to these search queries.[5] All advertising in relationship to Black girls for many years has been hypersexualized and pornographic, even if it purports to be just about dating or social in nature. Additionally, some of the results such as the UK rock band

Figure 2.4. Snapchat faced intense media scrutiny in 2016 for its "Bob Marley" and "yellowface" filters that were decried as racist stereotyping.

Black Girls lack any relationship to Black women and girls. This is an interesting co-optation of identity, and because of the band's fan following as well as possible search engine optimization strategies, the band is able to find strong placement for its fan site on the front page of the Google search.

Published text on the web can have a plethora of meanings, so in my analysis of all of these results, I have focused on the implicit and explicit messages about Black women and girls in both the texts of results or hits and the paid ads that accompany them. By comparing these to broader social narratives about Black women and girls in dominant U.S. popular culture, we can see the ways in which search engine technology replicates and instantiates these notions. This is no surprise when Black women are not employed in any significant numbers at Google. Not only are African Americans underemployed at Google, Facebook, Snapchat, and other popular technology companies as computer programmers, but jobs that could employ the expertise of people who understand the ramifications of racist and sexist stereotyping and misrepresentation and that require undergraduate and advanced degrees in ethnic, Black / African American, women and gender, American Indian, or Asian American studies are nonexistent.

One cannot know about the history of media stereotyping or the nuances of structural oppression in any formal, scholarly way through the traditional engineering curriculum of the large research universities from which technology companies hire across the United States. Ethics courses are rare, and the possibility of formally learning about the history of Black women in relation to a series of stereotypes such as the Jezebel, Sapphire, and Mammy does not exist in mainstream engineering programs. I can say that when I teach engineering students at UCLA about the histories of racial stereotyping in the U.S. and how these are encoded in computer programming projects, my students leave the class stunned that no one has ever spoken of these things in their courses. Many are grateful to at least have had ten weeks of discussion about the politics of technology design, which is not nearly enough to prepare them for a lifelong career in information technology. We need people designing technologies for society to have training and an education on the histories of marginalized people, at a minimum, and we need them working alongside people with rigorous training and preparation from the social sciences and humanities. To design technology for people, without a detailed and rigorous study of people and communities, makes for the many kinds of egregious tech designs we see that come at the expense of people of color and women.

In this effort to try and make sense of how to think through the complexities of race and gender in the U.S., I resist the notion of essentializing the racial and gender binaries; however, I do acknowledge that the discursive existence of these categories, "Black" and "women/girls," is shaped in part by power relations in the United States that tend to essentialize and reify such categories. Therefore, studying Blackness is, in part, guided by its historical construction against Whiteness as a social order and those who have power given their proximity to it. I make comparisons in this study of Blackness to Whiteness only for the purposes of making more explicit the discursive representations of Black girls' and women's identities against an often unnamed and unacknowledged background of a normativity that is structured around White-American-ness. I do believe that the results of my study on identities such as White men, boys, girls, and women deserve their own separate treatment using the extensive body of scholarship in the social construction of Whiteness and a critical Whiteness lens. This study does not deeply discuss those searches in this way. I am not arguing that Black women and girls are the only people maligned in search, although they were represented far worse than others when I began this research. The goal of studying representations of Black girls as a social identity is not to use such research to legitimize essentializing or naturalizing characterizations of people by biological constructions of race or gender; nor does this work suggest that discourses on race and gender in search engines reflect a particular "nature" or "truth" about people.

It is more interesting to think about the ways in which search engine results perpetuate particular narratives that reflect historically uneven distributions of power in society. Although I focus mainly on the example of Black girls to talk about search bias and stereotyping, Black girls are not the only girls and women marginalized in search. The results retrieved two years into this study, in 2011, representing Asian girls, Asian Indian girls, Latina girls, White girls, and so forth reveal the ways in which girls' identities are commercialized, sexualized, or made curiosities within the gaze of the search engine. Women and girls do not fare well in Google Search—that is evident. My goal is not to inform about this but to uncover new ways of thinking about search results and the power that such results have on our ways of knowing and relating. I do this by illuminating the case of Black girls, but undoubtedly, much could be written about the specific histories and contexts of these various identities of women and girls of color; and indeed, there is much still to question and advocate for around the commercialization of identity in search.

In order to fully interrogate this persistent phenomenon, a lesson on race and racialization is in order, as these processes are structured into every aspect of American work, culture, and knowledge production. To understand representations of race and gender in new media, it is necessary to draw on research about how race is constituted as a social, economic, and political hierarchy based on racial categories, how people are racialized, how this can shift over time without much disruption to the hierarchical order, and how White American identity functions as an invisible "norm" or "nothingness" on which all others are made aberrant.

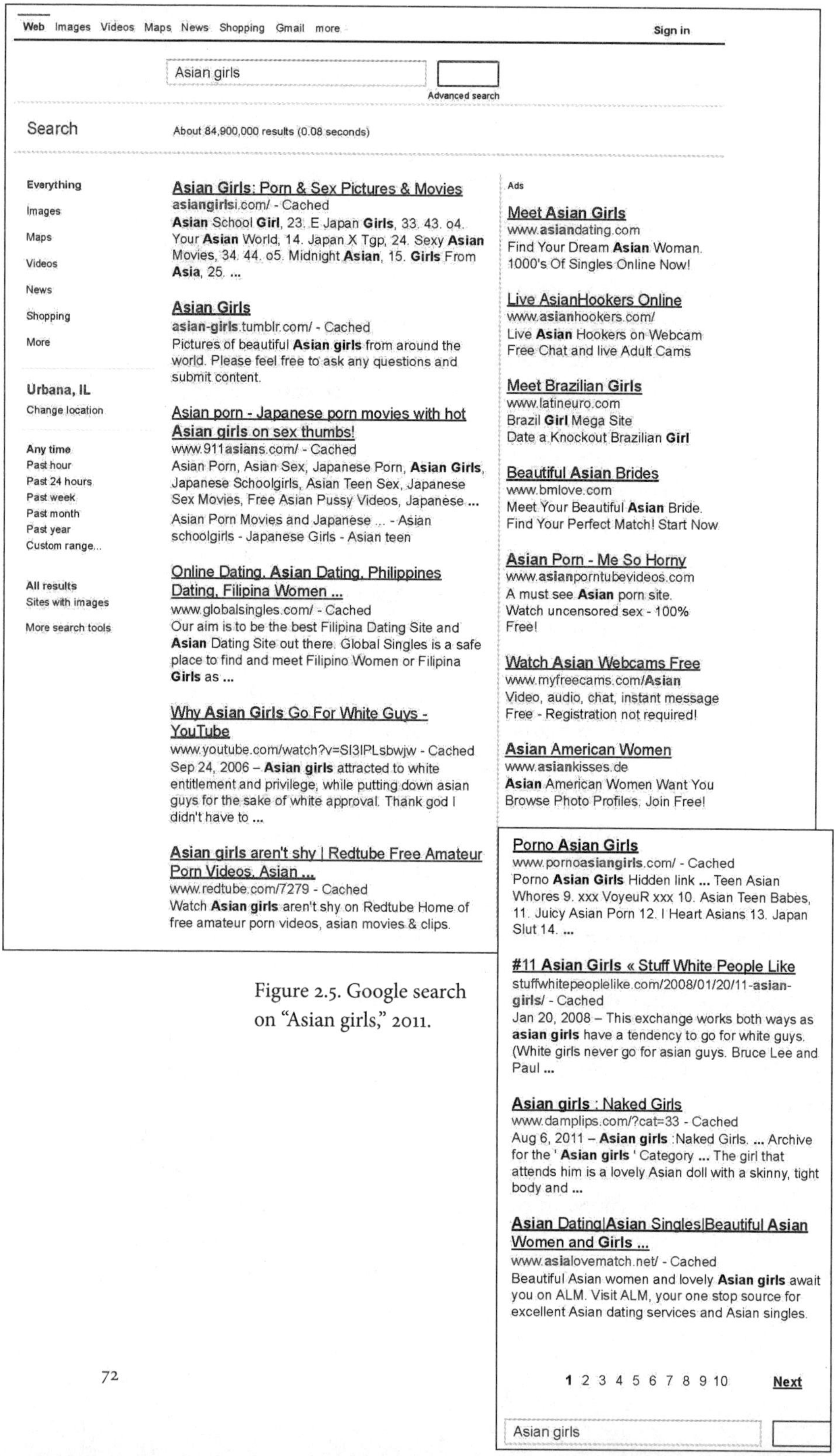
Web Images Videos Maps News Shopping Gmail more
Sign in
Asian girls
Advanced search
Search
About 84,900,000 results (0.08 seconds)
Everything
Images
Maps
Videos
News
Shopping
More
Urbana, IL
Change location
Any time
Past hour
Past 24 hours
Past week
Past month
Past year
Custom range...
All results
Sites with images
More search tools
Asian Girls: Porn & Sex Pictures & Movies
asiangirlsi.com/ - Cached
Asian School Girl, 23. E Japan Girls, 33. 43. o4. Your Asian World, 14. Japan X Tgp, 24. Sexy Asian Movies, 34. 44. o5. Midnight Asian, 15. Girls From Asia, 25. ...
Asian Girls
asian-girls.tumblr.com/ - Cached
Pictures of beautiful Asian girls from around the world. Please feel free to ask any questions and submit content.
Asian porn - Japanese porn movies with hot Asian girls on sex thumbs!
www.911asians.com/ - Cached
Asian Porn, Asian Sex, Japanese Porn, Asian Girls, Japanese Schoolgirls, Asian Teen Sex, Japanese Sex Movies, Free Asian Pussy Videos, Japanese ...
Asian Porn Movies and Japanese ... - Asian schoolgirls - Japanese Girls - Asian teen
Online Dating, Asian Dating, Philippines Dating, Filipina Women ...
www.globalsingles.com/ - Cached
Our aim is to be the best Filipina Dating Site and Asian Dating Site out there. Global Singles is a safe place to find and meet Filipino Women or Filipina Girls as ...
Why Asian Girls Go For White Guys - YouTube
www.youtube.com/watch?v=SI3IPLsbwjw - Cached
Sep 24, 2006 – Asian girls attracted to white entitlement and privilege, while putting down asian guys for the sake of white approval. Thank god I didn't have to ...
Asian girls aren't shy | Redtube Free Amateur Porn Videos, Asian ...
www.redtube.com/7279 - Cached
Watch Asian girls aren't shy on Redtube Home of free amateur porn videos, asian movies & clips.
Ads
Meet Asian Girls
www.asiandating.com
Find Your Dream Asian Woman.
1000's Of Singles Online Now!
Live AsianHookers Online
www.asianhookers.com/
Live Asian Hookers on Webcam
Free Chat and live Adult Cams
Meet Brazilian Girls
www.latineuro.com
Brazil Girl Mega Site
Date a Knockout Brazilian Girl
Beautiful Asian Brides
www.bmlove.com
Meet Your Beautiful Asian Bride.
Find Your Perfect Match! Start Now
Asian Porn - Me So Horny
www.asianporntubevideos.com
A must see Asian porn site.
Watch uncensored sex - 100% Free!
Watch Asian Webcams Free
www.myfreecams.com/Asian
Video, audio, chat, instant message
Free - Registration not required!
Asian American Women
www.asiankisses.de
Asian American Women Want You
Browse Photo Profiles. Join Free!
Porno Asian Girls
www.pornoasiangirls.com/ - Cached
Porno Asian Girls Hidden link ... Teen Asian Whores 9. xxx VoyeuR xxx 10. Asian Teen Babes, 11. Juicy Asian Porn 12. I Heart Asians 13. Japan Slut 14. ...
#11 Asian Girls « Stuff White People Like
stuffwhitepeoplelike.com/2008/01/20/11-asian-girls/ - Cached
Jan 20, 2008 – This exchange works both ways as asian girls have a tendency to go for white guys. (White girls never go for asian guys. Bruce Lee and Paul ...
Asian girls : Naked Girls
www.damplips.com/?cat=33 - Cached
Aug 6, 2011 – Asian girls :Naked Girls. ... Archive for the ' Asian girls ' Category ... The girl that attends him is a lovely Asian doll with a skinny, tight body and ...
Asian Dating|Asian Singles|Beautiful Asian Women and Girls ...
www.asialovematch.net/ - Cached
Beautiful Asian women and lovely Asian girls await you on ALM. Visit ALM, your one stop source for excellent Asian dating services and Asian singles.
1 2 3 4 5 6 7 8 9 10 Next
Asian girls

Figure 2.5. Google search on "Asian girls," 2011.

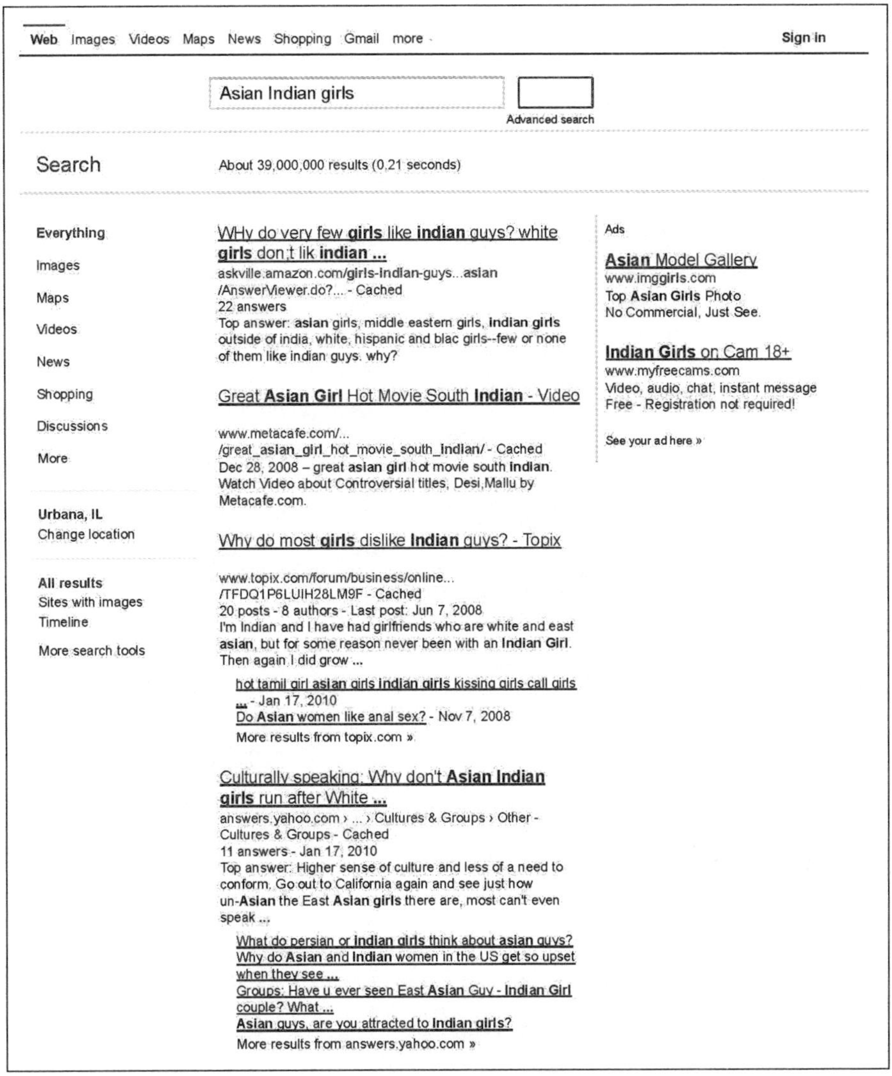

WHy do very few **girls** like **indian** guys? white
girls don;t lik **indian ...**
askville.amazon.com/girls-Indian-guys...asian
/AnswerViewer.do?... - Cached
22 answers
Top answer: asian girls, middle eastern girls, **indian girls**
outside of india, white, hispanic and blac girls--few or none
of them like indian guys. why?

Great **Asian Girl** Hot Movie South **Indian** - Video

www.metacafe.com/...
/great_asian_girl_hot_movie_south_Indian/ - Cached
Dec 28, 2008 – great **asian girl** hot movie south **indian**.
Watch Video about Controversial titles, Desi,Mallu by
Metacafe.com.

Why do most **girls** dislike **Indian** guys? - Topix

www.topix.com/forum/business/online...
/TFDQ1P6LUIH28LM9F - Cached
20 posts - 8 authors - Last post: Jun 7, 2008
I'm Indian and I have had girlfriends who are white and east
asian, but for some reason never been with an **Indian Girl**.
Then again I did grow ...

   hot tamil girl **asian girls indian girls** kissing girls call girls
   ... - Jan 17, 2010
   Do **Asian** women like anal sex? - Nov 7, 2008
   More results from topix.com »

Culturally speaking: Why don't **Asian Indian
girls** run after White **...**
answers.yahoo.com › ... › Cultures & Groups › Other -
Cultures & Groups - Cached
11 answers - Jan 17, 2010
Top answer: Higher sense of culture and less of a need to
conform. Go out to California again and see just how
un-**Asian** the East **Asian girls** there are, most can't even
speak ...

   What do persian or **indian girls** think about **asian guys?**
   Why do **Asian** and **Indian** women in the US get so upset
   when they see ...
   Groups: Have u ever seen East **Asian Guy** - **Indian Girl**
   couple? What ...
   Asian guys, are you attracted to **Indian girls?**
   More results from answers.yahoo.com »

Figure 2.6. Google search on "Asian Indian" girls in 2011.

73

Hispanic girls

Advanced search

Search

About 17,800,000 results (0.22 seconds)

Everything

Images

Maps

Videos

News

Shopping

More

Urbana, IL

Change location

All results

Sites with images

More search tools

Meet **Hispanic Girls** - **Hispanic** Dating And   Ad
Singles Site.
www.latinamericancupid.com/Dating
Browse Photos. Join Free Now!

Related searches: hispanic girls **gone wild**
mexican girls   hispanic girls **pictures**

Urban Dictionary: **hispanic girls**
www.urbandictionary.com/define.php?term=hispanic%20girls
The best **girls** there are. Them and **hispanic** women.
Because they have color, rhythm and they actually have full
figures, which means titty's and ass...

View **Hispanic Girls** - Rate Hispanic - The
Hispanic HOT or NOT site
www.ratehispanic.com/view.php?ut=1 - Cached
1 post - Last post: 17 hours ago
Email the webmaster · AIM the webmaster · Privacy Policy ·
Terms & Conditions. Pics View **Hispanic Girls** · View
Hispanic Guys · Top 50 Girls ...

°° **Hispanic/Latin Girls** -- ((100% Free
Hispanic/Latin Girls Chat)) °°
www.woome.com/people/girls/crowds/latin/ - Cached
°° **Hispanic/Latin Girls** Online // (100% Free **Hispanic/Latin**
Girls Chat) -- **Hispanic** /Latin Girl Chat Rooms, Meet a
Hispanic/Latin Girl Online Now!!

Ridiculously Hot **Hispanic Girl** Dancin' - YouTube

www.youtube.com/watch?v=iZ8KuYxljcw
4 min - Oct 23, 2007 - Uploaded by J1Goro
Amature **Hispanic Girls** Hot Butt Shakeby
DaneInJamaica6786 views; Featured Video.
Thumbnail 3:03. Add to. Ridiculously Hot
LATINA girl ...

Ask an Asian guy? Black and **Hispanic Girls**
part 2 of 2 - YouTube

www.youtube.com/watch?v=siF_WDDN6I4
8 min - Sep 15, 2007 -
Uploaded by CocoaAndMe
This video was mean as a joke. I am
obviously being facetious and absurd.
Episode 5 Do Asian guys date Black and
Hispanic girls?

More videos for **Hispanic girls** »

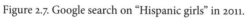

Figure 2.7. Google search on "Hispanic girls" in 2011.

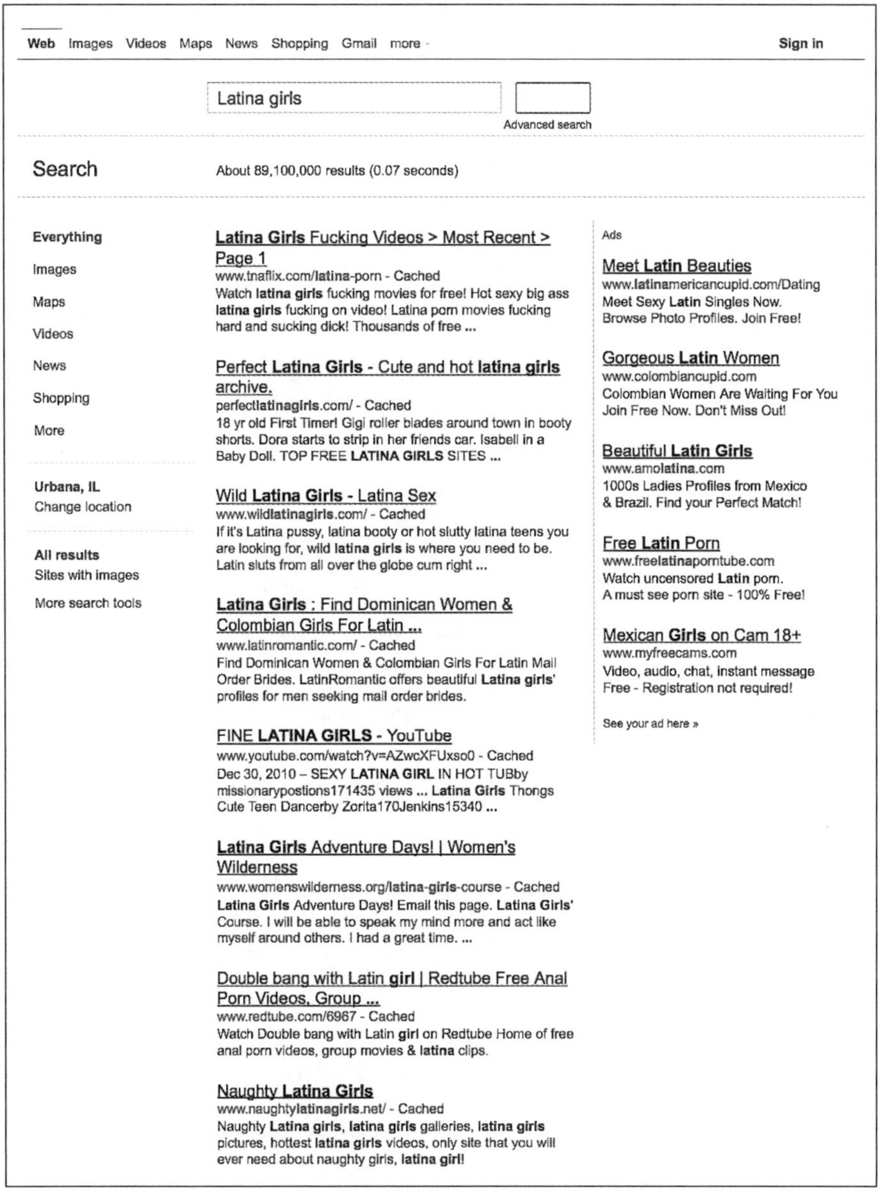

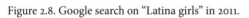

Figure 2.8. Google search on "Latina girls" in 2011.

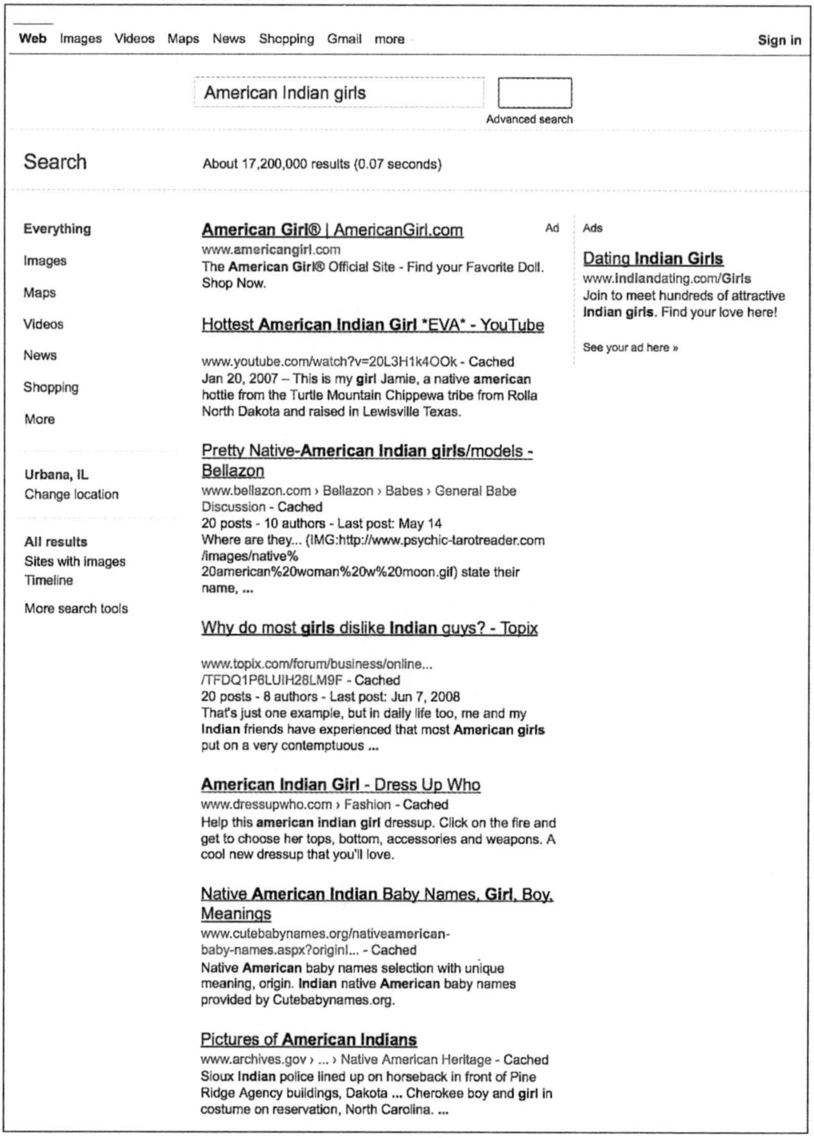
Web Images Videos Maps News Shopping Gmail more
Sign in
American Indian girls
Advanced search
Search
About 17,200,000 results (0.07 seconds)
Everything
Images
Maps
Videos
News
Shopping
More
Urbana, IL
Change location
All results
Sites with images
Timeline
More search tools
American Girl® | AmericanGirl.com
Ad
www.americangirl.com
The American Girl® Official Site - Find your Favorite Doll. Shop Now.
Hottest American Indian Girl *EVA* - YouTube
www.youtube.com/watch?v=20L3H1k4OOk - Cached
Jan 20, 2007 – This is my girl Jamie, a native american hottie from the Turtle Mountain Chippewa tribe from Rolla North Dakota and raised in Lewisville Texas.
Pretty Native-American Indian girls/models - Bellazon
www.bellazon.com › Bellazon › Babes › General Babe Discussion - Cached
20 posts - 10 authors - Last post: May 14
Where are they... (IMG:http://www.psychic-tarotreader.com/images/native%20american%20woman%20w%20moon.gif) state their name, ...
Why do most girls dislike Indian guys? - Topix
www.topix.com/forum/business/online.../TFDQ1P6LUIH28LM9F - Cached
20 posts - 8 authors - Last post: Jun 7, 2008
That's just one example, but in daily life too, me and my Indian friends have experienced that most American girls put on a very contemptuous ...
American Indian Girl - Dress Up Who
www.dressupwho.com › Fashion - Cached
Help this american indian girl dressup. Click on the fire and get to choose her tops, bottom, accessories and weapons. A cool new dressup that you'll love.
Native American Indian Baby Names, Girl, Boy, Meanings
www.cutebabynames.org/nativeamerican-baby-names.aspx?origin!... - Cached
Native American baby names selection with unique meaning, origin. Indian native American baby names provided by Cutebabynames.org.
Pictures of American Indians
www.archives.gov › ... › Native American Heritage - Cached
Sioux Indian police lined up on horseback in front of Pine Ridge Agency buildings, Dakota ... Cherokee boy and girl in costume on reservation, North Carolina. ...
Ads
Dating Indian Girls
www.indiandating.com/Girls
Join to meet hundreds of attractive Indian girls. Find your love here!
See your ad here »

Figure 2.9. Google search on "American Indian girls" in 2011.

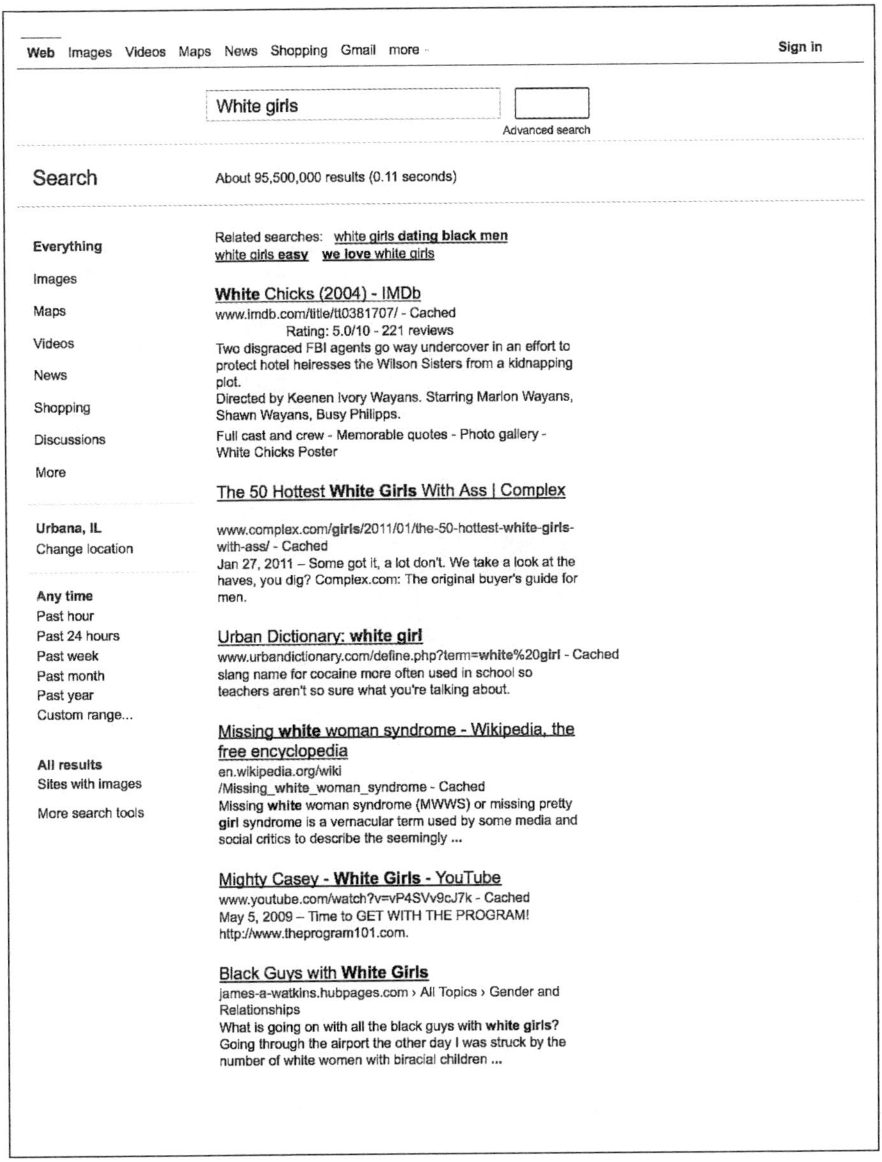
Web Images Videos Maps News Shopping Gmail more
Sign in
White girls
Advanced search
Search
About 95,500,000 results (0.11 seconds)
Everything
Images
Maps
Videos
News
Shopping
Discussions
More
Urbana, IL
Change location
Any time
Past hour
Past 24 hours
Past week
Past month
Past year
Custom range...
All results
Sites with images
More search tools
Related searches: white girls dating black men
white girls easy we love white girls
White Chicks (2004) - IMDb
www.imdb.com/title/tt0381707/ - Cached
Rating: 5.0/10 - 221 reviews
Two disgraced FBI agents go way undercover in an effort to protect hotel heiresses the Wilson Sisters from a kidnapping plot.
Directed by Keenen Ivory Wayans. Starring Marlon Wayans, Shawn Wayans, Busy Philipps.
Full cast and crew - Memorable quotes - Photo gallery - White Chicks Poster
The 50 Hottest White Girls With Ass | Complex
www.complex.com/girls/2011/01/the-50-hottest-white-girls-with-ass/ - Cached
Jan 27, 2011 – Some got it, a lot don't. We take a look at the haves, you dig? Complex.com: The original buyer's guide for men.
Urban Dictionary: white girl
www.urbandictionary.com/define.php?term=white%20girl - Cached
slang name for cocaine more often used in school so teachers aren't so sure what you're talking about.
Missing white woman syndrome - Wikipedia, the free encyclopedia
en.wikipedia.org/wiki /Missing_white_woman_syndrome - Cached
Missing white woman syndrome (MWWS) or missing pretty girl syndrome is a vernacular term used by some media and social critics to describe the seemingly ...
Mighty Casey - White Girls - YouTube
www.youtube.com/watch?v=vP4SVv9cJ7k - Cached
May 5, 2009 – Time to GET WITH THE PROGRAM! http://www.theprogram101.com.
Black Guys with White Girls
james-a-watkins.hubpages.com › All Topics › Gender and Relationships
What is going on with all the black guys with white girls? Going through the airport the other day I was struck by the number of white women with biracial children ...

Figure 2.10. Google search on “white girls” in 2011.

African-American girls

Advanced search

Search

About 59,500,000 results (0.14 seconds)

Everything

Images

Maps

Videos

News

Shopping

More

Urbana, IL
Change location

Any time
Past hour
Past 24 hours
Past week
Past 2 weeks
Past month
Past year
Custom range...

All results
Sites with images
Timeline

More search tools

American Girl® | AmericanGirl.com   Ads
www.**americangirl**.com
American Girl® - Celebrate girlhood Dolls, Outfits, Books,
Movie, More

African American Singles | eHarmony.com
www.eharmony.com/Black-Dating
Meet **African** Americans. Get Matched On 29 Dimensions of
Compatibility.

Black Girls and Modern-Day Slavery
www.theroot.com/views/**black**-**girls**-are-still-
enslaved - Cached
Apr 10, 2010 – The sexual trafficking of our young females is
happening at an alarming rate. Who will free them?

Images for African-American girls - Report images

**How Hair Affects African American Girls'
Self-Esteem**
jezebel.com/.../how-hair-affects-**african**-**american**-**girls**-
self+esteem - Cached
May 12, 2009 – Taking a cue from Chris Rock's
documentary Good Hair, today's Tyra examined how **black**
women — including little **girls** — feel about their hair, ...

[PDF] **Change It Up! Research Summary-What
African American Girls Say**
www.**girls**couts.org/research
/pdf/change_it_up_**african_american_girls**.pdf
File Format: PDF/Adobe Acrobat - Quick View
What follows is what **African American girls** are clearly
saying: We need to ... For **african american girls**, preferred
definitions of leadership imply personal ...

**How African American Girls/Women ... - What
About Our Daughters**
www.whataboutourdaughters.com/.../how-**african**-
american-**girls**women-...
How **African American Girls**/Women become freaks,
gold-diggers,. Date Monday, November 24, 2008 at 7:12AM
Author The Blogmother. We know what the ...

Figure 2.11. Google search on "African American girls" in 2011.

78

The leading thinking about race online has been organized along either theories of racial formation[6] or theories of hierarchical and structural White supremacy.[7] Scholars who study race point to the aggressive economic and social policies in the U.S. that have been organized around ideological conceptions of race as "an effort to reorganize and redistribute resources along particular racial lines."[8] Vilna Bashi Treitler, a professor of sociology and chair of the Department of Black Studies at the University of California, Santa Barbara, has written extensively about the processes of racialization that occur among ethnic groups in the United States, all of which are structured through a racial hierarchy that maintains Whiteness at the top of the social, political, and economic order. For Treitler, theories of racial formation are less salient—it does not matter whether one believes in race or not, because it is a governing paradigm that structures social logics. Race, then, is a hierarchical system of privilege and power that is meted out to people on the basis of perceived phenotype and heritage, and ethnic groups work within the already existent racial hierarchy to achieve more power, often at the expense of other ethnic groups. In Treitler's careful study of racialization, she notes that the racial binary of White versus Black is the system within which race has been codified through legislation and economic and public policy, which are designed to benefit White Americans. It is this system of affording more or less privileges to ethnic groups, including White Americans as the penultimate beneficiaries of power and privilege, that constitutes race. Ethnic groups are then "racialized" in the hierarchical system and vie for power within it. Treitler explains the social construction of race and the processes of racialization this way:

> Racial identities are obtained not because one is unaware of the choice of ethnic labels with which to call oneself, but because one is not allowed to be without a race in a racialized society. Race is a sociocultural hierarchy, and racial categories are social spaces, or positions, that are carved out of that racial hierarchy. The study of racial categories is important, because categories change labels and meanings, and we may monitor changes in the racial hierarchy by monitoring changes in the meaning and manifestations of racial categories.[9]

Treitler's work is essential to understanding that the reproduction of racial hierarchies of power online are manifestations of the same kinds of power systems that we are attempting to dismantle and intervene in—namely, eliminating discrimination and racism as fundamental organizing logics in our society. Tanya Golash-Boza, chair of sociology at the University of California, Merced, argues that critical race scholarship should expand the boundaries of simply marking where racialization and injustice occur but also must press the boundaries of public policy so that the understanding of the complex ways that marginalization is maintained can substantially shift.[10] Michael Omi and Howard Winant, two key scholars of race in the United States, distinguish the ways that racial rule has moved "from dictatorship to democracy" as a means of masking domination over racialized groups in the United States.[11] In the context of the web, we see the absolving of workplace practices such as the low level of employment of African Americans in Silicon Valley and the products that stem from it, such as algorithms that organize information for the public, not as matters of domination that persist in these realms but as democratic and fair projects, many of which mask the racism at play. Certainly, we cannot intervene if we cannot see or acknowledge these types of discriminatory practices. To help the reader see these practices, I offer here more examples of how racial algorithmic oppression works in Google Search.

On June 6, 2016, Kabir Ali, an African American teenager from Clover High School in Midlothian, Virginia, tweeting under the handle @iBeKabir, posted a video to Twitter of his Google Images search on the keywords "three black teenagers." The results that Google offered were of African American teenagers' mug shots, insinuating that the image of Black teens is that of criminality. Next, he changed one word—"black" to "white"—with very different results. "Three white teenagers" were represented as wholesome and all-American. The video went viral within forty-eight hours, and Jessica Guynn, from *USA Today*, contacted me about the story. In typical fashion, Google reported these search results as an anomaly, beyond its control, to which I responded again, "If Google isn't responsible for its algorithm, then who is?" One of Ali's Twitter followers later posted a tweak to the algorithm made by Google on a search for "three white teens" that now included a newly introduced "criminal" image of a White teen and more "wholesome" images of Black teens.

Figure 2.12. Kabir Ali's tweet about his searching for "three black teenagers" shows mug shots, 2016.

Figure 2.13. Kabir Ali's tweet about his searching for "three white teenagers" shows wholesome teens in stock photography, 2016.

What we know about Google's responses to racial stereotyping in its products is that it typically denies responsibility or intent to harm, but then it is able to "tweak" or "fix" these aberrations or "glitches" in its systems. What we need to ask is why and how we get these stereotypes in the first place and what the attendant consequences of racial and gender stereotyping do in terms of public harm for people who are the targets of such misrepresentation. Images of White Americans are persistently held up in Google's images and in its results to reinforce the superiority and mainstream acceptability of Whiteness as the default "good" to which all others are made invisible. There are many examples of this, where users of Google Search have reported online their shock or dismay at the kinds of representations that consistently occur. Some examples are shown in figures 2.14 and 2.15. Meanwhile, when users search beyond racial identities and occupations to engage concepts such as "professional hairstyles," they have been met with the kinds of images seen in figure 2.16. The "unprofessional hairstyles for work" image search, like the one for "three black teenagers," went viral in 2016, with multiple media outlets covering the story, again raising the question, can algorithms be racist?

Figure 2.14. Google Images search on "doctor" featuring men, mostly White, as the dominant representation, April 7, 2016.

Figure 2.15. Google Images search on "nurse" featuring women, mostly White, as the dominant representation, April 7, 2016.

Figure 2.16. Tweet about Google searches on "unprofessional hairstyles for work," which all feature Black women, while "professional hairstyles for work" feature White women, April 7, 2016.

Understanding technological racialization as a particular form of algorithmic oppression allows us to use it as an important framework in which to critique the discourse of the Internet as a democratic landscape and to deploy alternative thinking about the practices instantiated within commercial web search. The sociologist and media studies scholar Jessie Daniels makes a similar argument in offering a key critique of those scholars who use racial formation theory as an organizing principle for thinking about race on the web, arguing that, instead, it would be more potent and historically accurate to think about White supremacy as the dominant lens and structure through which sense-making of race online can occur. In short, Daniels argues that using racial formation theory to explain phenomena related to race online has been detrimental to our ability to parse how power online maps to oppression rooted in the history of White dominance over people of color.[12]

Often, group identity development and recognition in the United States is guided, in part, by ongoing social experiences and interactions, typically organized around race, gender, education, and other social factors that are also ideological in nature.[13] These issues are at the heart of a "politics of recognition,"[14] which is an essential form of redistributive justice for marginalized groups that have been traditionally maligned, ignored, or rendered invisible by means of disinformation on the part of the dominant culture. In this work, I am claiming that you cannot have social justice and a politics of recognition without an acknowledgment of how power—often exercised simultaneously through White supremacy and sexism—can skew the delivery of credible and representative information. Because Black communities live in material conditions that are structured physically and spatially in the context of a freedom struggle for recognition and resources, the privately controlled Internet portals that function as a public space for making sense of the distribution of resources, including identity-based information, have to be interrogated thoroughly.

In general, search engine users are doing simple searches consisting of one or more natural-language terms submitted to Google; they typically do not conduct searches in a broad or deep manner but rather with a few keywords, nor are they often looking past the first page or so of search engine results, as a general rule.[15] Search results as artifacts have symbolic and material meaning. This is true for Google, but I will revisit this idea in the conclusion in an interview with a small-business owner who uses the social network Yelp for her business and also finds herself forced from view by the algorithm. Search algorithms also function within the context of education: they are embedded in schools, libraries, and educational support technologies. They function in relationship to popular culture expressions such as "just Google it," which serves to legitimate the information and representations that are returned. Search algorithms function as an artifact of culture, akin to the ways that Cameron McCarthy describes informal and formal educational constructs:

> By emphasizing the relationality of school knowledge, one also raises the question of the ideological representation of dominant and subordinate groups in education and in the popular culture. By "representation," I refer not only to mimesis or the presence or absence of images of minorities and third-world people in textbooks; I refer also to the question of power that resides in the specific arrangement and deployment of subjectivity in the artifacts of the formal and informal culture.[16]

The Internet is an artifact, then, both as an extension of the formal educational process and as "informal culture," and thus it is a "deployment of subjectivity." This idea offers another vantage point from which to understand the ways that representation (and misrepresentation) in media are an expression of power relations. In the case of search engine results, McCarthy's analysis opens up a new way of thinking about the ways in which ideology plays a role in positioning the subjectivities of communities in dominant and subordinate ways.

This concept of informal culture embodied in media representations of popular stereotypes, of which search is an instance, is also taken up by the media scholars Jessica Davis and Oscar Gandy, Jr., who note,

> Media representations of people of color, particularly African Americans, have been implicated in historical and contemporary racial projects. Such projects use stereotypic images to influence the redistribution of resources in ways that benefit dominant groups at the expense of others. However, such projects are often typified by substantial tension between control and its opposition. Racial identity becomes salient when African American audiences oppose what they see and hear from an ideological position as harmful, unpleasant, or distasteful media representations.[17]

These tensions underscore the important dimensions of how search engines are used as a hegemonic device at the expense of some and to the benefit of dominant groups. The results of searches on "Jew," as we have already seen, are a window into this phenomenon and mark only the beginning of an important series of inquiries that need to be made about how dominant groups are able to classify and organize the representations of others, all the while neutralizing and naturalizing the agency behind such representations. My hope is that this work will increase the saliency of African American women and other women of color who want to oppose the ways in which they are collectively represented.

Google's enviable position as the monopoly leader in the provision of information has allowed its organization of information and customization to be driven by its economic imperatives and has influenced broad swaths of society to see it as the creator and keeper of information culture online, which I am arguing is another form of American imperialism that manifests itself as a "gatekeeper"[18] on the web. I make this claim on the basis of the previously detailed research of Elad Segev on the political economy of Google. The resistance to efforts by Google for furthering the international digital divide are partially predicated on the English-language and American values exported through its products to other nation-states,[19] including the Google Book Project and Google Search. Google's international position with over 770 million unique visitors across all of its properties, including YouTube, encompasses approximately half of the world's Internet users. Undoubtedly, Google/Alphabet is a broker of cultural imperialism that is arguably the most powerful expression of media dominance on the web we have yet to see.[20] It is time for the monopoly to be broken apart and for public search alternatives to be created.

How Pornification Happened to "Black Girls" in the Search Engine

Typically, webmasters and search engine marketers look for key phrases, words, and search terms that the public is most likely to use. Tools such as Google's AdWords are also used to optimize searches and page indexing on the basis of terms that have a high likelihood of being queried.

Information derived from tools such as AdWords is used to help web designers develop strategies to increase traffic to their websites. By studying search engine optimization (SEO) boards, I was able to develop an understanding of why certain terms are associated with a whole host of representational identities.

First, the pornography industry closely monitors the top searches for information or content, based on search requests across a variety of demographics. The porn industry is one of the most well-informed industries with sophisticated usage of SEO. A former SEO director for FreePorn.com has blogged extensively on how to elude Google and maximize the ability to show up in the first page of search results.[21] Many of these techniques include long-term strategies to co-opt particular terms and link them over time and in meaningful ways to pornographic content. Once these keywords are identified, then variations on these words, through what are called "long tail keywords," are created. This allows the industry to have users "self-select" for a variety of fetishes or interests. For example, the SEO board SEOMoz describes this process in the following way:

Most people use long tail keywords as an afterthought, or just assume these things will come naturally. The porn world though, actually investigates these "long tails," then expands off them. They have the unique reality of a lot of really weird people out there, who will search for specific things. Right now, according to Wordze, the most popular search featuring the word "grandma" is "grandma sex," with an estimated 16,148 searches per month. From there, there's a decent variety of long tails including things like "filipino grandma sex." For the phrase "teen sex," there are over 1000 recorded long tails that Wordze has, and in my experience, it misses a lot (it only shows things with substantial search volume). The main reason they take home as much traffic and profit at the end of the day as they do is that they actively embrace these long tail keywords, seeking them out and marketing towards them. Which brings us to reason #2. . . . When there is complete market saturation for a topic, the only way to handle it is to divide it into smaller, more easily approached niches. As stated above, they not only created sites with vague references to these things, but they targeted them specifically. If someone is ranking for a seemingly obscure phrase, it's because they went out there and created an entire site devoted to that long tail phrase.[22]

Furthermore, the U.S. dominates the number of pages of porn content, and so it exploits its ability to reach a variety of niches by linking every possible combination of words and identities (including grandmothers, as previously noted) to expand its ability to rise in the page rankings. The U.S. pornography industry is powerful and has the capital to purchase any keywords—and identities—it wants. If the U.S. has such a stronghold in supplying pornographic content, then the search for such content is deeply contextualized within a U.S.-centric framework of search terms. This provides more understanding of how a variety of words and identities that are based in the U.S. are connected in search optimization strategies, which are grounded in the development and expansion of a variety of "tails" and affiliations.

The information architect Peter Morville discusses the importance of keywords in finding what can be known in technology platforms:

> The humble keyword has become surprisingly important in recent years. As a vital ingredient in the online search process, keywords have become part of our everyday experience. We feed keywords into Google, Yahoo!, MSN, eBay, and Amazon. We search for news, products, people, used furniture, and music. And words are the key to our success.[23]

Morville also draws attention to what cannot be found, by stressing the long tail phenomenon on the web. This is the place where all forms of content that do not surface to the top of a web search are located. Many sites languish, undiscovered, in the long tail because they lack the proper website architecture, or they do not have proper metadata for web-indexing algorithms to find them—for search engines and thus for searchers, they do not exist.

Such search results are deeply problematic and are often presented without any alternatives to change them except through search refinement or changes to Google's default filtering settings, which currently are "moderate" for users who do not specifically put more filters on their results. These search engine results for women whose identities are already maligned in the media, such as Black women and girls,[24] only further debase and erode efforts for social, political, and economic recognition and justice.[25] These practices instantiate limited, negative portrayals of people of color in the media[26]—a defining and normative feature of American racism.[27] Media scholars have studied ways in which the public is directly impacted by these negative portrayals.[28] In the case of television, research shows that negative images of Blacks can adversely alter the perception of them in society.[29] Narissra M. Punyanunt-Carter, a communications scholar at Texas Tech University, has specifically researched media portrayals of African Americans' societal roles, which confirms previous studies about the effects of negative media images of Blacks on college students.[30] Thomas E. Ford found that both Blacks and Whites who view Blacks negatively on television are more likely to hold negative perceptions of them(selves).[31] Yuki Fujioka notes that in the absence of positive firsthand experience, stereotypical media portrayals of Blacks on television are highly likely to affect perceptions of the group.[32]

As we have seen, search engine design is not only a technical matter but also a political one. Search engines provide essential access to the web both to those who have something to say and offer and to those who wish to hear and find. Search is political, and at the same time, search engines can be quite helpful when one is looking for specific types of information, because the more specific and banal a search is, the more likely it is to yield the kind of information sought. For example, when one is searching for information such as phone numbers and local eateries, search engines help people easily find the nearest services, restaurants, and customer reviews (although there is more than meets the eye in these practices, which I discuss in the conclusion). Relevance is another significant factor in the development of information classification systems, from the card catalog to the modern search system or database, as systems seek to aid searchers in locating items of interest. However, the web reflects a set of commercial and advertising practices that bias particular ideas. Those industries and interests that are powerful, influential, or highly capitalized are often prioritized to the detriment of others and are able to control the bias on their terms.

Inquiries into racism and sexism on the web are not new. In many discourses of technology, the machine is turned to and positioned as a mere tool, rather than being reflective of human values.[33] Design is purposeful in that it forges both pathways and boundaries in its instrumental and cultural use.[34] Langdon Winner, Thomas Phelan Chair of Humanities and Social Sciences in the Department of Science and Technology Studies at Rensselaer Polytechnic Institute, analyzes the forms of technology, from the design of nuclear power plants, which reflect centralized, authoritarian state controls over energy, to solar power designs that facilitate independent, democratic participation by citizens. He shows that design impacts social relations at economic and political levels.[35] The more we can make transparent the political dimensions of technology, the more we might be able to intervene in the spaces where algorithms are becoming a substitute for public policy debates over resource distribution—from mortgages to insurance to educational opportunities.

Blackness in the Neoliberal Marketplace

Many people say to me, "But tech companies don't *mean* to be racist; that's not their intent." Intent is not particularly important. Outcomes and results are important. In my research, I do not look deeply at what advertisers or Google are "intending" to do. I focus on the social conditions that surround the lives of Black women living in the United States and where public information platforms contribute to the myriad conditions that make Black women's lives harder. Barney Warf and John Grimes explore the discourses of the Internet by naming the stable ideological notions of the web, which have persisted and are part of the external logic that buttresses and obscures some of the resistance to regulating the web:

> Much of the Internet's use, for commercialism, academic, and military purposes, reinforces entrenched ideologies of individualism and a definition of the self through consumption. Many uses revolve around simple entertainment, personal communication, and other ostensibly apolitical purposes . . . particularly advertising and shopping but also purchasing and marketing, in addition to uses by public agencies that legitimate and sustain existing ideologies and politics as "normal," "necessary," or "natural." Because most users view themselves, and their uses of the Net, as apolitical, hegemonic discourses tend to be reproduced unintentionally. . . . Whatever blatant perspectives mired in racism, sexism, or other equally unpalatable ideologies pervade society at large, they are carried into, and reproduced within, cyberspace.[36]

André Brock, a communications professor at the University of Michigan, adds that "the rhetorical narrative of 'Whiteness as normality' configures information technologies and software designs" and is reproduced through digital technologies. Brock characterizes these transgressive practices that couple technology design and practice with racial ideologies this way:

> I contend that the Western internet, as a social structure, represents and maintains White, masculine, bourgeois, heterosexual and Christian culture through its content. These ideologies are translucently mediated by the browser's design and concomitant information practices. English-speaking internet users, content providers, policy makers, and designers bring their racial frames to their internet experiences, interpreting racial dynamics through this electronic medium while simultaneously redistributing cultural resources along racial lines. These practices neatly recreate social dynamics online that mirror offline patterns of racial interaction by marginalizing women and people of color.[37]

What Brock points to is the way in which discourses about technology are explicitly linked to racial and gender identity—normalizing Whiteness and maleness in the domain of digital technology and as a presupposition for the prioritization of resources, content, and even design of information and communications technologies (ICTs).

Search engine optimization strategies and budgets are rapidly increasing to sustain the momentum and status of websites in Google Search. David Harvey, a professor of anthropology and geography at the Graduate Center of the City University of New York, and Norman Fairclough, an emeritus professor of linguistics at Lancaster University, point to the ways that the political project of neoliberalism has created new conditions and demands on social relations in order to open new markets.[38] I assert that this has negative consequences for maintaining and expanding social, political, and economic organization around common identity-based interests—interests not solely based on race and gender, although these are stable categories through which we can understand disparity and inequality. These trends in the unequal distribution of wealth and resources have contributed to a closure of public debate and a weakening of democracy. Both Harvey and Fairclough separately note the importance of the impact of what they call "new capitalism," a concept closely linked to the "informationalized capitalism" of Dan Schiller, retired professor from the University of Illinois at Urbana-Champaign, when viewed in the context of new media and the information age. What is important about new capitalism in the context of the web is that it is radically transforming previously public territories and spaces.[39] This expansion of capitalism into the web has been a significant part of the neoliberal justification for the commodification of information and identity. Identity markers are for sale in the commodified web to the highest bidder, as this research about keyword markers shows. It is critical that we engage with the ways that social relations are being transformed by new distributions of resources and responsibilities away from the public toward the private. For example, the hyperreliance on digital technologies has radically impacted the environment and global labor flows. Control over community identities are shifting as private companies on the web are able to manage and control definitions, and the very concept of community control on the web is increasingly becoming negligible as infusions of private capital into the infrastructure of the Internet has moved the U.S.-based web from a state-funded project to an increasingly privately controlled, neoliberal communication sphere.

Black Girls as Commodity Object

Part of the socialization of Black women as sexual object is derived from historical constructions of African women living under systems of enslavement and economic dependency and exploitation—systems that included the normalization of rape and conquest of Black bodies and the invention of fictions about Black women.[40] The constitution of rape culture, formed during the enslavement of Africans in the Americas, is at the intersection of patriarchy, slavery, and violence.[41] bell hooks's canonical essay "Selling Hot Pussy" in *Black Looks: Race and Representation* turned a Black feminist theoretical tradition toward the marketplace of culture, ideas, and representations of Black women. Her work details the ways in which Black women's bodies have been commodified and how these practices are normalized in everyday experiences in the cultural marketplace of our society.[42] Women's bodies serve as the site of sexual exploitation and representation under patriarchy, but Black women serve as the deviant of sexuality when mapped in opposition to White women's bodies.[43] It is in this tradition, then, coupled with an understanding of how racial and gender identities are brokered by Google, that we can help make sense of the trends that make women's and girls' sexualized bodies a lucrative marketplace on the web.

For Black women, rape has flourished under models of colonization or enslavement and what Joseph C. Dorsey, a professor of African American studies at Purdue University, calls "radically segmented social structures."[44] Rape culture is formed by key elements that include asserting male violence as natural, not making sexual violence illegal or criminally punishable, and differential legal consideration for victims and perpetrators of sexual violence on the basis of their race, gender, or class. Rape culture also fosters the notion that straight/heterosexual sex acts are commonly linked to violence.[45] I argue that these segmented social structures persist at a historical moment when Black women and children are part of the permanent underclass and represent the greatest proportion of citizens living in poverty.[46] The relative poverty rate in the United States—the distance between those who live in poverty and those at the highest income levels—is greatest between Black women and children and White men. Among either single or married households, the poverty rate of Blacks is nearly twice that of Whites.[47] Black people are three times more likely to live in poverty than Whites are, with 27.4% of Black people living below the poverty line, compared to 9.9% of Whites.[48] The status of women remains precarious across all social segments: 47.1% of all families headed by women, without the income, status, and resources of men, are living in poverty. In fact, Black and White income gaps have increased since 1974, after the gains of the civil rights movement. In 2004, Black families earned 58% of what White families earned, a significant decrease from 1974, when Black families earned 63% of what Whites earned.[49]

The feminist scholar Gilda Lerner has written the canonical documentary work on Black and White women in the United States. Her legacy is a significant contribution to understanding the racialized and gendered dynamics of patriarchy and how it serves to keep women subordinate. One of many conditions of a racialized and gendered social structure in the United States, among other aspects of social oppression, is the way in which Black women and girls are systemically disenfran-chised. Patriarchy, racism, and rape culture are part of the confluence of social practices that normalize Black women and girls as a sexual com-modity, an alienated and angry/pathetic other, or a subservient caretaker and helpmate to White psychosocial desires. Lerner points to the con-sequences of adopting the hegemonic narratives of women, particularly those made normative by the "symbol systems" of a society:

> Where there is no precedent, one cannot imagine alternatives to exist-ing conditions. It is this feature of male hegemony which has been most damaging to women and has ensured their subordinate status for mil-lennia. . . . The picture is false . . . as we now know, but women's progress through history has been marked by their struggle against this disabling distortion.[50]

Making sense of alternative identity constructions can be a tenuous pro-cess for women due to the erasures of other views of the past, according to Lerner. Meanwhile, the potency of commercial search using Google is that it functions as the dominant "symbol system" of society due to its prominence as the most popular search engine to date.[51]

Historical Categorizations of Racial Identity: Old Traditions Never Die

European fascination with African sexuality is well researched and heavily contested—most famously noted in the public displays of Sara Baartman, otherwise mocked as "The Venus Hottentot," a woman from South Africa who was often placed on display for entertainment and biological evidence of racial difference and subordination of African people.[52] Of course, this is a troubling aspect of museum practice that often participated in the curation and display of non-White bodies for European and White public consumption. The spectacles of zoos, cir-cuses, and world's fairs and expositions are important sites that predate the Internet by more than a century, but it can be argued and is in fact argued here that these traditions of displaying native bodies extend to the information age and are replicated in a host of problematic ways in the indexing, organization, and classification of information about Black and Brown bodies—especially on the commercial web.

Western scientific and anthropological quests for new discoveries have played a pivotal role in the development of racialization schemes, and scientific progress has often been the basis of justifying the mistreatment of Black women—including displays of Baartman during her life (and after). From these practices, stereotypes can be derived that focus on biological, genetic, and medical homogeneity.[53] Scientific classifications have played an important role in the development of racialization that persists into contemporary times:

> Historically created racial categories often carry hidden meanings. Until 2003 medical reports were cataloged in PubMed/MEDLINE and in the old Surgeon General's Index Catalogue using 19th century racial categories such as Caucasoid, Mongoloid, Negroid and Australoid. Originally suggesting a scale of inferiority and superiority, today such groupings continue to connote notions of human hierarchy. More importantly, PubMed's newer categories, such as continental population group and ancestry group, merely overlay the older ones.[54]

Inventions of racial categories are mutable and historically specific, such as the term "mulattoes" as a scientific categorization against which information could be collected to prove that "hybrid" people were biologically predisposed to "die out," and of course these categories are not stable across national boundaries; classifications such as "Colored," "Black," and "White" have been part of racial purification processes in countries such as South Africa.[55] Gender categorizations are no less problematic and paradoxical. Feminist scholars point to the ways that, at the same time that women reject biological classifications as essentializing features of sex discrimination, they are simultaneously forced to organize for political and economic resources and progress on the basis of gender.[56]

These conceptions and stereotypes do not live in the past; they are part of our present, and they are global in scope. In April 2012, Lena Adelsohn Liljeroth, the culture minister of Sweden, was part of a grotesque event to celebrate Sweden's World Art Day. The event included

Figure 2.17. Google search for Sara Baartman, in preparation for a lecture on Black women in film, January 22, 2013.

an art installation to bring global attention to the issue of female genital mutilation. However, to make the point, the artist Makode Aj Linde made a cake ripped straight from the headlines of White-supremacist debasement of Black women. Dressed in blackface, he adorned the top of a cake he made that was a provocative art experiment gone wrong, at the expense of Black women. These images are just one of many that make up the landscape of racist misogyny. After an outpouring of international disgust, Liljeroth denied any possibility that the project, and her participation, could be racist in tone or presentation.[57]

During slavery, stereotypes were used to justify the sexual victimization of Black women by their property owners, given that under the law, Black women were property and therefore could not be considered victims of rape. Manufacture of the Jezebel stereotype served an important role in portraying Black women as sexually insatiable and gratuitous. A valuable resource for understanding the complexity and problematic of racist and sexist narratives is the Jim Crow Museum of Racist Memorabilia at Ferris State University. The museum's work documents all of the informative and canonical writings about the ways that Black people have been misrepresented in the media and in popular culture as a means of subjugation, predating slavery in North America in the eighteenth century. It highlights the two main narratives that have con-

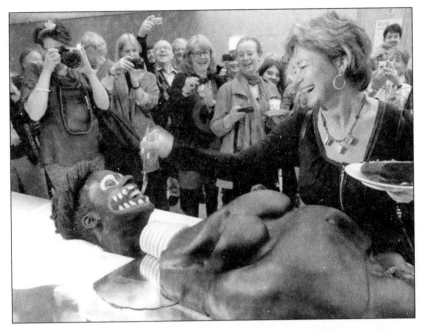

Figure 2.18. Lena Adelsohn Liljeroth, Swedish minister of culture, feeds cake to the artist Makode Aj Linde in blackface, at the Moderna Museet in Stockholm, 2012.

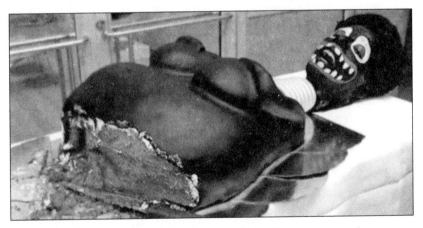

Figure 2.19. Makode Aj Linde's performance art piece at Moderna Museet. Source: www.forharriet.com, 2012.

tinued to besiege Black women: the exotic other, the Jezebel whore; and the pathetic other, the Mammy.[58] Notably, the pathetic other is too ugly, too stupid, and too different to elicit sexual attraction from reasonable men; instead, she is a source of pity, laughter, and derision. For example, the museum notes how seventeenth-century White European travelers to Africa found seminude people and indigenous practices and customs and misinterpreted various cultures as lewd, barbaric, and less than human, certainly a general sign of their own xenophobia.[59]

Researchers at the Jim Crow Museum have conducted an analysis of Jezebel images and found that Black female children are often sexually objectified as well, a fact that validates this deeper look at representations of Black girls on the web. During the Jim Crow era, for example, Black girls were caricatured with the faces of preteenagers and were depicted with adult-sized, exposed buttocks and framed with sexual innuendos. This stereotype evolved, and by the 1970s, portrayals of Black people as mammies, toms, tragic mulattoes, and picaninnies in traditional media began to wane as new notions of Black people as Brutes and Bucks emerged; meanwhile, the beloved creation of the White imagination, the Jezebel, persists. The Jezebel has become a mainstay and an enduring image in U.S. media. In 2017, these depictions are a staple of the 24/7 media cycles of Black Entertainment Television (BET), VH1, MTV, and across the spectrum of cable television. Jezebel is now known as the video vixen, the "ho," the "around the way girl," the porn star—and she remains an important part of the spectacle that justifies the second-class citizenship of Black women.[60] "Black women" searches offer sites on "angry Black women" and articles on "why Black women are less attractive." These narratives of the exotic or pathetic Black woman, rooted in psychologically damaging stereotypes of the Jezebel,[61] Sapphire, and Mammy,[62] only exacerbate the pornographic imagery that represents Black girls, who are largely presented in one of these ways. The largest commercial search engine fails to provide culturally situated knowledge on how Black women and girls have traditionally been discriminated against, denied rights, or violated in society and the media even though they have organized and resisted on many levels.

Figure 2.20. One dominant narrative stereotype of Black women, the Jezebel Whore, depicted here over more than one hundred years of cultural artifacts. Source: Jim Crow Museum of Racist Memorabilia at Ferris State University, www.ferris.edu.

Reading the Pornographic Representation

This study highlights misrepresentation in Google Search as a detailed example of the power of algorithms in controlling the image, concepts, and values assigned to people, by featuring a detailed look at Black girls. I do not intend to comprehensively evaluate the vast range of representations and cultural production that exists on the Internet for Black women and girls, some portion of which indeed reflects individual agency in self-representation (e.g., selfie culture). However, the nature of representation in commercial search as primarily pornographic for Black women is a distinct form of sexual representation that is commercialized by Google. Pornography is a specific type of representation that denotes male power, female powerlessness, and sexual violence. These pornographic representations of women and people of color have been problematized by many scholars in the context of mass media.[63] Rather than offer relief, the rise of the Internet has brought with it ever more commodified, fragmented, and easily accessed pornographic depictions that are racialized.[64] In short, biased traditional media processes are being replicated, if not more aggressively, around problematic representations in search engines. Here, I am equally focused on "the pornography of representation,"[65] which is less about moral obscenity arguments about women's sexuality and more about a feminist critique of how women are represented as pornographic objects:

> Representations are not just a matter of mirrors, reflections, key-holes. Somebody is making them, and somebody is looking at them, through a complex array of means and conventions. Nor do representations simply exist on canvas, in books, on photographic paper or on screens: they have a continued existence in reality as objects of exchange; they have a genesis in material production.[66]

Some people argue that pornography has been understudied given its commercial viability and persistence.[67] Certainly, the technical needs of the pornography industry have contributed to many developments on the web, including the credit card payment protocol; advertising and promotion; video, audio, and streaming technologies.[68]

In library studies, discussions of the filtering of pornographic content out of public libraries and schools are mainstream professional discourse.[69] Tremendous focus on pornography as a legitimate information resource (or not) to be filtered out of schools, public libraries, and the reach of children has been a driving element of the discussions about the role of regulation of the Internet.

Black feminist scholars are also increasingly looking at how Black women are portrayed in the media across a host of stereotypes, including pornography. Jennifer C. Nash, an associate professor of African American studies and gender and sexuality studies at Northwestern University, foregrounds the complexities of theorizing Black women and pornography in ways that are helpful to this research:

> Both scholarly traditions pose the perennial question "is pornography racist," and answer that question in the affirmative by drawing connections between Baartman's exhibition and the contemporary display of

black women in pornography. However, merely affirming pornography's alleged racism neglects an examination of the ways that pornography mobilizes race in particular social moments, under particular techno-logical conditions, to produce a historically contingent set of racialized meanings and profits.[70]

Nash focuses on the ways in which Black feminists have aligned with antipornography rhetoric and scholarship. While my own project is not a specific study of the nuances of Black women's agency in net porn, the Black feminist media scholar Mireille Miller-Young has covered in detail the virtues and problematics of pornography.[71] This research is helpful in explaining how women are displayed as pornographic search results. I therefore integrate Nash's expanded views about racial iconography into a Black feminist framework to help interpret and evaluate the results.

In the field of Internet and media studies, the research interest and concern of scholars about harm in imagery and content online has been framed mostly around the social and technical aspects of addressing Internet pornography but less so around the existence of commercial porn:

> The relative invisibility of commercial pornography in the field has more to do with cultural hierarchies and questions of taste: as a popular genre, pornography has considerably low cultural status as that which, accord-ing to various US court decisions, lacks in social, cultural, or artistic value. Furthermore, the relatively sparse attention to porn is telling of an attachment to representations and exchanges considered novel over more familiar and predictable ones.[72]

As such, Black women and girls are both understudied by scholars and also associated with "low culture" forms of representation.[73] There is a robust political economy of pornography, which is an important site of commerce and technological innovation that includes file-sharing networks, video streaming, e-commerce and payment processing, data compression, search, and transmission.[74] The antipornography activist and scholar Gail Dines discusses this web of relations that she character-izes as stretching "from the backstreet to Wall Street":

Porn is embedded in an increasingly complex and extensive value chain, linking not just producers and distributors but also bankers, software, hotel chains, cell phone and Internet companies. Like other businesses, porn is subject to the discipline of capital markets and competition, with trends toward market segmentation and industry concentration.[75]

Dines's research particularly underscores the ways in which Black women are more racialized and stereotyped in pornography—explicitly playing off the media misrepresentations of the past and leveraging the notion of the Black woman as "ho" through the most graphic types of porn in the genre.

Miller-Young underscores the fetishization of Black women that has created new markets for porn, explicitly linking the racialization of Black women in the genre:

Within this context of the creation and management of racialized desire as both transgressive and policed, pornography has excelled at the production, marketing, and dissemination of categories of difference as special subgenres and fetishes in a form of "racialized political theater." Empowered by technological innovations such as video, camcorders, cable, satellite, digital broadband, CD-ROMs, DVDs, and the internet, the pornography business has exploited new media technology in the creation of a range of specialized sexual commodities that are consumed in the privacy of the home.[76]

hooks details the ways that Black women's representations are often pornified by White, patriarchally controlled media and that, while some women are able to resist and struggle against these violent depictions of Black women, others co-opt these exploitative vehicles and expand upon them as a site of personal profit: "Facing herself, the black female realizes all that she must struggle against to achieve self-actualization. She must counter the representation of herself, her body, her being as expendable."[77] Miller's research on the political economy of pornography, bolstered by the hip-hop music industry, is important to understanding how Black women are commodified through the "'pornification' of hip-hop and the mainstreaming and 'diversification' of pornography."[78]

Figure 2.21. Google video search results on "black girls," June 22, 2016.

Although Google changed its algorithm in late summer 2012 and suppressed pornography as the primary representation of Black girls in its search results, by 2016, it had also modified the algorithm to include more diverse and less sexualized images of Black girls in its image search results, although most of the images are of women and not of children or teenagers (girls). However, the images of Black girls remain troubling in Google's video search results, with narratives that mostly reflect user-generated content (UGC) that engages in comedic portrayals of a range stereotypes about Black / African American girls. Notably, the White nationalist Colin Flaherty's work, which the Southern Poverty Law Center has described as propaganda to incite racial violence and White anxiety, is the producer of the third-ranked video to represent Black girls.

Porn on the Internet is an expansion of neoliberal capitalist interests. The web itself has opened up new centers of profit and pushed the boundaries of consumption. Never before have there been so many points for the transmission and consumption of these representations of Black women's bodies, largely trafficked outside the control and benefit of Black women and girls themselves.

Providing Legitimate Information about Black Women and Girls

Seeing the Internet as a common medium implies that there may be an expectation of increased legitimacy of information to be found there.[79] Recognizing the credibility of online information is no small task because commercial interests are not always apparent,[80] and typical measures of credibility are seldom feasible due to the complexity of the web.[81] If the government, industry, schools, hospitals, and public agencies are driving users to the Internet as a means of providing services, then this confers a level of authority and trust in the medium itself. This raises questions about who owns identity and identity markers in cyberspace and whether racialized and gendered identities are ownable property rights that can be contested. One can argue, as I do, that social identity is both a process of individual actors participating in the creation of identity and also a matter of social categorization that happens at a socio-structural level and as a matter of personal definition and external definition.[82]

According to Mary Herring, Thomas Jankowski, and Ronald Brown, Black identity is defined by an individual's experience of common fate with others in the same group.[83] The question of specific property rights to naming and owning content in cyberspace is an important topic.[84] Racial markers are a social categorization that is both imposed and adopted by groups,[85] and thus racial identity terms could be claimed as the property of such groups, much the way Whiteness has been constituted as a property right for those who possess it.[86] This is a way of thinking about how mass media have co-opted the external definitions of identity[87]—racialization—which also applies to the Internet and its provision of information to the public: "Our relationships with the mass media are at least partly determined by the perceived utility of the information we gather from them. . . . Media representations play an important role in informing the ways in which we understand social, cultural, ethnic, and racial difference."[88] Media have a tremendous impact on informing our understandings of race and racialized others as an externality, but this is a symbiotic process that includes internal definitions that allow people to lay claim to racial identity.[89] In addition, the Internet and its landscape offer up and eclipse traditional media distribution channels and serve as a new infrastructure for delivering all forms of prior media: television, film, and radio, as well as new media that are more social and interactive. Taking these old and new media together, it can be argued that the Internet has significant influence on forming opinions on race and gender.

What We Find Is Meaningful

Because most of Google's revenue is derived from advertising, it is important to consider advertising as a media practice with tremendous power in shaping culture and society.[90] The transmission of stereotypes about women in advertising creates a "limited 'vocabulary of intention,'" encouraging people to think and speak of women primarily in terms of their relationship to men, family, or their sexuality.[91] Research shows how stereotypical depictions of women and minorities in advertising impact the behavior of those who consume it.[92] Therefore, it is necessary to cast a deeper look into the effects of the content and trace the kinds of hegemonic narratives that situate these results.

The feminist media scholar Jean Kilbourne has carefully traced the impact of advertising on society from a feminist perspective. She researches the addictive quality of advertising and its ability to cause feelings and change perspectives, regardless of a consumer's belief that he or she is "tuning out" or ignoring the persuasiveness of the medium:

> Advertising corrupts relationships and then offers us products, both as solace and as substitutes for the intimate human connection we all long for and need. Most of us know by now that advertising often turns people into objects. Women's bodies, and men's bodies too these days, are dismembered, packaged, and used to sell everything from chain saws to chewing gum. But many people do not fully realize that there are terrible consequences when people become things. Self-image is deeply affected. The self-esteem of girls plummets as they reach adolescence, partly because they cannot possibly escape the message that their bodies are objects, and imperfect objects at that. Boys learn that masculinity requires a kind of ruthlessness, even brutality. Violence becomes inevitable.[93]

In the case of Google, its purpose is to "pull eyeballs" toward products and services, as evidenced in its products such as AdWords and the ways in which it has already been proven to bias its own properties over its competitors. This complicates the way to think about search engines and reinforces the need for significant degrees of digital literacy for the public.

Using a Black feminist lens in critical information studies entails contextualizing information as a form of representation, or cultural production, rather than as seemingly neutral and benign data that is thought of as a "website" or "URL" that surfaces to the top in a search. The language and terminologies used to describe results on the Internet in commercial search engines often obscure the fact that commodified forms of representation are being transacted on the web and that these commercial transactions are not random or without meaning as simply popular websites. Annette Kuhn, an emeritus professor of film studies at Queen Mary University of London, challenges feminist thinkers to interrogate gender, race, and representation in her book *The Power of the Image: Essays on Representation and Sexuality*:

> In order to challenge dominant representations, it is necessary first of all to understand how they work, and thus where to seek points of possible

productive transformation. From such understanding flow various politics and practices of oppositional cultural production, among which may be counted feminist interventions. . . . There is another justification for a feminist analysis of mainstream images of women: may it not teach us to recognize inconsistencies and contradictions within dominant traditions of representation, to identify points of leverage for our own intervention: cracks and fissures through which may be captured glimpses of what in other circumstances might be possible, visions of "a world outside the order not normally seen or thought about"?[94]

In this chapter, I have shown how women, particularly Black women, are misrepresented on the Internet in search results and how this is tied to a longer legacy of White racial patriarchy. The Internet has also been a contested space where the possibility of organizing women along feminist values in cyberspace has had a long history.[95] Information and communication technologies are posited as the domain of men, not only marginalizing the contributions of women to ICT development but using these narratives to further instantiate patriarchy.[96] Men, intending to or not, have used their control and monopoly over the domain of technology to further consolidate their social, political, and economic power in society and rarely give up these privileges to create structural shifts in these inheritances. Where men shape technology, they shape it to the exclusion of women, especially Black women.[97]

The work of the feminist scholars Judy Wajcman and Anna Everett is essential to parsing the historical development of narratives about women and people of color, specifically African Americans in technology. Each of their projects points to the specific ways in which technological practices prioritize the interests of men and Whites. For Wajcman, "people and artifacts co-evolve, reminding us that 'things could be otherwise,' that technologies are not the inevitable result of the application of scientific and technological knowledge. . . . The capacity of women users to produce new, advantageous readings of artefacts is dependent upon the broader economic and social circumstances."[98] Adding to the historical tracings that Everett provides about early African American contributions to cyberspace, she notes that these contributions have been obscured by "colorblindness" in mainstream and scholarly media that erases the contributions of African Americans.[99] Institutional relations predicated on gender and race situate women and people of color outside the power systems from which technology arises. This is how colorblind ideology is mechanized in Silicon Valley: through denial of the existence of both racial orders and contributions from non-Whites.

This fantasy of postracialism has been well documented by Jessie Daniels, who has written about the problems of colorblind racism in tech industries.[100] This tradition of defining White and Asian male dominance in the tech industries as a matter of meritocracy is buttressed by myths of Asian Americans as a model minority. The marginalization of women and non-Whites is a by-product of such entrenchments, design choices, and narratives about technical capabilities.[101] Rayvon Fouché, the American studies chair at Purdue University, underscores the importance of Black culture in shaping the technological systems. He argues that technologies could "be more responsive to the realities of black life in the United States" by organizing around the sensibilities of the Black community. Furthermore, he problematizes the dominant narratives of technology "for" Black people:

> Americans are continually bombarded with seemingly endless self-regenerating progressive technological narratives. In this capitalist-supported tradition, the multiple effects that technology has on African American lives go underexamined. This uplifting rhetoric has helped obfuscate the distinctly adversarial relationships African Americans have had with technology.[102]

In this work on the politics of search engines and their representations of women and girls of color, I have documented how certain searches on keywords point information seekers to an abundance of pornography using the default "moderate" setting in Google Search, and I have offered more examples of how Silicon Valley defends itself by continuing to underemploy people who have expertise in these important fields of ethnic and gender studies. The value of this exploration is in showing how gender and race are socially constructed and mutually constituted through science and technology. The very notion that technologies are neutral must be directly challenged as a misnomer.

Whether or not one cares about the specific misrepresentations of women and girls of color or finds the conceptual representations of teenagers, professors, nurses, or doctors problematic, there is certain evidence that the way that digital media platforms and algorithms control the narrative about people can have dire consequences when taken to the extreme.

Searching for People and Communities $\qquad$ Q

On the evening of June 17, 2015, in Charleston, South Carolina, a twenty-one-year-old White nationalist, Dylann "Storm" Roof, opened fire on unsuspecting African American Christian worshipers at "Mother" Emanuel African Methodist Episcopal Church in one of the most heinous racial and religious hate crimes of recent memory.[1] His racist terrorist attack led to the deaths of South Carolina state senator Rev. Clementa Pinckney, who was also the pastor of the church, along with librarian Cynthia Hurd, Tywanza Sanders, Rev. Sharonda Singleton, Myra Thompson, Ethel Lance, Susie Jackson, Rev. Daniel Simmons Sr., and Rev. DePayne Middleton Doctor. There were three survivors of the attack, Felecia Sanders, her eleven-year-old granddaughter, and Polly Sheppard. The location of the murders was not chosen in vain by Roof; Emanuel AME stood as one of the oldest symbols of African American freedom in the United States. It was organized by free and enslaved Black/African people in 1791, with its membership growing into the thousands, only to be burned down in 1822 by White South Carolinians who heard that the church member Denmark Vessey was leading an effort to organize enslaved Blacks to revolt against their slave masters. For over two hundred years, Emanuel AME has been a site and symbol of a struggle for freedom from White supremacy and a place where organizing for civil rights and full participation of African Americans has been foregrounded by its members and supporters from across the country.

The massacre was a tragedy of epic proportions. Reports of the racist-motivated murders came on the heels of many months and years of news reports about hundreds of African Americans murdered by police officers, security guards, and self-appointed neighborhood watchmen. As news of the massacre hit social media sites, a Twitter user by the name of @HenryKrinkIe tweeted that a "racist manifesto" had been found at www.lastrhodesian.com, which documented the many thoughts informing the killer's understanding of race relations in the U.S. The first responder to a tweeted request for forty-nine dollars to access the site was @EMQuangel, who offered to pay for the "Reverse WhoIs" database report in order to verify that the site did in fact belong to Dylann Roof. Within a few hours, several news outlets began reporting on Roof's many writings at the website, where he allegedly shared the following:

> The event that truly awakened me was the Trayvon Martin case. I kept hearing and seeing his name, and eventually I decided to look him up. I read the Wikipedia article and right away I was unable to understand what the big deal was. It was obvious that Zimmerman was in the right. But more importantly this prompted me to type in the words "black on White crime" into Google, and I have never been the same since that day. The first website I came to was the Council of Conservative Citizens. There were pages upon pages of these brutal black on White murders. I was in disbelief. At this moment I realized that something was very wrong. How could the news be blowing up the Trayvon Martin case while hundreds of these black on White murders got ignored?
>
> From this point I researched deeper and found out what was happening in Europe. I saw that the same things were happening in England and France, and in all the other Western European countries. Again I found myself in disbelief. As an American we are taught to accept living in the melting pot, and black and other minorities have just as much right to be here as we do, since we are all immigrants. But Europe is the homeland of White people, and in many ways the situation is even worse there. From here I found out about the Jewish problem and other issues facing our race, and I can say today that I am completely racially aware.[2]

According to the manifesto, Roof allegedly typed "black on White crime" in a Google search to make sense of the news reporting on Trayvon Martin, a young African American teenager who was killed and whose killer, George Zimmerman, was acquitted of murder. What Roof found was information that confirmed a patently false notion that Black violence on White Americans is an American crisis.

Roof reportedly reached the Council of Conservative Citizens (CCC) when he searched Google for real information that would help him make sense of the high-profile Martin case. For Roof, CCC was a legitimate information resource purporting to be a conservative news media organization. Yet the foremost national authority on hate organizations, the Southern Poverty Law Center, tracks and describes the CCC this way:

> The Council of Conservative Citizens (CCC) is the modern reincarnation of the old White Citizens Councils, which were formed in the 1950s and 1960s to battle school desegregation in the South. Among other things, its Statement of Principles says that it "oppose[s] all efforts to mix the races of mankind." Created in 1985 from the mailing lists of its predecessor organization, the CCC, which initially tried to project a "mainstream" image, has evolved into a crudely white supremacist group whose website has run pictures comparing the late pop singer Michael Jackson to an ape and referred to black people as "a retrograde species of humanity." The group's newspaper, Citizens Informer, regularly publishes articles condemning "race mixing," decrying the evils of illegal immigration, and lamenting the decline of white, European civilization. Gordon Baum, the group's founder, died in March of 2015.[3]

To verify what might be possible to find in the post–Dylann Roof murders of nine African Americans, I too conducted a search of the term "black on white crimes." In these search scenarios from August 3 and 5, 2015, in Los Angeles, California, and Madison, Wisconsin, NewNation. org was the first result, followed by a number of conservative, White-nationalist websites that foster hate toward African Americans and Jewish people. I conducted the searches in similar fashion to searching for "black girls" and other girls of color, signed out of all platforms, and I cross-verified the search results (figure 3.2) with another researcher on a different computer. NewNation.org's website promoted so much anti-Black racist hatred that in 2013, its founder was the subject of a distributed denial of service (DDOS) attack by @Anon_Dox_323, a member of the hacker group Anonymous, which often targets individuals and organizations through a variety of "hacktivist" online takedowns, as seen in figure 3.3.[4]

What is compelling about the alleged information that Roof accessed is how his search terms did not lead him to Federal Bureau of Investigation (FBI) crime statistics on violence in the United States, which

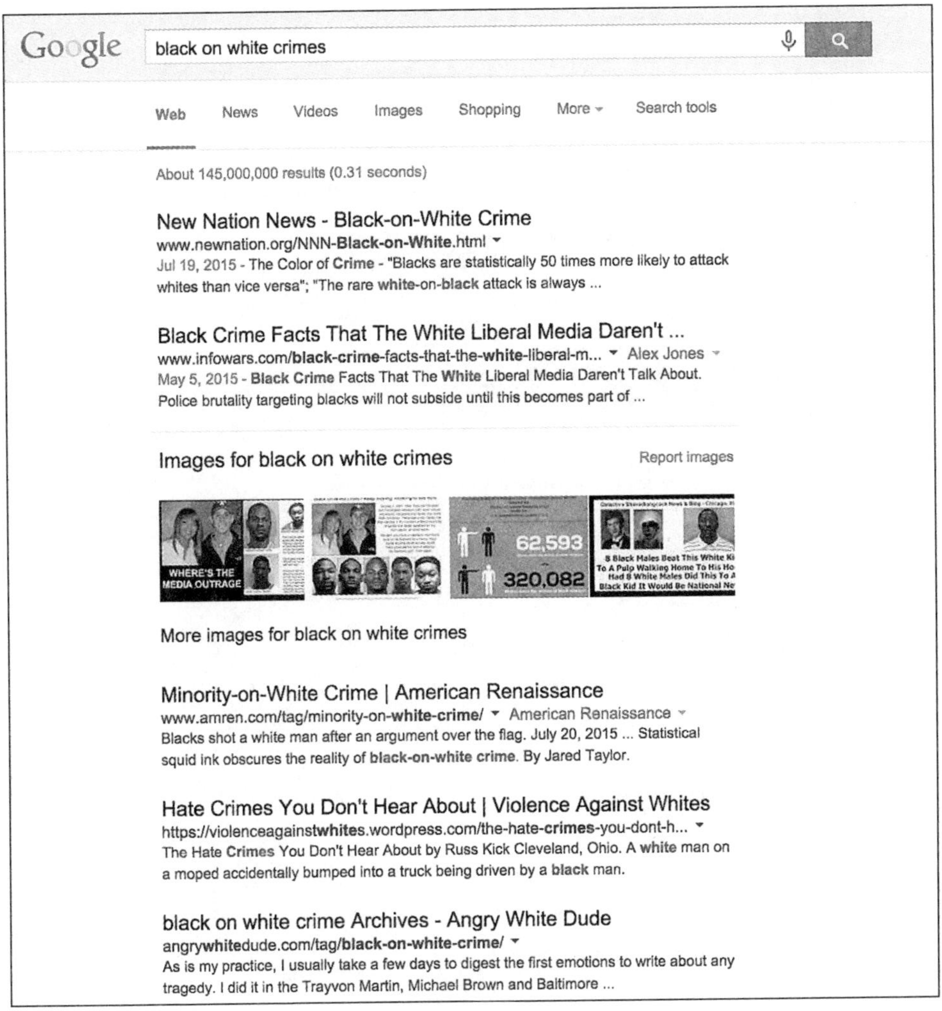

Figure 3.1. Google search on the phrase "black on white crimes" in Los Angeles, CA, August 3, 2015.

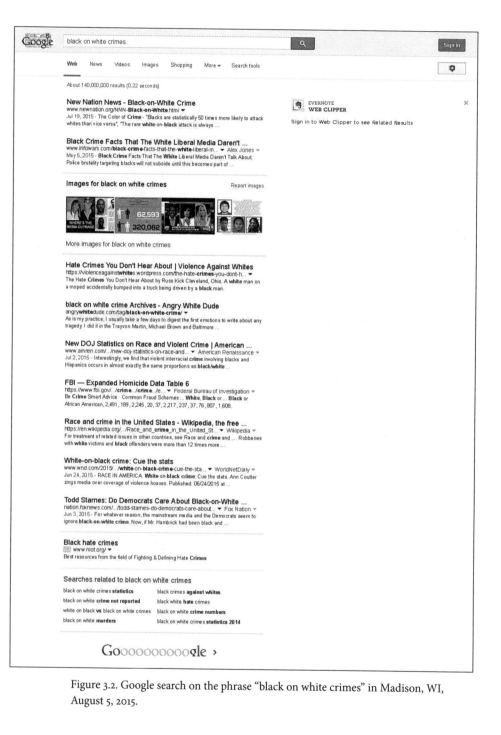

Figure 3.2. Google search on the phrase "black on white crimes" in Madison, WI, August 5, 2015.

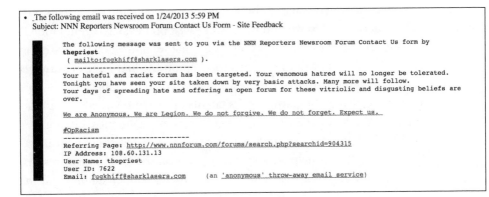

- .The following email was received on 1/24/2013 5:59 PM
Subject: NNN Reporters Newsroom Forum Contact Us Form - Site Feedback

The following message was sent to you via the NNN Reporters Newsroom Forum Contact Us form by
thepriest
(mailto:fuqkhiff@sharklasers.com).

Your hateful and racist forum has been targeted. Your venomous hatred will no longer be tolerated.
Tonight you have seen your site taken down by very basic attacks. Many more will follow.
Your days of spreading hate and offering an open forum for these vitriolic and disgusting beliefs are
over.

We are Anonymous. We are Legion. We do not forgive. We do not forget. Expect us.

#OpRacism

Referring Page: http://www.nnnforum.com/forums/search.php?searchid=904315
IP Address: 108.60.131.13
User Name: thepriest
User ID: 7622
Email: fuqkhiff@sharklasers.com   (an 'anonymous' throw-away email service)

Figure 3.3. On May 14, 2014, NewNation.org published this notice on its website to alert its members to the hack.

point to how crime against White Americans is largely an intraracial phenomenon. Most violence against White Americans is committed by White Americans, as most violence against African Americans is largely committed by other African Americans. White-on-White crime is the number-one cause of homicides against White Americans, as violent crime is largely a matter of perpetration by proximity to those who are demographically similar to the victim.[5] Homicides across racial lines do not nearly happen in the ways White supremacist organizations purport. A search on the phrase "black on white crimes" does not lead to any experts on race or to any universities, libraries, books, or articles about the history of race in the United States and the invention of racist myths in service of White supremacy, such as "black on white crime." It does not point to any information to dispel stereotypes trafficked by White supremacist organizations. It is critical that we think about the implications of people who are attempting to vet information in the news media about race and race relations and who are led to fascist, conservative, anti-Black, anti-Jewish, and/or White supremacist websites. The power of search engines to lead people to a breadth and depth of information cannot be more powerfully illustrated than by looking at Dylann Roof's own alleged words about using Google to find information about the Trayvon Martin murder, which led to his racial identity development.

There can be no doubt that what commercial search engines provide at the very top of the results ranking (on the first page) can have deleterious effects as much as it can also be harmless, depending on the concepts being queried. What we find when we search on racial and gender identities is profitable to Google, as much as what we find when we search on racist concepts. Recall that what shows up on the first page of search is typically highly optimized advertising-related content, because Google is an advertising company and its clients are paying Google for placement on the first page either through direct engagement with Google's AdWords program or through a gray market of search engine optimization products that help sites secure a place on the first page of results. Jessie Daniels's book *Cyber Racism: White Supremacy Online and the New Attack on Civil Rights* is the most comprehensive and important research to date on the ways that "cloaked websites," or websites that purport to be one thing, such as a viable news source or a legitimate social and cultural organization, operate as fronts for organizations such as the CCC, the Ku Klux Klan, and thousands of hate-based websites, which also pay to play. Daniels names the mainstream process of making sense of online information a "white racial frame,"[6] which allows many White Americans to essentially segregate online into spaces that question the legitimacy and viability of cultural pluralism and racial equality.

In the case of Dylann Roof's alleged Google searches, his very framing of the problems of race relations in the U.S. through an inquiry such as "black on white crime" reveals how search results belie any ability to intercede in the framing of a question itself. In this case, answers from conservative organizations and cloaked websites that present news from a right-wing, anti-Black, and anti-Jewish perspective are nothing more than propaganda to foment racial hatred.

What we find in search engines about people and culture is important. They oversimplify complex phenomena. They obscure any struggle over understanding, and they can mask history. Search results can reframe our thinking and deny us the ability to engage deeply with essential information and knowledge we need, knowledge that has traditionally been learned through teachers, books, history, and experience. Search results, in the context of commercial advertising companies, lay the groundwork, as I have discussed throughout this book, for implicit bias: bias that is buttressed by advertising profits. Search engine results also function as a type of personal record and as records of communities, albeit unstable ones. In the context of commercial search, they signal

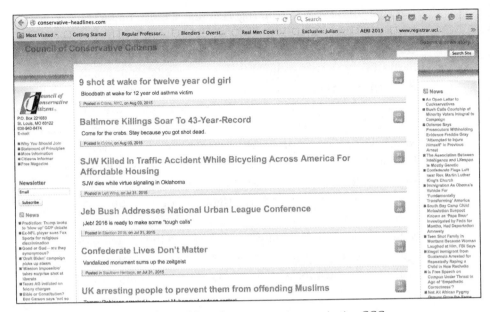

Figure 3.4. Cloaked "news" website of the White supremacist organization CCC, August 5, 2015.

what advertisers think we want, influenced by the kinds of information algorithms programmed to lead to popular and profitable web spaces. They galvanize attention, no matter the potential real-life cost, and they feign impartiality and objectivity in the process of displaying results, as detailed in chapter 1. In the case of the CCC, 579 websites link into the CCC's URL www.conservative-headlines.com from all over the world, including from sites as prominent as yahoo.com, msn.com, reddit.com, nytimes.com and huffingtonpost.com.

A straight line cannot be drawn between search results and murder. But we cannot ignore the ways that a murderer such as Dylann Roof, allegedly in his own words, reported that his racial awareness was cultivated online by searching on a concept or phrase that led him to very narrow, hostile, and racist views. He was not led to counterpositions, to antiracist websites that could describe the history of the CCC and its articulated aims in its Statement of Principles that reflect a long history of anti-Black, anti-immigrant, antigay, and anti-Muslim fervor in the United States. What we need is a way to reframe, reimagine, relearn, and remember the struggle for racial and social justice and to see how information online in ranking systems can also impact behavior and thinking offline. There is no federal, state, or local regulation of the psychological impact of the Internet, yet big-data analytics and algorithms derived from it hold so much power in overdetermining decisions. Algorithms that rank and prioritize for profits compromise our ability to engage with complicated ideas. There is no counterposition, nor is there a disclaimer or framework for contextualizing what we get. Had Dylann Roof asked an expert on the rhetoric of the CCC and hate groups in the U.S., such as the Southern Poverty Law Center, he would have found a rich, detailed history of how White supremacist organizations work to undermine democracy and civil rights, and we can only hope that education would have had an impact on his choices. But search results are not tied to a multiplicity of perspectives, and the epistemology of "ranking" from one to a million or more sites suggests that what is listed first is likely to be the most credible and trustworthy information available.

Searching for Protections from Search Engines 🔍

On January 16, 2013, a California court decided that a middle school science teacher was unfit for the classroom because material from her nine-month stint in the pornography industry had been discovered on the Internet. *USA Today* reported on January 16, 2013, that Judge Julie Cabos-Owen wrote in her opinion, "Although [the woman's] pornography career has concluded, the ongoing availability of her pornographic materials on the Internet will continue to impede her from being an effective teacher and respected colleague."[1] The teacher was fired, although she testified that she engaged in this work after her boyfriend left her and she faced financial hardship. In every interview with school district officials reported in the media, the teacher was deemed immoral and incapable of being an excellent role model for her students. News outlets began reporting on March 9, 2011, that a St. Louis high school teacher was fired from her job when a student discovered her previous work as an exotic dancer in the pornography industry in the 1990s. Though she reported that working in the industry was one of the greatest regrets of her life, she was unable to keep her job. School officials decided that her work from nearly two decades before was too much of a distraction to keep her employed. A band teacher in Ohio resigned when her participation in the adult entertainment industry was discovered. A surgical tech was treated with disdain and disrespected at the hospital where she worked when an anesthesia tech recognized her from her adult entertainment films. A real estate salesperson was let go after a coworker recognized her from adult films on the Internet. A freshman at Duke University was eviscerated by her peers when it was discovered that she did porn to pay her way through school. She was trying to pay a $60,000 annual tuition at her dream school because her parents could not afford to cover it. She was threatened and bullied online and on campus after a member of a Greek fraternity outed her to hundreds of men on campus. An award-winning high school principal took sexually provocative photos with her husband over the course of many years, and during their divorce, he sent hundreds of photos to the school board, which summarily demoted her after threats to end her long and excellent teaching career. What was privately shared in a marriage became a case of revenge porn that threatened to destroy all that she had earned. Their intimate acts, of which he was a participant, were only used against her. In 2010, the website IsAnyoneUp.com allowed users to post anonymous sexually explicit, nude images of men and women that included their name, address, and social media profiles from Facebook or Twitter. The founder of the site, Hunter Moore, faced multiple lawsuits that eventually forced the closure of the site in 2012, but he alleged the website had more than thirty million page views per month.[2] During the height of his websites "success," Moore managed to circumvent a number of legal actions because he never claimed *ownership* of the material posted to his site. Copyright claims by victims of revenge porn have been the most viable means for securing take-down notices in the courts and the primary way of getting images down from the web, predicated on lack of consent for distribution. Danny Gold, writing for TheAwl.com, interviewed a woman who shared what it felt like to have her images up at the site:

> I was submitted to isanyoneup.com by my ex-boyfriend. I am confronted by friends, family and strangers that they have seen me naked online everyday. . . . You may think it's funny but sometimes [I] don't want to leave my house and go to the mall with my family because I fear somebody will come up to me while I'm with my mother and mention it. My sisters . . . are ashamed to be related with me and want to lie to their friends that they are my sisters. I am a disgrace to my family. . . . My self worth has gone out the window and I worry I may never get it back. This keeps me one step away from happiness every single day. I don't know what to do anymore.[3]

The circulation of sexually explicit material has prompted thirty-four states to enact "revenge porn" laws, or laws that address nonconsensual pornography (NCP), defined by the Cyber Civil Rights Initiative as the distribution of sexually graphic images of individuals without their consent.[4] Laws currently range from misdemeanors to felonies, depending on the nature of the offense. On December 4, 2015, the first conviction under the California "revenge porn" law, of Noe Iniguez, was reported by the *Los Angeles Times*. Iniguez posted to Facebook a topless photo of his ex-girlfriend, including a series of slurs that included encouraging her employer to fire her.[5] In December 2015, Hunter Moore of *IsAnyoneUp. com* was sentenced to two and a half years in prison after pleading guilty to "one count of unauthorized access to a protected computer to obtain information for purposes of private financial gain and one count of aggravated identity theft," according to the *Washington Post*.[6]

What does it mean that one's past is always determining one's future because the Internet never forgets?

On the Right to Be Forgotten

These cases in the U.S. are typical, but there are many scenarios that have prompted people to call for expanded protections online. In 2014, the European Court of Justice ruled in the case of *Google Spain v. AEPD and Mario Costeja González*[7] that people have the right to request delisting of links to information about them from search engines, particularly if that information on the web may cause them personal harm. The pivotal legal decision was not without substantive prior effort at securing "the right to delete," "the right to forget or be forgotten," "the right to oblivion," or "the right to erasure," all of which have been detailed in order to better distinguish the rights that European citizens have in controlling information about themselves on the web.[8] In 2009, the French government signed the "Charter of good practices on the right to be forgotten on social networks and search engines,"[9] which stands as a marker of the importance of personal control over information on the web.[10] Since then, considerable debate and pushback from Google has ensued, highlighting the tensions between corporate control over personal information and public interest in the kinds of records that Google keeps.

At the center of the calls for greater transparency over the kinds of information that people are requesting removal of from the Internet is a struggle over power, rights, and notions of what constitutes freedom, social good, and human rights to privacy and the right to futures unencumbered by the past. The rulings against Google that support the "right to be forgotten" law currently affects only the European Union. Such legal protections are not yet available in the United States, where greater encroachments on personal information privacy thrive and where vulnerable communities and individuals are less likely to find recourse when troublesome or damaging information exists and is indexed by a commercial search engine. However, Google is still indexing and archiving links about people and groups within the EU on its domains outside of Europe, such as on google.com, opening up new challenges to the notion of national boundaries of the web and to how national laws extend to information that is digitally available beyond national borders. These laws, however, generally ignore the record keeping that Google does on individuals and organizations that are archived and shared with third parties beyond Google's public-facing search results.

I am not talking solely about the harmful effects of search results for groups of people. I am also concerned about the logic and harm caused by our reliance on large corporations to feed us information, information that ultimately leads us somewhere, often to places unexpected and unintended. In the case of the web results, this means communicating erroneous, false, or downright private information that one would otherwise not want perceived as the "official record" of the self on Google, the effects of which can be devastating. A difficult aspect of challenging *group* versus individual representations online is that there are no protections or basis for action under our current legal regime. Public records, of which web results can be included, whether organized by the state or vis-à-vis corporations, work in service of a privatized public good. Google and other large monopolies in the information and communications technology sector have a responsibility to communities, as much as they do to individuals. Currently, there is key legislation that challenges Google's records of information it provides about individuals, much of which is being discussed through legislative reforms such as the "right to be forgotten" policies in the European Union,[11] and new laws in the U.S. are emerging around "revenge porn." These tensions need to be taken up by and for communities and groups, particularly marginalized racial minorities in the United States and abroad, whose collective experiences, rights, and representations are not sufficiently protected online. Search results are records, and the records of human activity are a matter of tremendous contestation; they are a battleground over the identity, control, and boundaries of legitimate knowledge. Records, in the form of websites, and their visibility are power. Ultimately, both individuals and communities are not sufficiently protected in Google's products and need the attention of legislators in the United States.

At a time when state funding for public goods such as universities, schools, libraries, archives, and other important memory institutions is in decline in the U.S., private corporations are providing products, services, and financing on their behalf. With these trade-offs comes an exercising of greater control over the information, which is deeply consequential for those who are already systematically oppressed, as noted by the many scholars I have discussed in this book. They are also of incredible consequence for young people searching for information and ideas who are not able to engage their ideas with teachers, professors, librarians, and experts from a broad range of perspectives because of structural barriers such as the skyrocketing cost of college tuition and the incredible burdens of student debt. If advertising companies such as Google are the go-to resource for information about people, cultures, ideas, and individuals, then these spaces need the kinds of protections and attention that work in service of the public.

In the context of searching for racialized and gendered identities in Google's search engine, the right to control what information or records can exist and persist is important. It is even more critical because the records are presented in a ranking order, and research shows that the public in the U.S. believes that search results are credible and trustworthy.[12] As already noted in the previous chapters, Google exercises considerable discursive and hegemonic control over identity at the group and cultural levels, and it also has considerable control over personal identity and what can circulate in perpetuity, or be forgotten, through take-downs or delisting of bad information. Searches on keywords about minoritized, marginalized, and oppressed groups can yield all kinds of information that may or may not be credible or true, but they surface in a broader culture of implicit bias that already exists against minority groups. The right to be forgotten is an incredibly important mechanism for thinking through whether instances of misrepresentation can be impeded or stopped.

Our worst moments are also for sale, as police database mug shots are the fodder of online platforms that feature pictures of people who have been arrested. This is a practice that disproportionately impacts people of color, particularly African Americans, who are overarrested in the United States for crimes that they may not be convicted of in court. New platforms such as Mugshots.com and UnpublishArrest.com are services that promise, for a fee of $399 (one arrest) up to $1,799 (for five arrests), to remove mug shots from the Mugshots.com database across all major search engines. UnpublishArrest.com notes, "As a courtesy, when permanent unpublishing is chosen and information is unpublished for The Mugshots.com Database; requests will be submitted to Google to have the inactive links (dead links) and mugshots associated with the arrest(s) and Mugshots.com removed from the Google search results. Google results are controlled by Google and as such; courtesy Google submissions are not guaranteed nor are they part of the optional paid service provided. Google's removal lead times average 7–10 days and can take as long as 4–6 weeks."[13] Proponents of this practice, including lawmakers and public-interest organizations, argue that this is a public safety issue and that the public has a right to know who potential criminals are in their communities. Opponents of the practice argue that it is a privacy issue and a matter that inflames the public, particularly people who are not found guilty but who appear guilty given the titillating nature of the pubic display of these photos.

Research shows just how detrimental the lack of control over identity is. In the 2012 work of Latanya Sweeney, a professor of government and technology at Harvard University and the director of the Data Privacy Lab in the Institute of Quantitative Social Science at Harvard, she showed that Google searches on African American–sounding names are more likely to produce criminal-background-check advertisements than are White-sounding names.[14] Time and again, the research shows that racial bias is perpetuated in the commercial information portals that the public relies on day in and day out. Yet, as I have noted in previous chapters, the prioritization and circulation of misrepresentative and even derogatory information about people who are oppressed and maligned in the larger body politic of a nation, as are African Americans, Native Americans, Latinos, and other peoples of color, is an incredible site of profit for media platforms, including Google. We need to think about delisting or even deprioritizing particular types of representative records. How do we reconcile the fact that ethnic and cultural communities have little to no control over being indexed in ways that they may not want? How does a group resolve the ways that the pubic engages with Google as if it is the arbiter of truth?

The recording of human activity is not new. In the digital era, the recordings of human digital engagements are a matter of permanent record, whether known to people or not. Memory making and forgetting through our digital traces is not a choice, as information and the recording of human activities through digital software, hardware, and infrastructure are necessary and vital components of the design and profit schemes of such actions. The information studies scholars Jean-François Blanchette and Deborah Johnson suggest that the tremendous capture and storage of data, without plans for data disposal, undermines our "social forgetfulness," a necessary new beginning or "fresh start," that should be afforded people in the matter of their privacy record keeping. They argue that much policy and media focus has been on the access and control that corporations have over our personal information, but less attention had been paid to the retention of our every digital move.[15]

The Edward Snowden revelations in 2014 made some members of the public aware that governments, through multinational corporations such as Verizon and Google, were not only collecting but also storing private records of digital activity of millions of people around the world. The threats to democracy and to individual privacy rights through the recording of individuals' information must be taken up, particularly in the context of persistent racialized oppression.

I foreground previous work about why we should be concerned about data retention in the digital world and the ways in which the previous paper-based information-keeping processes by institutions faced limits of space and archival capacity. These limits of space and human labor in organization and preservation presupposed a type of check, or "institutional forgetfulness,"[16] that was located in the storage medium itself, rather than relating to policy limits on holding information for long periods of time. Oscar Gandy, Jr., aptly characterizes the nature of why forgetting should be an important, protected right:

> The right to be forgotten, to become anonymous, and to make a fresh start by destroying almost all personal information, is as intriguing as it is extreme. It should be possible to call for and to develop relation-

ships in which identification is not required and in which records are not generated. For a variety of reasons, people have left home, changed their identities, and begun their lives again. If the purpose is non-fraudulent, is not an attempt to escape legitimate debts and responsibilities, then the formation of new identities is perfectly consistent with the notions of autonomy I have discussed.[17]

These rights to become anonymous include our rights to become who we want to be, with a sense of future, rather than to be locked into the traces and totalizing effect of a personal history that dictates, through the record, a matter of truth about who we are and potentially can become. The record, then, plays a significant ontological role in the recognition of the self by existing, or not, in an archived body of information.[18] In the case of Google, though not an archive of specific intent organized in the interest of a particular concern, it functions as one of the most ubiquitous and powerful record keepers of digital engagement. It records our searches or inquiries, our curiosities and thoughts.

The record, then, in the context of Google, is never ending. Its data centers, as characterized in a recent YouTube video produced by Google,[19] keep copies of our personal information on at least two servers, with "more important data" on digital tape. The video does not explain which data is considered most important, nor does it state how long data is stored on Google's servers. In many ways, Google's explanations about how it manages data storage speaks to and assuages the sensitivity to issues about Web 2.0 transactions such as credit card protections or secure information (Social Security numbers, passwords) transmitted over the Internet that might be used for online financial or highly private transactions.

Google says,

> We safeguard your data.
>
> Rather than storing each user's data on a single machine or set of machines, we distribute all data—including our own—across many computers in different locations. We then chunk and replicate the data over multiple systems to avoid a single point of failure. We randomly name these data chunks as an extra measure of security, making them unreadable to the human eye.

While you work, our servers automatically back up your critical data. So when accidents happen—if your computer crashes or gets stolen—you can be up and running again in seconds.

Lastly, we rigorously track the location and status of each hard drive in our data centers. We destroy hard drives that have reached the end of their lives in a thorough, multi-step process to prevent access to the data.

Our security team is on-duty 24x7.

Our full-time Information Security Team maintains the company's perimeter defense systems, develops security review processes, and builds our customized security infrastructure. It also plays a key role in developing and implementing Google's security policies and standards.

At the data centers themselves, we have access controls, guards, video surveillance, and perimeter fencing to physically protect the sites at all times.[20]

The language of privacy and security, as articulated by Google's statements on data protection, does not address what happens when you want your data to be deleted or forgotten. Indeed, Google suggests that when you delete data from an application, it is wiped from the Google servers:

Deleted Data

After a Google Apps user or Google Apps administrator deletes a message, account, user, or domain, and confirms deletion of that item (e.g., empties the Trash), the data in question is removed and no longer accessible from that user's Google Apps interface.

The data is then deleted from Google's active servers and replication servers. Pointers to the data on Google's active and replication servers are removed. Dereferenced data will be overwritten with other customer data over time.[21]

But these explanations do not address the myriad ways that records are created and circulated through Google's products and how we lose control over information about ourselves. Recently, Darlene Storm wrote an article for *ComputerWorld* citing researchers who purchased twenty mobile phones from Craigslist and eBay only to find thousands of photos, emails, and texts—including deleted messages through

Facebook—after doing factory resets of their data.[22] The most acute breaches of personal security were on Android smartphones, after using Google's software to allegedly wipe them clean. Personal information at the level of device and infrastructure is not forgotten and can be circulated with ease.

The ways in which our human activities are recorded and stored are vast, and the value of social forgetfulness is not just good for individuals but is good for society. We should frame it as a public or social good:

> A world in which there is no forgetfulness—a world in which everything one does is recorded and never forgotten—is not a world conducive to the development of democratic citizens. It is a world in which one must hesitate over every act because every act has permanence, may be recalled and come back to haunt one, so to speak. Of course, the opposite is equally true: A world in which individuals are not held accountable over time for the consequences of their actions will not produce the sense of responsibility that is just as necessary to a democratic society. Thus, achieving the appropriate degree of social forgetfulness is a complex balancing act, ever in tension between the need to hold accountable, and the need to grant a "fresh start."[23]

Google's position about forgetting has stood in stark contrast to previous conceptions of memory and forgetting, as Napoleon Xanthoulis of the Dickson Poon School of Law at King's College London articulated in his important article theorizing the rights of individuals to control their data privacy as a fundamental human rights issues: a "right to cyber-oblivion." He notes that Google's chief privacy officer, Peter Fleisher, has argued against cyber-oblivion, or record wiping, as "an attempt to give people the right to wash away digital muck, or delete the embarrassing stuff."[24] Indeed, Google's position has been that the recording of everything we do is a matter of the cultural record of humanity, "even if it's painful."[25] Both Xanthoulis and Blanchette and Johnson argue that it is important that bad actors, violators of the public trust, and ill-intentioned public officials not necessarily be allowed to erase their deeds from the digital record. This has been Google's general disposition toward erasures of information from its records. However, Google has begun to respond to pressures to change its algorithm. On August

10, 2012, Google announced on its blog that it would be pushing further down in its ranking websites with valid complaints about copyright infringement.[26] Google suggested that this would help users find more credible and legitimate content from the web. This decision was met with much commendation from powerful media companies—many of which are Google's advertising customers. These companies want to ensure that their copyrighted works are prioritized and that pirated works are not taking prominence in Google's web results.

* * *

There are many troubling issues to contend with when our every action in the digital record is permanently retained or is retained for some duration so as to have a lasting impact on our personal lives. Privacy and identity ownership are constructed within a commercial web space such as Google, and Google controls the record. Subjects and publics are documented through Google's algorithms, and displays of search results are decidedly opportunistic and profitable. While tremendous focus on "right to be forgotten" legislation is on control of records that are publicly visible on the web (e.g., websites, images, audio files, etc.), more attention needs to be paid to information that is collected and archived by Google that is not visible to the public. These records are conveyed by Google as necessary for its product development and for enhanced consumer experiences (see Google's privacy policy). However, Google's record keeping has its genesis in providing information shared across its networked services for its clients, which include U.S.-based national security agencies, as well as Google's commercial partners. Increased attention must be paid to both the visible and invisible ways that identity information and records of activity can be archived through Internet infrastructures, buttressed by Google's monopoly on information services in the United States. Inevitably, the power differentials between the record keepers, in this case a private company such as Google, and those who are recorded are insurmountable. Google's power is only buttressed by its work on behalf of the U.S. government, which has outsourced its data collection and unconstitutional privacy invasions to the company.[27]

The goal of elevating these conversations is to recognize and name the neoliberal communication strategies used by Google to circumvent or suppress its record keeping of the public through surveillance, particularly in its privacy policies and responses to "right to be forgotten" public policy. Google's control and circumvention of privacy and the right to be forgotten intensifies damage to vulnerable populations. As I have previously argued, Google is, at one moment, implicated in prioritizing predatory misrepresentations of people, such as algorithmically privileging sexualized information about women and girls, because it is profitable. In another moment, it is providing our records to third parties. While Google has consistently argued that "right to oblivion" laws are unfairly shifting the record of real-world human activity, which it believes the public has a right to know, recent leakages of requests for take-down notices were reported in the British media, showing that the nature of take-down requests is much more personal and relevant to everyday people, rather than public figures skirting responsibility to some alleged public interest.

On July 14, 2015, the *Guardian* reported that "less than 5% of nearly 220,000 individual requests made to Google to selectively remove links to online information concern criminals, politicians and high-profile public figures . . . with more than 95% of requests coming from everyday members of the public."[28] What is critical to this new revelation is that previously Google's statements about the nature of "right to be forgotten" requests have been exaggerated or unknown because delisting information from its records has not been transparent, despite calls for information about the nature of the requests from over eighty academics in a letter authored by Ellen P. Goodman, a professor of law at Rutgers University, and Julia Powles, a researcher at the University of Cambridge Faculty of Law.[29] In an open letter to Google, the scholars not only argue that the public has a right to have information taken out of Google's search engine and all other engines subject to data protection rulings, but they also state,

> Google and other search engines have been enlisted to make decisions about the proper balance between personal privacy and access to information. The vast majority of these decisions face no public scrutiny, though they shape public discourse. What's more, the values at work in this process will/should inform information policy around the world. A fact-free debate about the RTBF [right to be forgotten] is in no one's interest.[30]

Challenging content on the web under the auspices of the right to be forgotten must extend beyond the take down of personal information and beyond erasing the memory of past acts from the web. The right to be forgotten must include the recognition of all forms of records that Google is archiving and sharing with third parties, both visible and invisible to the public.

The discussion about the right to be forgotten has largely lived in the frameworks of contesting neoliberal control and encroachments on social and public life organized around unstable notions of a public sphere. In the academics' letter, calls for transparency about delisting requests point to the ways that ideologies of transparency privilege a kind of fact-based, information-oriented gathering of evidence to make clear and thoughtful decisions within the context of how privacy should operate within the records of Google. The questions about who controls the records of our social life and how they can be forgotten must move to the fore in the United States. They are explicitly tied to who can own identity markers and how we can reclaim them at both the individual and community level.

Librarians and information professionals are particularly implicated in these projects. In 2016, the librarian Tara Robertson wrote an important blog post to the profession about why all information should not be digitized and made available on the open web. Robertson's point is that people share material, thoughts, and communications with each other in closed communities, as in the case of the digitization of *On Our Backs*, a lesbian porn publication that had a limited print run and circulated from 1984 to 2004, prior to the mainstreaming and commercialization of content on the web that we see today. People who participated in the publication did so before there was an Internet, before digitization would make the material public.[31] Robertson raises the important ethical issues, as have many other researchers, about what should be digitized and put on the open web and what belongs to communities with shared values, to be shared within a community:

> In talking to some queer pornographers, I've learned that some of their former models are now elementary school teachers, clergy, professors, child care workers, lawyers, mechanics, health care professionals, bus drivers and librarians. We live and work in a society that is homopho-

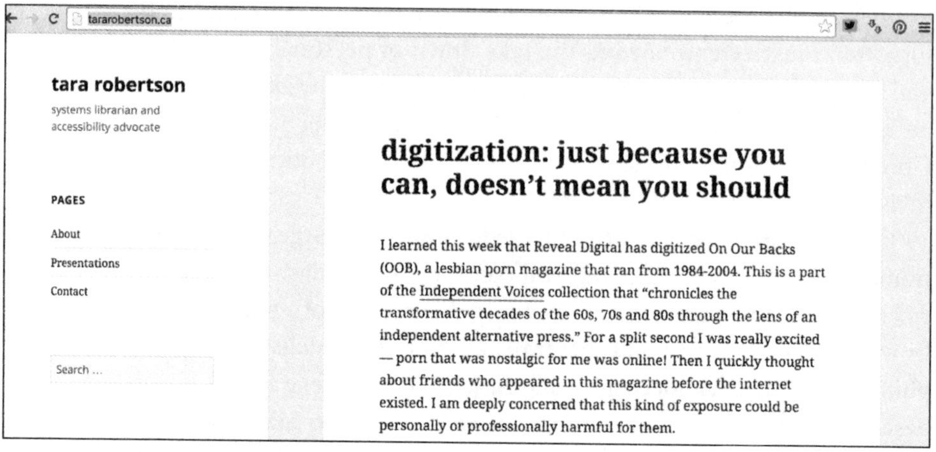

Figure 4.1. Call to librarians not to digitize sensitive information that was meant to be private, by Tara Robertson.

bic and not sex positive. Librarians have an ethical obligation to steward this content with care for both the object and with care for the people involved in producing it.[32]

On Our Backs has an important history. It is regarded as the first lesbian erotica magazine to be run by women, and its title was a cheeky play on the name of a second-wave, and often antipornography, feminist newspaper named *Off Our Backs*. *On Our Backs* stood in the sex-positive margin for lesbians who were often pushed out of the mainstream feminist and gay liberation movements of the 1970s–1990s. What Robertson raises are the ethical considerations that arise when participants in marginalized communities are unable to participate in the decision making of having content they create circulate to a far wider, and outsider, audience. These are the kinds of issues facing information workers, from the digitization of indigenous knowledge from all corners of the earth that are not intended for mass public consumption, to individual representations that move beyond the control of the subject. We cannot ignore the long-term consequences of what it means to have everything subject to public scrutiny, out of context, out of control.

Ultimately, what I am calling for is increased regulation that is undergirded by research that shows the harmful effects of deep machine-learning algorithms, or artificial intelligence, on society. It is not just a matter of concern for Google, to be fair. These are complex issues that span a host of institutions and companies. From the heinous effects manifested from Dylann Roof's searching on false concepts about African Americans that may have influenced his effort to spark a race war, to the ways in which information can exist online about people and communities that can be nearly impossible to correct, to the owning of identity by the highest bidder—public policy must address the many increasing problems that unregulated commercial search engines pose. In addition to public policy, we can reconceptualize the design of indexes of the web that might be managed by librarians and information institutions and workers to radically shift our ability to contextualize information. This could lead to significantly greater transparency, rather than continuing to make the neoliberal capitalist project of commercial search opaque.

The Future of Knowledge in the Public   Q

Student protests on college campuses have led to calls for increased support of students of color, but one particular request became a matter of national policy that led to a threat to the Library of Congress's budget in the summer of 2016. In February 2014, a coalition of students at Dartmouth College put forward "The Plan for Dartmouth's Freedom Budget: Items for Transformative Justice at Dartmouth" (the "Freedom Plan"),[1] which included a line item to "ban the use of 'illegal aliens,' 'illegal immigrants,' 'wetback,' and any racially charged term on Dartmouth-sanctioned programming materials and locations." The plan also demanded that "the library search catalog system shall use undocumented instead of 'illegal' in reference to immigrants." Lisa Peet, reporting for *Library Journal*, noted,

> The replacement of the subject heading was the culmination of a two-year grassroots process that began when Melissa Padilla, class of 2016, first noticed what she felt were inappropriate search terms while researching a paper on undocumented students at Dartmouth's Baker-Berry Library in 2013. While working with research and instruction services librarian Jill Baron, Padilla told LJ [*Library Journal*], she realized that nearly every article or book she looked at was categorized with the subject heading "Illegal aliens."[2]

The Dartmouth College librarians became deeply engaged in petitioning the Library of Congress. According to Peet, "Baron, DeSantis, and research and instruction services librarian Amy Witzel proposed that the students gather documentation to prove that 'Illegal aliens' is not a preferred term, and to find evidence that better terms—such as 'Undocumented immigrant,' which was their initial suggestion for a replacement—were in common use. At that point news organizations such as the Associated Press, *USA Today*, ABC, the *Chicago Tribune*, and the *LA Times* had already committed not to use the term 'Illegal' to describe an individual."[3] Though unsuccessful in 2015, the librarians' case to the Library of Congress had gained traction, and the librarian and professor Tina Gross at St. Cloud State University began organizing caucuses and committees in the American Libraries Association, including the subject analysis committee, social responsibilities round table, and REFORMA, which advocates for library services for Latinos and those who speak Spanish. Social media campaigns ensued, organized under the Twitter hashtags #DropTheWord and #NoHumanBeingIsIllegal.[4] By March 29, 2016, Dartmouth College's student-led organization the Coalition for Immigration Reform, Equality (CoFired) and DREAMers announced in a press release that after a two-year battle, in partnership with campus librarians and the American Libraries Association, "the Library of Congress will replace the term 'illegal aliens' with 'noncitizens' and 'unauthorized immigrants' in its subject headings."[5]

"Illegal Alien" Revisited

The struggle over reclassifying undocumented immigrants was part of a long history of naming members of society as problem people. In many ways, this effort to eliminate "illegal alien" was similar to the ways that Jewish people were once classified by the Library of Congress as the "Jewish question," later to be reclassified in 1984 as "Jews," and Asian Americans were once classified as the "Yellow Peril."[6] Control over identity is political and often a matter of public policy. Almost as soon as the successful change was approved, House Republicans introduced HR 4926 on April 13, 2016, also known as the "Stopping Partisan Policy at the Library of Congress Act," sponsored by Rep. Diane Black (R-TN). In essence, the bill threatened the Library's budget, and Black suggested that the effort to change the Library of Congress Subject Headings (LCSH) was a matter of "caving to the whims of left-wing special interests and attempting to mask the grave threat that illegal immigration poses to our economy, our national security, and our sovereignty."[7]

The battle over how people are conceptualized and represented is ongoing and extends beyond the boundaries of institutions such as the Library of Congress or corporations such as Alphabet, which owns and manages Google Search. Jonathan Furner, a professor of information studies at UCLA, suggests that information institutions and systems, which I argue extend from state-supported organizations such as the Library of Congress to the Internet, are participating in "legitimizing the ideology of dominant groups" to the detriment of people of color.[8] His case study of the Dewey Decimal Classification (DDC) system, for example, underscores the problematic conceptualizations of race and culture and efforts to "deracialize" the library and classification schemes.[9] Furner offers several strategies for thinking about how to address these issues, using critical race theory as the guiding theoretical and methodological model. I believe these strategies are of great value to thinking about the information studies issues at hand in this research:

- admission on the part of designers that bias in classification schemes exists, and indeed is an inevitable result of the ways in which they are currently structured;
- recognition that adherence to a policy of neutrality will contribute little to eradication of that bias and indeed can only extend its life; [and]
- construction, collection and analysis of narrative expressions of the feelings, thoughts, and beliefs of classification-scheme users who identify with particular racially-defined populations.[10]

While the web-indexing process is not the same as classification systems such as DDC, the application of the theoretical model is still valid for thinking about conceptualizing algorithms and indexing models that could actively intervene in the default normativity of racism and sexism in information resources.

Problems in Classifying People

The idea of classification as a social construct is not new. A. C. Foskett suggests that classificationists are the products of their times.[11] In the work of Nicholas Hudson of the University of British Columbia on the origins of racial classification in the eighteenth century, he suggests that during the Enlightenment, Europeans began to construct "imagined communities," citing Benedict Anderson's term.[12] He says, "This mental image of a community of like-minded individuals, sharing a 'general will' or a common national 'soul,' was made possible by the expansion of print-culture, which stabilized national languages and gave wide access to a common literary tradition."[13] Classification systems, then, are part of the scientific approach to understanding people and societies, and they hold the power biases of those who are able to propagate such systems. The invention of print culture accelerated the need for information classification schemes, which were often developing in tandem with the expansion of popular, scholarly, and scientific works.[14] Traces of previous works defining the scientific classification of native peoples as "savage" and claims about Europeans as the "superior race," based on prior notions of peoples and nations, began to emerge and be codified in the eighteenth century. Extensive histories have been written of how racial classification emerged in the eighteenth and nineteenth centuries in North America as a paradigm of differentiation that would support the exclusion of native and African people from social and political life.

By the nineteenth century, the processes involved in the development of racial classification marked biological rather than cultural difference and were codified to legally deny rights to property ownership and citizenship. These historical practices undergird the formation of racial classification, which is both assumed and legitimated in classification systems. Without an examination of the historical forces at play in the development of such systems, the replication and codification of people of African descent into the margins goes uncritically examined. This process can be seen in knowledge organization that both privileges and subordinates through information hierarchies such as catalogs and classification systems. The field of library science has been implicated in the organization of people and critiqued for practices that perpetuate power by privileging some sectors of society at the expense of others.

Traditional library and information science (LIS) organization systems such as subject cataloging and classification are an important part of understanding the landscape of how information science has inherited and continues biased practices in current system designs, especially on the web.

Opportunities abound for the interdisciplinarity of LIS to extend more deeply into cultural and feminist studies, because these social science fields provide powerful and important social context for information about people that can help frame how that information is organized

and made available. To date, much of the attention to information organization, storage, and retrieval processes has been influenced and, more
importantly, funded by scientific research needs stemming from World
War II and the Cold War.[15] The adoption of critical race theory as a
stance in the field would mean examining the beliefs about the neutrality and objectivity of the entire field of LIS and moving toward undoing racist classification and knowledge-management practices. Such a
stance would be a major contribution that could have impact on the
development of new approaches to organizing and accessing knowledge
about marginalized groups.

If the information-retrieval priority of making access to recorded information efficient and expedient is the guiding process in the development of technical systems, from databases to web search engines, then
what are the distinguishing data markers that define information about
racialized people and women in the United States? What have primarily
been missing from the field of information science, and to a lesser degree library science, are the issues of representation that are most often
researched in the fields of African American studies, gender studies,
communications, and increasingly digital media studies. Information
organization is a matter of sociopolitical and historical processes that
serve particular interests.

A Short History of Misrepresentation in Classifying People

In order to understand how racial and gender representations in Google
Search express the same traditional bias that exists in other organizational systems, an overview of how women and non-Whites have been
historically represented in information categorization environments
is in order. The issue of misrepresentations of women and people of
color in classification systems has been significantly critiqued.[16] Hope
A. Olson, an associate dean and professor at the School of Information
Studies at the University of Wisconsin, Milwaukee, has contributed
among the most important theories on the social construction of classification that many of us in the field assign to our students as a way of
fostering greater awareness about the power that library, museum, and
information professionals hold. Those who have the power to design
systems—classification or technical—hold the ability to prioritize

hierarchical schemes that privilege certain types of information over others. An example of these biases include the cataloging of people as subjects in the Library of Congress Subject Headings (LCSH), which serve as a foundational and authoritative framework for categorizing information in libraries in the United States. The LCSH have been noted to be fraught with bias, and the radical librarian Sanford Berman details the ways that this bias has reflected Western perspectives:

> Since the first edition of *Library of Congress Subject Headings* appeared 60 years ago, American and other libraries have increasingly relied on this list as the chief authority—if not the sole basis—for subject cataloging. There can be no quarrel about the practical necessity for such labor-saving, worry-reducing work, nor—abstractly—about its value as a global standardizing agent, as a means for achieving some uniformity in an area that would otherwise be chaotic. . . . But in the realm of headings that deal with people and cultures—in short, with humanity—the LC list can only "satisfy" parochial, jingoistic Europeans and North Americans, white-hued, at least nominally Christian (and preferably Protestant) in faith, comfortably situated in the middle- and higher-income brackets, largely domiciled in suburbia, fundamentally loyal to the Established Order, and heavily imbued with the transcendent, incomparable glory of Western Civilization.[17]

Eventually the LCSH abolished labels such as "Yellow Peril" and "Jewish Question" or made substitutions in the catalog, changing "Race Question" or "Negroes" to "Race Relations" and "Afro-Americans,"[18] but the establishment of such headings and the subsequent decade-long struggles to undo them underscored Berman's point about Western racial bias. (In fact, it was Berman who led the field in calling for anti-racist interventions into library catalogs in the 1970s.) Patriarchy, like racism, has been the fundamental organizing point of view in the LCSH. The ways in which women were often categorized was not much better, with headings such as "Women as Accountants" in lieu of the now-preferred "Women Accountants"; women were consistently an aberration to the assumed maleness of a subject area.[19]

Furthermore, efforts at self-identity from the perspective of marginalized and oppressed groups such as the Roma or Romanies cannot escape the stigmatizing categorization of their culture as "Gypsies," even though their "see also" designation to "rogues and vagabonds" was finally dropped from the LCSH.[20] A host of other problematic naming conventions including "Oriental" instead of "Asian" and the location of Christianity at the top of the religious hierarchy, with all deviations moving toward the classification of "Primitive," suggests that there is still work to be done in properly addressing and classifying groups of people around identity.[21] Olson says, "the problem of bias in classification can be linked to the nature of classification as a social construct. It reflects the same biases as the culture that creates it."[22] These types of biases are often seen in offline information practices where conquest is a means of erasing the history of one dynasty or culture by the subsequent regime.[23] Olson's research has already shown that classifications reflect the philosophical and ideological presumptions of dominant cultures over subordinate cultures or groups. For example, in traditional Dewey Decimal Classification (DDC), over 80% of its religion section is devoted exclusively to Christianity, even though there are greater numbers of other religious texts and literature.[24] Olson points to the Library of Congress Classification (LCC) and its biases toward North American and European countries in volumes on the law, with far fewer allocations of space for Asia, Eurasia, Africa, the Pacific area, and Antarctica, reflecting the discourse of the powerful and the presumption of marginality for all others.[25]

In this respect, Olson reminds us that the ordering of information provided in classification schemes "tends to reflect the most mainstream version of these relationships" because "classificatory structures are developed by the most powerful discourses in a society. The result is the marginalization of concepts outside the mainstream."[26] In other words, the most mainstream (e.g., White, heterosexual, Christian, middle-class) controlling regimes in society will privilege themselves and diminish or subdue all others in the organization of what constitutes legitimate knowledge. When we inherit privilege, it is based on a massive knowledge regime that foregrounds the structural inequalities of the past, buttressed by vast stores of texts, images, and sounds saved in archives, museums, and libraries. Certainly, classification systems have some boundaries and limits, as they are often defined in whole by what is included and what is excluded.[27] In the case of most library databases in the United States, Eurocentrism will dominate the canons of knowledge. Knowledge management reflects the same social biases that exist in society, because human beings are at the epicenter of information curation. These practices of the past are part of the present, and only committed and protracted investments in repairing knowledge stores to reflect and recenter all communities can cause a shift toward equality and inclusion in the future. This includes reconciling our brutal past rather than obscuring or minimizing it. In this way, we have yet to fully confront our histories and reconstitute libraries and museums toward reconciliation and reparation.

Search engines, like other databases of information, are equally bounded, limited to providing only information based on what is indexed within the network. Who has access to provide information in the network certainly impacts whether information can be found and surfaced to anyone looking for it. Olson's research points to the ways that some discourses are represented with more power, even if their social classifications are relatively small:

> In North American society, taking away women, African Americans, Hispanic Americans, French Canadians, Native peoples, Asian Americans, lesbians and gay men, people with disabilities, anyone who is not Christian, working class and poor people, and so forth, one is left with a very small "core." An image that shows the complexity of these overlapping categories is that of a huge Venn diagram with many sets limited by Boolean ANDs. The white AND male AND straight AND European AND Christian AND middle-class AND able-bodied AND Anglo mainstream becomes a very small minority . . . , and each set implies what it is not. The implication of this image is that not every person, not every discourse, not every concept, has equal weight. Some discourses simply wield more power than others.[28]

Arguably, if education is based in evidence-based research, and knowledge is a means of liberation in society, then the types of knowledge that widely circulate provide a crucial site of investigation. How oppressed people are represented, or misrepresented, is an important element of engaging in efforts to bring about social, political, and economic justice.

Figure 5.1. Google autocorrects to "himself" rather than "herself." Search sent to me by a colleague, June 16, 2016.

We have to ask ourselves what it means in practical terms to search for concepts about gender, race, and ethnicity only to find information lacking or misrepresentative, whether in the library database or on the open web. Olson's notion that cultural metaphor is the basis of the construction of classification systems means these cultural metaphors are profoundly represented in the notions of the "Jewish Question" or the "Race Question." These subject headings suggest both an answer and a point of view from which the problems of Jews and race are presupposed. Simply put, to phrase "Jewish" or "race" as a question or problem to be answered suggests a point of view on the part of the cataloger that is quite different from how a Jewish person or a racialized person might frame themselves. It is here that the context and point of view of library and information science professionals who are responsible for framing people and communities as "problems" and "questions" is important. By examining the ways that Black people specifically have been constructed in the knowledge schemes, the African American studies professor and philosopher Cornel West aptly describes the positionality of how this community is depicted in the West:

> Black people as a problem-people rather than people with problems;
> black people as abstractions and objects rather than individuals and persons; black and white worlds divided by a thick wall (or a "Veil") . . . ;
> black rage, anger, and fury concealed in order to assuage white fear and anxiety; and black people rootless and homeless on a perennial journey

to discover who they are in a society content to see blacks remain the permanent underdog.[29]

The library scholar Joan K. Marshall points to the way this idea was expressed in the Library of Congress when "N*ggers" was a legitimate subject category, reflecting the "social backgrounds and intellectual levels" of users, concretizing oppressive race relations.[30] Difference, in the case of the Library of Congress, is in direct relation to Whiteness as the norm. No one has made this more clear than Berman, whose groundbreaking work on Library of Congress Subject Headings has forever changed the field. He notes that in the case of both Jews and the representations of race, these depictions are not without social context:

> For the image of the Jew to arouse any feelings, pro or con, he [sic] had to be generalized, abstracted, depersonalized. It is always possible for the personal, individual case to contradict a general assertion by providing living, concrete proof to the contrary. For the Jews to become foils of a mass movement, they had to be converted into objectified symbols so as to become other than human beings.[31]

In the case of Google, because it is a commercial enterprise, the discussions about its similar information practices are situated under the auspices of free speech and protected corporate speech, rather than being posited as an information resource that is working in the public domain, much like a library. An alternative possibility could be that corporate free speech in the interests of advertisers could be reprioritized against the harm that sexist and racist speech on the Internet could have on those who are harmed by it. This is the value of using critical race theory—considering that free speech may in fact not be a neutral notion but, rather, a conception that when implemented in particular ways silences many people in the interests of a few.

The disclaimer by Google for the problem of searching for the word "Jew" leading to White supremacist, Holocaust-denial web results is surprisingly similar to the construction of Jewish identity in the LCSH. Both systems reflect the nature of the relationship between Jewish and non-Jewish Europeans and North Americans. This is no surprise, given that hyperlinking and indexing are directly derived from library science

citation-analysis practices. This linkage between the indexing practices of the World Wide Web and the traditional classification systems
of knowledge structures such as the Library of Congress is important.
Both systems rely on human decisions, whether given over en masse
to artificial intelligence and algorithms or left to human beings to catalog. The representation of people and cultures in information systems
clearly reflects the social context within which the subjects exist. In the
case of search engines, not unlike cataloging systems, the social context
and histories of exploitation or objectification are not taken into explicit
consideration—rather, they are disavowed. What can be retrieved by information seekers is mediated by the technological system—be it a catalog or an index of web pages—by the system design that otherizes. In the
case of the web, old cataloging and bibliometric practices are brought
into the modern systems design.

Library science scholars know that bibliographic and naming controls
are central to making knowledge discoverable.[32] Part of the issue is trying to understand who the audience is for knowledge and naming and
organizing information in ways that can be discovered by the public.
Berman cites Joan Marshall's critiques of the underlying philosophy of
the Library of Congress's subject-cataloging practices and the ways that
they constitute an audience through organizational bias, wherein a "majority reader" is established as a norm and, in the case of the Library of
Congress, is often "white, Christian (usually Protestant) and male."[33] Indeed, these scholars are taking note of the influence that categorization
systems have on knowledge organization and access. What is particularly important in the interrogation of these marginalizing information-
management systems is Berman's reference to the Algerian psychologist
Franz Fanon's articulation of the mechanics of cultural "brain washing"
that occurs through racist cataloging practices.[34] Berman underscores
that the problems of racial representation and racism are deeply connected to words and images and that a racist worldview is embedded
in cataloging practices that serve to bolster the image and domination
of Western values and people (i.e., White, European, and North Americans over people of African descent). The library practitioner Matthew
Reidsma gave a recent gift to the profession when he blogged about library discovery systems, or search interfaces, that are just as troubled
as commercial interfaces. In his blog post, he details the limitations of

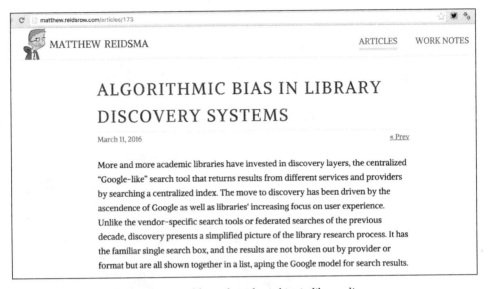

matthew.reidsrow.com/articles/173

MATTHEW REIDSMA   ARTICLES   WORK NOTES

ALGORITHMIC BIAS IN LIBRARY DISCOVERY SYSTEMS

March 11, 2016   « Prev

More and more academic libraries have invested in discovery layers, the centralized "Google-like" search tool that returns results from different services and providers by searching a centralized index. The move to discovery has been driven by the ascendence of Google as well as libraries' increasing focus on user experience. Unlike the vendor-specific search tools or federated searches of the previous decade, discovery presents a simplified picture of the library research process. It has the familiar single search box, and the results are not broken out by provider or format but are all shown together in a list, aping the Google model for search results.

Figure 5.2. A call to the profession to address algorithmic bias in library discovery systems by Matthew Reidsma attempts to influence the field of information studies. Source: Reidsma, 2016.

databases, the kinds of gender biases that are present in discovery tools, and how little innovation has been brought to bear in resolving some of the contradictions we know about.[35]

I sought to test the call that Reidsma made to the profession to interrogate library information management tools by conducting searches in a key library database. I looked in the largest library image database available to academic libraries, ArtStor, and found troublesome practices of metadata management there too. Undoubtedly, these kinds of cataloging stances can be evaluated in the context of the field of library science, which is largely averse to teaching and talking about race and the White racial gaze on information. I have published several articles with colleagues about the challenges of teaching about race in the library and information studies classroom and the importance of integrating theory and training of information workers around issues of social justice in the profession. I interpret these kinds of cataloging mishaps as a result of the investment of the profession in colorblind ideology. Unable and unequipped to think through the complexities of systems of racialization, the profession writ large struggles to find frameworks to

Figure 5.3. Search in ArtStor for "black history" features the work of a series of European and White American artists, March 2, 2016. The first result is work by Thomas Waterman Wood.

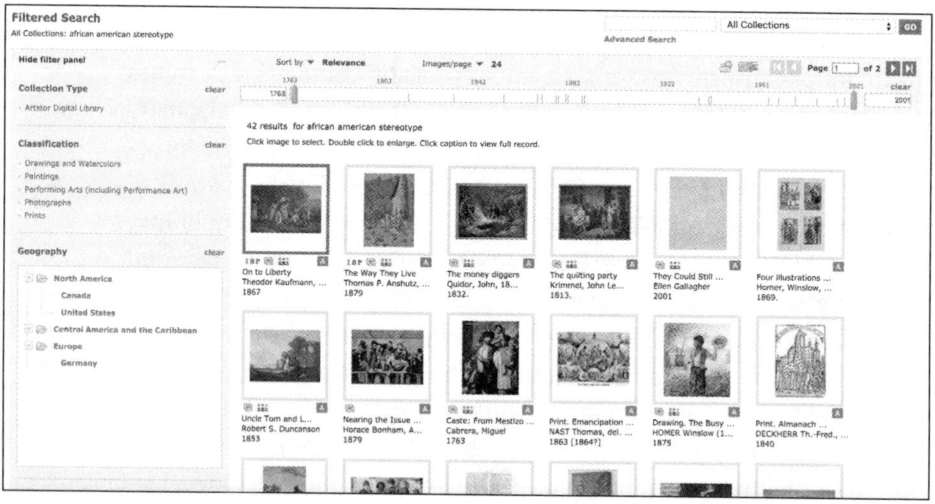

Figure 5.4. *On to Liberty*, an oil on canvas by Theodore Kauffman, a German painter, is the first item under "African American stereotype."

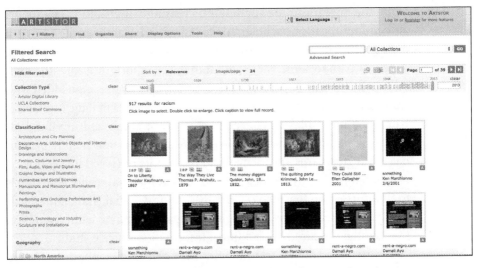

Figure 5.5. A satirical piece by the artist Damali Ayo and her online piece *Rent-A-Negro*, which is a critique of liberal racial ideologies that tokenize African Americans. The work is cataloged as "racism."

think critically about the long-term consequences of misidentification of people and, in this case, concepts about works of art.

Search as a Source of Reality

Indeed, problematic results in ArtStor are just a small window into a long and troubled history of misrepresentation in library subject cataloging and classification systems, which are faithful reflections of the problematic representations in mainstream U.S. culture. Our ability to recognize these challenges can be enhanced by asking questions about how technological practices are embedded with values, which often obscure the social realities within which representations are formed. The interface of the search engine as a mechanism for accessing the Internet is not immune, nor impartial, to the concerns of embedded value systems. Search is also more than the specific mathematical algorithms and deep-machine learning developed by computer scientists and software engineers to index upward of a trillion pages of information and move some from the universal data pile to the first page of results on a computer screen. The interface on the screen presents an information reality, while the operations are rendered increasingly invisible.[36] The media and communications scholar Alex Galloway destabilizes the idea that digital technologies are transparent, benign windows or doors providing a view or path to somewhere and in themselves insignificant—the digital interface is a material reality structuring a discourse, embedded with historical relations, working often under the auspices of ludic capitalism, where a kind of playful engagement of labor is masked in vital digital media platforms such as Google.[37] Search does not merely present pages but structures knowledge, and the results retrieved in a commercial search engine create their own particular material reality. Ranking is itself information that also reflects the political, social, and cultural values of the society that search engine companies operate within, a notion that is often obscured in traditional information science studies.

Further, new digital technologies may constitute containers for old media discourses, and the web interface (such as a plain Google search box) is a transitional format from previous media forms.[38] Certainly in the case of digital technology such as commercial search engines, the interface converges with the media itself. Commercial search, in the case of Google, is not simply a harmless portal or gateway; it is in fact a creation or expression of commercial processes that are deeply rooted in social and historical production and organization processes. John Battelle, who has carefully traced the history of Google, describes search as the product of our needs and desires, aggregated by companies:

> Link by link, click by click, search is building possibly the most lasting, ponderous, and significant cultural artifact in the history of humankind: the Database of Intentions. The Database of Intentions is simply this: the aggregate results of every search ever entered, every result list ever tendered, and every path taken as a result. . . . This information represents the real-time history of post-Web culture—a massive clickstream database of desires, needs, wants, and preferences that can be discovered, subpoenaed, archived, tracked and exploited for all sorts of ends.[39]

Undoubtedly, search is also pivotal in the development of artificial intelligence. In many ways, Google Search is an attempt to use computer science as a basis for sorting and making decisions about the relevance and quality of information rather than human sorting and web-indexing practices—practices that search engine companies such as Yahoo! and those of the past invested in heavily and that were both expensive to implement and limited and less responsive in real time.[40]

Providing Context for Information about People

In a narrow sense, information is a series of signals and messages that can be expressed through mathematics, algorithms, and statistical probabilities. In a broader sense, however, Tefko Saracevic, a professor emeritus of information science at Rutgers, suggests that information is constituted through "cognitive processing and understanding."[41] There is a pivotal relationship between information and users that is dependent on human understanding. It is this point that I want to emphasize in the context of information retrieval: information provided to a user is deeply contextualized and stands within a frame of reference. For this reason, it is important to study the social context of those who are organizing information and the potential impacts of the judgments inherent in informational organization processes. Information must be treated in a context; "it involves motivation or intentionality, and therefore it is connected to the expansive social context or horizon, such as culture, work, or problem-at-hand," and this is fundamental to the origins of information science and to information retrieval.[42] Information retrieval as a practice has become a highly commercialized industry, predicated on federally funded experiments and research initiatives, leading to the formation of profitable ventures such as Yahoo! and Google, and a focus on information relevance continues to be of importance to the field. Information science is essentially deeply entwined with the history of library science and has primarily been concerned with the collection, storage and retrieval, and access to and use of information. Saracevic notes that "the domain of information science is the transmission of the universe of human knowledge in recorded form, centering on manipulation (representation, organization, and retrieval) of information, rather than knowing information."[43] This foregrounds the ways that representations in search engines are decontextualized in one specific type of information-retrieval process, particularly for groups whose images, identities, and social histories are framed through forms of systemic domination. Although there is a long, broad, and historical context for addressing categorizations, the impact of learning from these traditions has not yet been fully realized.[44]

Attention to "the universe of human knowledge" is suggestive for contextualizing information-retrieval practices this way, leading to inquiries into the ways current information-retrieval practices on the web, via commercial search engines, make some types of information available and suppress others. The present focus on the types of information presented in identity-based searches shows that they are removed from the social context of the historical representations and struggles over disempowering forms of representation. These critiques have been levied toward other media practices such as television and print culture. Whether human beings believe that the information delivered in search is relevant has consistently been the basis of judgment about information quality,[45] but what is underdiscussed is that retrieval of information in commercial platforms such as web-based search engines is not unique to the individual searcher. A web-based commercial search engine does not entirely "know" who a user is, and it is not customizing everything to our personal and political tastes, although it is aggregating us to people it thinks are similar to us on the basis of what is known through our digital traces.

Finding Culturally Situated Information on the Web

The field of LIS is significantly engaged in information classification and organization work, which can inform the framework for thinking about developing ICTs that are focused on surfacing prioritized results, such as the search engine. Critical race theory in this process of developing information-organization tools is of great value, particularly when thinking about the phenomenon of excessive recall of documents on the web that are irrelevant or decontextualized. Responses to the kinds of problematic biases in large commercial search engines are part of the growing motivation behind a host of culturally situated search engines that are emerging, particularly Blackbird (www.blackbirdhome.com), a Mozilla Firefox browser designed to help surface content of greater relevance to African Americans. Blackbird has been met with mixed reviews, from support and interest to wholesale rejection.[46] In any case, organizations and individuals are responding to the limits of traditional commercial search engines through the development of such search engines. Identity-focused websites, a combination of web-based browsers and web directories, are emerging to prioritize the interests of specific communities on the basis of the human-curated practices of the past and can be seen in search engines such as BlackWebPortal (www. blackwebportal.com); GatewayBlackPortal (www.gatewayblack.com), which is based on international models such as JGrab, a Jewish search engine; BlackFind.com (www.blackfind.com); and Blackbird. Sites such as Jewogle (www.jewogle.com), which serves as an online encyclopedia of the accomplishments of Jewish people; Jewish.net (http://jewish. net/), which is used to "search the Jewish Web"; JewGotIt (www.jewgotit. com); and Maven Search (www.maven.co.il), which catalogs over fifteen thousand Jewish websites, have emerged in the hundreds, some tongue in cheek, across religion, culture, and national origin. Much of this is a response of communities that are seeking control over relevant content and representation, as well as access to quality information within racial or group identity.

One of the fundamental challenges for these culturally situated search engines is the way in which they make visible the contradictions and biases in search engines, which André Brock discusses in relationship to Blackbird. He notes that "Blackbird's efforts to foreground African American content were seen as an imposition on the universal appeal of the internet, highlighting the perception of the browser as a social structure limited by Black representation."[47] Brock's work indicates that though there is a demand for culturally relevant Internet browsing that will help surface content of interest to Black people, its value works against norms on the web, making it less desirable.

Reproducing Social Relations through Information Technologies

Online racial disparities cannot be ignored because they are part of the context within which ICTs proliferate, and the Internet is both reproducing social relations and creating new forms of relations based on our engagement with it. Technologies and their design do not dictate racial ideologies; rather, they reflect the current climate. As users engage with technologies such as search engines, they dynamically co-construct content and the technology itself.[48] Online information and content available in search is also structured systemically by the infusion of advertising revenue and the surveillance of user searches, which the subjects of such practices have very little ability to reshape or reformulate. Lack of attention to the current exploitative nature of online keyword searches only further entrenches the problematic identities in the media for women of color, identities that have been contested since the advent of commercial media such as broadcast, print, and radio. Noticeably absent in the discussions of search is the broader social and technical interplay that exists dynamically in the way technology is increasingly mediating public access to information, from libraries to the search engine.

Now, more than ever, a new conception of information access and quality rooted in historical, economic, and social relations could have a transformational effect on the role and consequences of search engines. It is my goal through this research to ensure that traditionally underrepresented ideas and perspectives are included in the shaping of the field—to surface counternarratives that would allow for a questioning of the normalization of such practices. Rather than prioritize the dominant narratives, Internet search platforms and technology companies could allow for greater expression and serve as a democratizing tool for the public. This is rendered impossible with the current commercial practices.

What we need are public search engine alternatives, united with public-interest journalism and librarianship, to ensure that the public has access to the highest quality information available.

The Future of Information Culture   Q

In March 2010, the U.S. Federal Communications Commission (FCC) put forward its ten-year broadband plan, wherein it called for high-speed Internet to become the common medium of communications in the United States.[1] This plan still governs the information landscape. The FCC envisioned that the Internet, as the common medium, would potentially displace current telecommunications and broadcast television systems as the primary communications vehicle in the public sphere. According to the report, "almost two-thirds of the time users spend online is focused on communication, information searching, entertainment or social networking."[2] The plan called for increased support for broadband connectivity to facilitate Americans' ability to access vital information, and it is focused on infrastructure, devices, accessibility, and connectivity. However, the plan made no mention of the role of search engines in the distribution of information to the public, with the exception of noting that the plan itself will be archived and made available in perpetuity in the archives of the Internet. Primary portals to the Internet, whether connecting through the dwindling publicly funded access points in libraries and schools or at home, serve as a gateway to information and cannot be ignored. Access to high-quality information, from journalism to research, is essential to a healthy and viable democracy. As information moves from the public sphere to private control by corporations, a critical juncture in the quality of information available and the public's ability to sift and use it is at stake, as the noted political economist Herbert Schiller forewarned:

> The American economy is now hostage to a relatively small number of giant private companies, with inter-locking connections, that set the national agenda. This power is particularly characteristic of the communication and information sector where the national cultural-media agenda is provided by a very small (and declining) number of integrated private

combines. The development has deeply eroded free individual expression, a vital element of a democratic society.[3]

An increasingly de- and unregulated commercially driven Internet raises significant issues about how information is accessed and made available. This is exacerbated by the gamification of news and headlines, as Nicole Cohen of the Institute of Communication, Culture, Information, and Technology at the University of Toronto, Mississauga, has documented in her ethnography of journalists who write for online news outlets. In her book *Writers' Rights: Freelance Journalism in a Digital Age*, she documents the increasing tensions between journalists and commercial news media organizations.[4] In some cases, journalists are facing screens that deliver real-time analytics about the virality of their stories. Under these circumstances, journalists are encouraged to modify headlines and keywords within a news story to promote greater traction and sharing among readers. The practices Cohen details are precisely the kind of algorithmically driven analytics that place pressure on journalists to modify their content for the express purposes of increasing advertising traffic. Undoubtedly, in this case, big-data analytics have potential to significantly compromise the quality of reporting to the public.

As quality information typically provided by the public sector moves into more corporate and commercial spaces, the ability of the public to ensure protections that are necessary in a democracy is eroded, due to the cost of access. Organizations such as FreePress.org are showing how the rise of advertising and commercial interests have bankrupted the quality and content of journalism, heretofore considered a fundamental and necessary component of a democratic society. The media scholars Robert McChesney and John Nichols have noted in great historical detail and with abundant concrete evidence the importance of information in a democratic society—free from commercial interests.[5] These rapid shifts over the past decade from the public-interest journalism environment prior to the 1990s, along with the corporate takeover of U.S. news media, have eroded the quality of information available to the public. Similarly, the move of the Internet from a publicly funded, military-academic project to a full-blown commercial endeavor has also impacted how information is made available on the web.

Media stereotypes, which include search engine results, not only mask the unequal access to social, political, and economic life in the United States as broken down by race, gender, and sexuality; they maintain it.[6] This suggests that commercial search engines, in order to opt out of such traditional racist representations, might want, at minimum, to do something like a "disclaimer" and, at maximum, to produce a permanent "technical fix" to the proliferation of racist or sexist content. Veronica Arreola wondered as much on the *Ms.* blog in 2010 when Google Instant, a new search-enhancement tool, initially did not include the words "Latinas," "lesbian," and "bisexual" because of their X-rated front-page results: "You're Google. . . . I think you could figure out how to put porn and violence-related results, say, on the second page?"[7]

It is these kinds of practices that mark the consequences of the rapid shift over the past decade from public-interest information to the corporate takeover of U.S. news media, which has made locating any kind of alternative information increasingly difficult and pushed the public toward the web. Equally, media consolidations have contributed to the erosion of professional standards such as fact checking, not misrepresenting people or situations, avoiding imposing cultural values on a group, and distinguishing between commercial and advertising interests versus editorial decisions—all of which can be applied to information provision on the web.[8] As the search arena is consolidated under the control of a handful of corporations, it is even more crucial to pay close attention to the types of processes that are shaping the information prioritized in search engines. In practice, the higher a web page is ranked, the more it is trusted. Unlike the vetting of journalists and librarians, who are entrusted to fact check and curate information for the public according to professional codes of ethics, the legitimacy of websites' ranking and credibility is simply taken for granted. The take-home message is that, when it comes to online commercial search engines, it is no longer enough to simply share news and education on the web; we must ask ourselves how the things we want to share are found and how the things we find have appeared.

A Monopoly on Information

Not enough attention has been paid to Google's monopoly on information in the most recent debates about network control. The focus on net neutrality in the U.S. is largely invested in concerns over the movement of packets of data across commercial networks owned by the telecommunications and cable giants, which include AT&T, Verizon, DirecTV, and Comcast. Much of the debate has focused on maintaining an open Internet, free from traffic-routing discrimination. In this context, discrimination refers to the movement of data and the rights of content providers not to have their traffic delayed or managed across the network regardless of size or content. Focus on content prioritization processes should enter the debates over net neutrality and the openness of the web when mediated by search engines, especially Google. Over the past few years, consumer watchdog organizations have been enhancing their efforts to provide data about Google's commercial practices to the public, and the Federal Trade Commission is investigating everything from Wi-Fi data harvesting of consumer data to Google's horizontal ownership and dominance of web-based services such as YouTube, AdSense, Google Maps, Blogger, Picasa, Android, Feedburner, and so on. Internet service providers have been set back by the recent U.S. court of appeals decision to protect the rights of consumers via maintaining the FCC stance on protecting net neutrality. The decision prevents Comcast from prioritizing or discriminating in traffic management over its networks. Organizations such as the Open Internet Coalition have been at the fore in lobbying Congress for protections from the prioritization of certain types of lawful Internet traffic that multinational telecommunications companies are able to promote, while simultaneously blocking access to their networks by competitors. Quietly, companies such as Google, Facebook, and Twitter that have high volumes of traffic have backed the Open Internet Coalition in an effort to ensure that they will have the necessary bandwidth to support their web-based assets that draw millions of users a day to their sites with tremendous traffic.

Outside the United States, Google has faced a host of complaints about representations of material culture and identity. In the realm of public information, the former Harvard University librarian Robert

Darnton outlined the problematic issues that arose from the Google book-digitization project. In this project, Google digitized millions of books, over ten million as of the close of 2009, opening up considerable speculation about the terms on which readers will be able to access these texts. The legal issues at play at the height of the legal battle included potential violations of antitrust law and whether public interests would prevail against monopolistic tendencies inherent in one company's control and ownership of such a large volume of digital content.[9] Proponents of Google's project suggested that the world's largest library will make previously out-of-print and unavailable texts accessible to a new generation of readers/consumers. Opponents were fearful that Google would control the terms of access, unlike public libraries, on the basis of shareholder interests. Further challenges to this project were leveled by France and Germany, which rejected the ownership of their material culture by a U.S.-based company, claiming it is impinging on their national and cultural works.[10] They suggested that the digitization of works by their national citizens of the past is an infringement on the public good, which is threatened by Google's monopoly on information. In 2013, U.S. Circuit Court Judge Denny Chin ruled that the Google book project was "fair use," serving a blow to critics, and in 2015, a hearing of the case was rejected by the U.S. Supreme Court.[11] An appeal to the Second Circuit, New York, affirmed Google's right to claim fair use. Despite Darnton's critique, underscored by media scholars such as Siva Vaidhyanathan, a professor of media studies and law at the University of Virginia, who has written substantially on the threats of the decision to the legal concept of "fair use," the verdict underscores the power of Google's capital and its influence, to the detriment of nations that cannot withstand its move to create the largest digital repository in the world. This includes the ability to own, categorize, and determine the conditions or terms of access to such content. In support of the position against the project before the European Commission, concerns were presented by France that "a large portion of the world's heritage books in digital format will be under the control of a single corporate entity."[12]

Closer to home, with the exception of the Anti-Defamation League's previously mentioned letter, many protests of Google's information and website representation have not been based on the way cultural identities are presented, but rather the focus has been on commercial interests in patents, intellectual property, and even page ranking. For example, in 2003, an early lawsuit against Google focused on its prioritization of high-paying advertisers that were competing against small businesses and entities that do not index pages on the basis of the pay-per-click advertising model that has come to dominate experiences of the Internet in the United States. The lawsuit by Search King and PR Network against Google alleged that Google decreased the page rank of its clients in a direct effort to annihilate competition.[13] Since Bob Massa, the president of Search King and PR Ad Network, issued a statement against Google's biased ranking practices, Google's business practices have been under increased scrutiny, both in the U.S. and globally.

Why Public Policy Matters

Given the controversies over commercial, cultural, and ethnic represen-tations of information in PageRank, the question that the Federal Trade Commission might ask today, however, is whether search engines such as Google should be regulated over the values they assign to racial, gen-dered, and sexual identities, as evidenced by the types of results that are retrieved. At one time, the FCC enforced decency standards for media content, particularly in television, radio, and print. Many political inter-ventions over indecency and pornography on the web have occurred since the mid-1990s, with the 1996 Communications Decency Act (CDA) being the most visible and widely contested example, particu-larly section 230 with respect to immunity for online companies, which cannot be found liable for content posted by third parties. Section 230 is specifically designed to protect children from online pornography, while granting the greatest rights to freedom of expression, which it does by not holding harm toward Internet service providers, search engines, or any other Internet site that is trafficking content from other people, organizations, or businesses—companies such as Google, Facebook, Verizon, AT&T, Wordpress, and Wikipedia—all of which are exempt from liability under the act.[14] These were the same protections afforded to Hunter Moore and his revenge-porn site discussed in chapter 4.

The attorney Gregory M. Dickinson describes the important prece-dents set by a court ruling against the Internet service provider Prodigy. He suggests that the court's interpretation of Prodigy's market position was that of a "family-friendly, carefully controlled and edited Internet provider," which engaged in processes to filter or screen offensive content in its message boards; as such, it "had taken on the role of a newspaper-like publisher rather than a mere distributor and could therefore be held liable."[15] He underscores the importance of the court ruling in *Stratton Oakmont, Inc. v. Prodigy Services Co.* (1995) that Prodigy's engagement in some level of filtering content of an objectionable nature meant that Prodigy was responsible and liable. This, he argues, was not Congress's intent—to hold harmless any platform providing content that is obscene, pornographic, or objectionable by community standards of decency.

Commercial search engines, at present, have been able to hide behind disclaimers asserting that they are not responsible for what happens in their search engine technologies. Yet Dickinson's study of the law with respect to Prodigy raises interesting legal issues that could be explored in relationship to search engines, particularly Google, now that it has admitted to engaging in filtering practices. What is most apparent since the passage of the CDA in 1996 is that decency standards on the web and in traditional media have been fodder for "the culture wars," and by all apparent measures, indecency is sanctioned by Congress, the FCC, and media companies themselves. These protections of immunity are mostly upheld by the *Zeran v. America Online, Inc.* (1997) ruling in the U.S. Court of Appeals for the Fourth Circuit, which found that companies are not the responsible parties or authors of problematic material distributed over their hardware, software, or infrastructure, even though section 230 was intended to have these companies self-censor indecent material. Instead, the courts have ruled that they cannot hold companies liable for not self-censoring or removing content. Complicating the issues in the 1996 act is the distinction between "computer service providers" (nonmediated content) and "information providers" (mediated content).[16]

During the congressional hearings that led to the Federal Trade Commission investigation of Google, the reporter Matthew Ingram suggested in a September 2011 article that "it would be hard for anyone to prove that the company's free services have injured consumers."[17] But Ingram is arguably defining "injury" a little too narrowly. Searching for "Latinas" or "Asian women" brings about results that focus on porn, dating, and fetishization. What is strikingly similar in the cases of searching for "Jew" and for "black girls" is that objectionable results materialized in Google's page-ranking algorithm—results that might not reflect the social or historical context of the lives of each group or their desire to be represented this way. However, what is strikingly dissimilar is that Black teenagers and girls of color have far less social, political, or economic agency than the Anti-Defamation League does. Public policy must open up avenues to explore and assess the quality of group identity information that is available to the public, a project that will certainly be hotly contested but that should still ensue.

The Web as a Source of Opportunity

The web is characterized as a source of opportunity for oppressed and marginalized people, with tremendous focus put on closing the hardware, software, and access gaps on the Internet for various communities. Among the most prevalent ideas about the political aspects of technology disenfranchisement and opportunity are theories that center on the concept of the "digital divide," a term coined in a series of speeches and surveys by the Clinton-Gore administration and the National Telecommunications Infrastructure Administration. Digital-divide narratives have focused on three key aspects of disempowerment that have led to technological deficits between Whites and Blacks: access to computers and software, development of skills and training in computer technologies, and Internet connectivity—most recently characterized by access to broadband.[18]

However true the disparities between Whites and non-Whites or men and women in the traditional articulations of the digital divide, often missing from this discourse is the framework of power relations that precipitate such unequal access to social, economic, and educational resources.[19] Thus, the context for discussing the digital divide in the U.S. is too narrow a framework that focuses on the skills and capabilities of people of color and women, rather than questioning the historical and cultural development of science and technology and representations prioritized through digital technologies, as well as the uneven and exploitive global distribution of resources and labor in the information and communication ecosystem. Certainly, the digital divide was an important conceptual framework to deeper engagement for poor people and people of color, but it also created new sites of profit for multinational corporations.[20] Closing the digital divide through ubiquitous access, training, and the provisioning of hardware and software does address the core criticisms of the digital technology have and have-not culture in the U.S.; but much like the provisioning of other technological goods such as the telephone, it has not altered the landscape of power relations by race and gender.

Search needs to be reconciled with the critical necessity of closing the digital divide, since search is such a significant part of mediating the online experience. Digital-divide scholars have argued that increased culturally relevant engagements with technology, web presence, and skill building will contribute to greater inclusion and to greater social, political, and economic agency for historically underrepresented, marginalized, and oppressed groups.[21] This is the thrust of the neoliberal project of "uplift" and "empowerment"—by closing the skill-based gaps in computer programming, for example. These approaches do not account for the political economy and corporate mechanisms at play, and we must ask how communities can intervene to directly shape the practices of market-dominant and well-established technology platforms that are mediating most of our web interaction.[22] They also often underexamine the diasporic labor conditions facing Black women who are engaged in the raw-mineral extraction process to facilitate the manufacture of computer and mobile phone hardware. I raise this issue because research on the global digital divide, and Google's role in it,[23] must continue to expand to include a look at the ways that Black people in the U.S. and abroad are participating and, in the case of the United States, *not* participating to a significant degree in information and communication technology industries.[24] This makes calls for "prosumer" participation,[25] as a way of conceptualizing how Black people can move beyond being simple consumers of digital technologies to producers of technological output, a far more complex discussion.

George Ritzer and Nathan Jurgenson at the University of Maryland characterize this emphasis of merging the consumptive and productive aspects of digital engagement as "a trend toward unpaid rather than paid labor and toward offering products at no cost, and the system is marked by a new abundance where scarcity once predominated."[26] The critical communications scholar Dallas Smythe describes this type of prosumerism as "the audience as commodity," where users are sold to advertisers as a commodity and, in return for "free" services, users are explicitly exposed to advertising.[27] Christian Fuchs, the director of the Communication and Media Research Institute and Westminster Institute for Advanced Studies, discusses this accumulation strategy, bolstered by Google's users, as a process of both prosumer commodity and audience commodity by virtue of the decentralized nature of the web.[28] The intensive participation of people in uploading, downloading, sharing, tagging, browsing, community building, and content generation allows for mass distribution and one-to-many or many-to-many engagements in a way that traditional media could not have done due to its centralized nature.[29] In Fuchs's work on the political economy of Google, he characterizes the unpaid, user-generated content provided by its users as the basis for Google's ability to conduct keyword searching because it indexes all user-generated content and "thereby acts as a meta-exploiter of all user-generated content producers."[30] Surplus labor is created for Google through users' engagements with its products, from Gmail to Google Scholar, the reading of blogs in Blogger/Blogspot, the use of Google Maps or Google Earth, or the watching of videos on YouTube, among many of the company's services.[31] The vertical offerings of Google are so great,[32] coupled with its prioritization of its own properties in keyword searches, that mere use of any of these "free" tools creates billion-dollar profits for Google—profits generated from both unpaid labor from users and the delivery of audiences to advertisers. Fuchs's work explicitly details how Google's commodities are not its services such as Gmail or YouTube; its commodities are all of the content creators on the web whom Google indexes (the prosumer commodity) and users of their services who are exposed to advertising (audience commodity).

We are the product that Google sells to advertisers.

These aspects of software and hardware development are important, and decreased engagements of women and people of color in the high-tech design sector, coupled with increased marginalized participation in the most dangerous and volatile parts of the information and communication technology labor market, have impact on the artifacts such as search results themselves. According to U.S. Department of Labor workforce data obtained by the *Mercury News* through a Freedom of Information request, of the 5,907 top managers in the Silicon Valley offices of the ten largest high-tech companies in 2005, 296 were Black or Hispanic, a 20% decline from 2000.[33] Though the scope of this book does not include a formal interrogation of Black manufacturing labor migration to outsourced ICT manufacturing outside the United States, it is worth noting that this phenomenon has implications for participation in industries that shape everything from hardware to software design, of which Google is playing a primary role. As of July 1, 2016, Google's own diversity scorecard shows that only 2% of its workforce is African American, and Latinos represent 3%. With all of the aberrations and challenges that tech companies face in charges of data discrimination, the possibility of hiring recent graduates and advanced-degree holders in Black studies, ethnic studies, American Indian studies, gender and women's studies, and Asian American studies with deep knowledge of history and critical theory could be a massive boon to working through the kinds of complex challenges facing society, if this is indeed the goal of the technocracy. From claims of Twitter's racist trolling that drives people from its platform[34] to charges that Airbnb's owners openly discriminate against African Americans who rent their homes[35] to racial profiling at Apple stores in Australia[36] and Snapchat's racist filters,[37] there is no shortage of projects to take on in sophisticated ways by people far more qualified than untrained computer engineers, whom, through no fault of their own, are underexposed to the critical thinking and learning about history and culture afforded by the social sciences and humanities in most colleges of engineering nationwide. The lack of a diverse and critically minded workforce on issues of race and gender in Silicon Valley impacts its intellectual output.

Google is a powerful and important resource for organizing information and facilitating social cooperation and contact, while it simultaneously reinforces hegemonic narratives and exploits its users. This has widely been characterized by critical media scholars as a dialectic that has less to do with Google's technologies and services and more to do with the organization of labor and the capitalist relations of production.[38] The notion that Google/Alphabet has the potential to be a democratizing force is certainly laudable, but the contradictions inherent in its projects must be contextualized in the historical conditions that both create it and are created by it. Thinking about the specifics of who benefits from these practices—from hiring to search results to technologies of surveillance—these are problems and projects that are not equally experienced. I have written, for example, with my colleague Sarah T. Roberts about the myriad problems with a project such as Google Glass and the problems of class privilege that directly map to the failure of the project and the intensifying distrust of Silicon Valley gentrifiers in tech corridors such as San Francisco and Seattle.[39] The lack of introspection about the public wanting to be surveilled at the level of intensity that Google Glass provided is part of the problem: centuries-old concepts of conquest and exploration of every landscape, no matter its inhabitants, are seen as emancipatory rather than colonizing and totalizing for people who fall within its gaze. People on the street may not characterize Google Glass as a neocolonial project in the way we do, but they certainly know they do not like seeing it pointed in their direction; and the visceral responses to Google Glass wearers as "Glassholes" is just one indicator of public distrust of these kinds of privacy intrusions.

The neocolonial trajectories are not just in products such as search or Google Glass but exist throughout the networked economy, where some people serve as the most exploited workers, including child and forced laborers,[40] in such places as the Democratic Republic of Congo, mining ore called columbite-tantalite (abbreviated as "coltan") to provide raw materials for companies such as Nokia, Intel, Sony, and Ericsson (and now Google)[41] that need such minerals in the production of components such as tantalum capacitors, used to make microprocessor chips for computer hardware such as phones and computers.[42] Others in the digital-divide network serve as supply-chain producers for hardware companies such as Apple[43] or Dell,[44] and this outsourced labor from the U.S. goes to low bidders that provide the cheapest labor under neoliberal economic policies of globalization.

To review, in the ecosystem, Black people provide the most grueling labor for blood minerals, and they do the dangerous, toxic work of dismantling e-waste in places such as Ghana, where huge garbage piles of poisonous waste from discarded electronics from the rest of the world are shipped. In the United States, Black labor is for the most part bypassed in the manufacturing sector, a previous site of more stable unionized employment, due to electronics and IT outsourcing to Asia. African American identities are often a commodity, exploited as titillating fodder in a network that traffics in racism, sexism, and homophobia for profit. Meanwhile, the onus for change is placed on the backs of Black people, and Black women in the United States in particular, to play a more meaningful role in the production of new images and ideas about Black people by learning to code, as if that alone could shift the tide of Silicon Valley's vast exclusionary practices in its products and hiring.

Michele Wallace, a professor of English at the City College of New York and the Graduate Center of the City University of New York (CUNY), notes the crisis in lack of management, design, and control that Black people have over the production of commercial culture. She states that under these conditions, Black people will be "perpetual objects of contemplation, contempt, derision, appropriation, and marginalization."[45] Janell Hobson at the University of Albany draws important attention to Wallace's commentary on Black women as creative producers and in the context of the information age. She confirms this this confluence of media production on the web is part of the exclusionary terrain for Black women, who are underrepresented in many aspects of the information industry.[46] I would add to her argument that while it is true that the web can serve as an alternative space for conceiving of and sharing empowered conceptions of Black people, this happens in a highly commercially mediated environment. It is simply not enough to be "present" on the web; we must consider the implications of what it means to be on the web in the "long tail" or mediated out of discovery and meaningful participation, which can have a transformative impact on the enduring and brutal economic and social disenfranchisement of African Americans, especially among Black women.

Social Inequality Will Not Be Solved by an App

An app will not save us. We will not sort out social inequality lying in bed staring at smartphones. It will not stem from simply sending emails to people in power, one person at a time. New, neoliberal conceptions of individual freedoms (especially in the realm of technology use) are oversupported in direct opposition to protections realized through large-scale organizing to ensure collective rights. This is evident in the past thirty years of active antilabor policies put forward by several administrations[47] and in increasing hostility toward unions and twenty-first-century civil rights organizations such as Black Lives Matter. These proindividual, anticommunity ideologies have been central to the anti-democratic, anti-affirmative-action, antiwelfare, antichoice, and antirace discourses that place culpability for individual failure on moral failings of the individual, not policy decisions and social systems.[48] Discussions of institutional discrimination and systemic marginalization of whole classes and sectors of society have been shunted from public discourse for remediation and have given rise to viable presidential candidates such as Donald Trump, someone with a history of misogynistic violence toward women and anti-immigrant schemes. Despite resistance to this kind of vitriol in the national electoral body politic, society is also moving toward greater acceptance of technological processes that are seemingly benign and decontextualized, as if these projects are wholly apolitical and without consequence too. Collective efforts to regulate or provide social safety nets through public or governmental intervention are rejected. In this conception of society, individuals make choices of their own accord in the free market, which is normalized as the only legitimate source of social change.[49]

It is in this broader social and political environment that the Federal Communications Commission and Federal Trade Commission have been reluctant to regulate the Internet environment, with the exception of the Children's Internet Protection Act[50] and the Child Safe Viewing Act of 2007.[51] Attempts to regulate decency vis-à-vis racist, sexist, and homophobic harm have largely been unaddressed by the FCC, which places the onus for proving harm on the individual. I am trying to make the case, through the mounting evidence, that unregulated digital platforms cause serious harm. Trolling is directly linked to harassment offline, to bullying and suicide, to threats and attacks. The entire experiment of the Internet is now with us, yet we do not have enough intense scrutiny at the level of public policy on its psychological and social impact on the public.

The reliability of public information online is in the context of real, lived experiences of Americans who are increasingly entrenched in the shifts that are occurring in the information age. An enduring feature of the American experience is gross systemic poverty, whereby the largest percentages of people living below the poverty line suffering from un- and underemployment are women and children of color. The economic crisis continues to disproportionately impact poor people of color, especially Black / African American women, men, and children.[52] Furthermore, the gap between Black and White wealth has become so acute that a recent report by Brandeis University found that this gap quadrupled between 1984 and 2007, making Whites five times richer than Blacks in the U.S.[53] This is not the result of moral superiority; this is directly linked to the gamification of financial markets through algorithmic decision making. It is linked to the exclusion of Blacks, Latinos, and Native Americans from the high-paying jobs in technology sectors. It is a result of digital redlining and the resegregation of the housing and educational markets, fueled by seemingly innocuous big-data applications that allow the public to set tight parameters on their searches for housing and schools. Never before has it been so easy to set a school rating in a digital real estate application such as Zillow.com to preclude the possibility of going to "low-rated" schools, using data that reflects the long history of separate but equal, underfunded schools in neighborhoods where African Americans and low-income people live. These data-intensive applications that work across vast data sets do not show the microlevel interventions that are being made to racially and economically integrate schools to foster educational equity. They simply make it easy to take for granted data about "good schools" that almost exclusively map to affluent, White neighborhoods. We need more intense attention on how these types of artificial intelligence, under the auspices of individual freedom to make choices, forestall the ability to see what kinds of choices we are making and the collective impact of these choices in reversing decades of struggle for social, political, and economic equality. Digital technologies are implicated in these struggles.

These dramatic shifts are occurring in an era of U.S. economic policy that has accelerated globalization, moved real jobs offshore, and decimated labor interests. Claims that the society is moving toward greater social equality are undermined by data that show a substantive decrease in access to home ownership, education, and jobs—especially for Black Americans.[54] In the midst of the changing social and legal environment, inventions of terms and ideologies of "colorblindness" disingenuously purport a more humane and nonracist worldview.[55] This is exacerbated by celebrations of multiculturalism and diversity that obscure structural and social oppression in fields such as education and information sciences, which are shaping technological practices.[56] Research by Sharon Tettegah, a professor of education at the University of Nevada, Las Vegas, shows that people invested in colorblindness are also less empathetic toward others.[57] Making race the problem of those who are racially objectified, particularly when seeking remedy from discriminatory practices, obscures the role of government and the public in solving systemic issues.[58]

Central to these "colorblind" ideologies is a focus on the inappropriateness of "seeing race." In sociological terms, colorblindness precludes the use of racial information and does not allow any classifications or distinctions.[59] Yet, despite the claims of colorblindness, research shows that those who report higher racial colorblind attitudes are more likely to be White and more likely to condone or not be bothered by derogatory racial images viewed in online social networking sites.[60] Silicon Valley executives, as previously noted, revel in their embrace of colorblindness as if it is an asset and not a proven liability. In the midst of reenergizing the effort to connect every American and to stimulate new economic markets and innovations that the Internet and global communications infrastructures will afford, the real lives of those who are on the margin are being reengineered with new terms and ideologies that make a discussion about such conditions problematic, if not impossible, and that place the onus of discriminatory actions on the individual rather than situating problems affecting racialized groups in social structures.[61]

Formulations of postracialism presume that racial disparities no longer exist, a context within which the colorblind ideology finds momentum.[62] George Lipsitz, a critical Whiteness scholar and professor at the University of California, Santa Barbara, suggests that the challenge to recognizing racial disparities and the social (and technical) structures that instantiate them is a reflection of the possessive investment in Whiteness—which is the inability to recognize how White hegemonic ideas about race and privilege mask the ability to see real social problems.[63] I often challenge audiences who come to my talks to consider that at the very historical moment when structural barriers to employment were being addressed legislatively in the 1960s, the rise of our reliance on modern technologies emerged, positing that computers could make better decisions than humans. I do not think it a coincidence that when women and people of color are finally given opportunity to participate in limited spheres of decision making in society, computers are simultaneously celebrated as a more optimal choice for making social decisions. The rise of big-data optimism is here, and if ever there were a time when politicians, industry leaders, and academics were enamored with artificial intelligence as a superior approach to sense-making, it is now. This should be a wake-up call for people living in the margins, and people aligned with them, to engage in thinking through the interventions we need.

Conclusion

Algorithms of Oppression

We have more data and technology than ever in our daily lives and more social, political, and economic inequality and injustice to go with it. In this book, I have sought to critique the political-economic framework and representative discourse that surrounds racial and gendered identities on the web, but more importantly, I have shined a light on the way that algorithms are value-laden propositions worthy of our interrogation. I am particularly mindful of the push for digital technology adoption by Black / African Americans, divorced from the context of how digital technologies are implicated in global racial power relations. I have tried to show how traditional media misrepresentations have been instantiated in digital platforms such as search engines and that search itself has been interwoven into the fabric of American culture. Although rhetoric of the information age broadly seeks to disembody users, or at least to minimize the hegemonic backdrop of the technological revolution, African Americans have embraced, modified, and contextualized technology into significantly different frameworks despite the relations of power expressed in the socio-algorithms. This book can open up a dialogue about radical interventions on socio-technical systems in a more thoughtful way that does not further marginalize people who are already in the margins. Algorithms are, and will continue to be, contextually relevant and loaded with power.

Toward an Ethical Algorithmic Future

This book opens up new lines of inquiry using what I believe can be a black feminist technology studies (BFTS) approach to Internet research. BFTS could be theorized as an epistemological approach to researching gendered and racialized identities in digital and analog media studies, and it offers a new lens for exploring power as mediated by intersectional identities. More research on the politics, culture, and values embedded in search can help frame a broader context of African American digital technology usage and early adoption, which is largely underexamined, particularly from the perspectives of women and girls. BFTS is a way to bring more learning beyond the traditional discourse about technology consumption—and lack thereof—among Black people. Future research using this framework can surface counternarratives about Black people and technology and can include how African American popular cultural practices are influencing non–African American youth.[1] Discourses about African Americans and women as technologically illiterate are nothing new, but dispelling the myth of Blacks / African Americans as marginal to the broadest base of digital technology users can help us define new ways of thinking about motivations in the next wave of technology innovation, design, and, quite possibly, resistance.

Algorithms and Invisibility: My Interview with Kandis

Most of the attention to the protection of online information has been argued legally as a matter of "rights." Rights are a type of property, or entitlement, that function on the web through a variety of narratives, such as "free speech" and "freedom of expression," all of which are constitutionally protected in the United States. The framing of web content and ownership of web URLs as "property" afforded private protections is of consequence for individuals, as noted in Jessie Daniels's aforementioned work, which documents the misrepresentation of Dr. Martin Luther King Jr. at the site martinlutherking.org, a cloaked website managed by neo-Nazis and White supremacists at Stormfront.[2] Private ownership of identity on the web is a matter of who can pay and who lines up quickly enough to purchase identity markers that establish a type of official record about a person or a group of people. Indeed, anyone can own anyone else's identity in the current digital landscape. The right to control over group and personal identity and memory must become a matter of concern for archivists, librarians, and information workers, and a matter of internet regulation and public policy.

In concluding this book, I want to extend an example beyond Google to look closely at the consequences of the lack of identity control on another platform: Yelp.

Kandis has been in business for thirty years, and her primary clients are African American. This is her story, which elucidates in a very personal way how algorithmic oppression works and is affecting her very quality of life as a small business owner who runs the only local African American hair salon within a predominantly White neighborhood, located near a prestigious college town in the United States:

When I first came and opened up my shop here, there was a strong African American community. There were Black sororities and fraternities, and they had step shows, which no loner exist anymore! The Black Student Union organization was very strong; it was the '80s. Everyone felt like family, and everyone knew each other. Even though I only worked in this part of town, it was almost like I went to school there too. We all knew each other, and everyone celebrated each other's success.

I often get invited to participate in the major events and celebrations—from marriages to their parents' funerals. For instance, I have several clients from the '80s who I still service to this day. Here it is twenty years later, and now I'm servicing their sons' and daughters' hair, who may or may not attend the same university. The relationships are intact and so strong. It's not uncommon, even if we aren't always in touch for the past several years, for clients who may live on the other side of the country to send a recommendation my way! I have worked in this community for thirty years. I know a lot of people. They all have to get their hair done.

I asked Kandis how has that changed:

Well, prior to the changes the Internet brought about, I never had to do much advertising because my name carried weight through the campus and the graduate school. So, if you were a Black prelaw or premed student, I would know who you were, pretty much as you were coming into the school, because people would tell them about me, and then they would book an appointment with me.

But now, since there are only a small number of African Americans at the university, and those few people aren't looking up at each other, we are losing the art of conversation and how we used to verbally pass information. So my name started dying down. It kind of reminds me of how in elementary school, there are songs that kids sing, and they continue through generations. All kids know certain nursery rhymes and songs, even the ones their parents sang when they were little. It's like those song are trapped in time.

We, as African Americans, are storytellers. My name is not being talked about anymore, because young people don't talk to each other anymore. I was able to afford a modest lifestyle. Prior to these changes, from the stock market crashing and now this way of doing business through technology, life has become an uphill battle, and I felt like I was drowning. I've actually considered leaving, but where would I go? Where would I go?

Look, I'm very much used to diversity, but when the campus stopped admitting so many Blacks, I became a minority in a way that I had never felt before. You think of the university as being a part of the community, and the community would benefit from the university. But I don't think they thought about would happen to all the businesses who supported those students. Where would the students and faculty go to get their needs met, like their hair cared for? I mean, other students can go down the street to anyone, but the Black students have to have a car to travel thirty minutes across town? Why are they required have to have a car or transportation when no one else needs that to get their hair done?

Kandis was directly impacted by the shifts away from affirmative action that decimated the admission of African Americans to colleges and universities over the past twenty years:

Sometimes people are in a highly competitive arena, and they need to go to a nonjudgmental place where they can be themselves and where they don't have to apologize for the way they speak or their culture or wonder if they go to a Caucasian hair stylist, if they can handle their hair.

To be a Black woman and to need hair care can be an isolating experience.

The quality of service I provide touches more than just the external part of someone. It's not just about their hair. A lot of people are away from their families, and they need someone to trust who will support them. People do like to be recommended to someone they can trust.

I asked Kandis how the Internet changed things for her and her business:

Back then, when I had many more clients, there was no Internet. A personal computer was almost like a concept but not a reality for most people. At the beginning, you had a lot of younger people on the cutting edge of computers or who were more computer savvy and up on the current trend. My generation was a little bit slower to comprehend and participate. The Internet has also developed a new age of the infomercial and the how-to-do-it-yourself university!

The Internet is now showing everyone how to do it themselves and how to cut out the middleman. They have created the new consumers. New consumers have less value for small businesses; they think just because they watch the new infomercial, they can do it themselves, buy it themselves, make it themselves. Also, because you can purchase everything for yourself, the new consumers now feel entitled. They feel no shame with coming in and snapping photographs. They collect your hard work, all your information in two seconds, by taking pictures of all of my products so they can go and purchase them online instead of from me.

When things started changing so fast technologically, using the computer was an easier transition for me, because I had taken a few computer [Mac] classes on campus, and I was able to adapt to what was going on. Because of this, I was familiar, and I was comfortable with exploring the unknown.

I quickly realized the Internet/Yelp told people that I did not exist.

I think algorithms don't take into consideration communities of color and their culture of trusting in the web with our personal information and that we are dealing with things that won't even allow us to give someone a review. We don't like to give our personal information out like that. And just because I don't have reviews doesn't mean that I have no value. Because the computer, or I guess the Internet/Yelp, is redefining who is valuable and where the value lies, and I believe this is false. It's not right.

The algorithm shouldn't get to decide whether I exist or not. So I had to figure it out, within my financial limitations, because now it becomes another financial burden to stay relevant in eyes of what the web is telling people about who is valuable. I had to be creative and spend a lot of time on the computer trying to figure what was the least expensive way to be visible with the most impact.

So, when I discovered Yelp and it's alleged benefits—because I don't think it really benefited me—I was forced to participate in Yelp.

I asked what that participation with Yelp was like.

They tell you that everything is free, like they are doing a community service, but later on, it's basically pay to play. They call on a regular basis to get you to spend a few hundred dollars a month to advertise with them, and if you don't, they are going to push you further down their pile. I can be sitting in my chair searching for myself and not find me or find me ten pages later. I can type in every keyword, like "African American," "Black," "relaxer," natural," as keywords, and White businesses, White hairdressers, or White salons would clearly come up before me—along with people who have not been in business as long as me. I think they need to put in how long someone has been in business in that algorithm, because I don't think it's fair that people who are brand new are popping up before those of us who may or may not be on the Internet but have more experience and are more established.

And another thing, Black people don't "check in" and let people know where they're at when they sit in my chair. They already feel like they are being hunted; they aren't going to tell The Man where they are. I have reviews from real clients that they put into a filter because it doesn't meet their requirements of how they think someone should review me.

I asked her to tell me more about that.

I think Yelp looks at people as *their* clients, not mine. If they are your clients who are loyal to your business and you, they are not interested. They want to market to my clients, and if you review me and you've never reviewed any other businesses, they are not going to take you as a serious voice on Yelp. What is that about? They are selling to the reviewers. Since I am the only Black person in this neighborhood doing hair, that should tip the scale in my favor, but it doesn't. If they were honest, it would mean I would go to the top. But they are promoting and biasing the lay of the land in this area, which is causing me more harm by making it look like I don't exist.

I have been on Facebook and pulled up some folks who work at Yelp, and from my perspective and from what I saw, there weren't that many Black people. It wasn't diverse. You can see everyone on FB, and these people are not Black people. And that's a problem, because how would they know to even consider the needs of a minority or what our language is? You are telling us we have to use certain keywords, and you don't even know our language, because you think that "Black hair" means hair *color*, not *texture*! We don't call each other African American; society calls us that. Do you know what I mean? We are Black.

You know, they locked me out of Yelp. When I sent them an email asking them why I wasn't on the first page of Yelp and why, when I'm sitting in my chair, I can't find myself and why, when I used certain keywords, I couldn't find myself. I told them that by doing that, they are suggesting I don't exist. At that time, they put most of my reviews in a filter and locked me out for about four months. Every time you make a change on Yelp, there is someone checking you. If you go into your page, there is someone looking at what you are doing. I know that because if you get people inquiring about you, Yelp will call you and try to get advertising from you. And they will say that they see people trying to connect with you through Yelp, and then they will try to sell you advertising. They will try to show their value by saying they can help you get more business.

I used to have my own page, but now you have a third of a page with people who are similar to you. And if they don't choose you, they are showing your competition. For a fee, they will remove your competition, but otherwise they are showing your competition on your own page! You don't have your own page anymore; you are on a page with advertising and your competition, who are similar to your style, and they will put you up against them while searching on your own business.

They'd rather put other salons in other parts of the city to avoid driving the clients to someone who is not paying for advertisement. So I would do something like put up a picture of myself, as this was something that they suggested, and I use keywords to be found, but that doesn't help now.

Before, Yelp would encourage the business owner to upload a photo of themselves, and that was great for me. This is when being in the minority would help me stand out. That didn't last long because they stopped showing your head shot, and now they put up a map instead of allowing you to use your own your image. Your own image isn't shown. Before you get to my photos and my reviews, there are suggestions to other people who could be as far as five miles or more away. The first one is laser hair removal and extensions. I don't do hair removal or extensions.[3]

Kandis pulled out her mobile phone and walked me through her Yelp page and showed me how it works.

They are already advertising against me. At the end of the page, there are more competitors. I have to pay to take that off. My reviews are in the middle. You can't control the photos anymore. They have a "people who viewed this also viewed . . ." section, and it goes to other businesses. I have to pay to get that taken off. They have a few reviews now that are blocked, that they felt that I had asked my clients to do, and because these people haven't reviewed other people, they don't show.

So if you get two reviews in one day and haven't had any in six months, they think you have done something, and they block my reviews.[4] The basic principle of Yelp is to supposedly lead people with unbiased decisions when choosing a good business. How? You tell me? Can they honestly do this when they're in the business of selling the advertisement?

They control the algorithm, which controls who can write the reviews. All this has a major influence on where you're placed on the list. You hope and pray that your customers, who may be from a different generation or culture, will participate in their construct. It just isn't as random as one may think.

There is no algorithm that can replace human dignity. They created a system that simulates a value, based on their own algorithm, so Yelp can be the number-one beneficiary. When companies like Yelp shake the tree for low-hanging fruit, this affects mostly small businesses and the livelihoods of real people who will never work for corporate America. The key is to be independent of these companies, because they never stop. They have new goals, and they come back with new visions. And it's not like a real contract where you can argue and negotiate. The scale is unbalanced; you can't negotiate.

I verified all of the claims that Kandis was making by visiting her page and the pages of other small business to see how they placed her competitors. Indeed, several times when I thought I was clicking on reviews of her small business or getting more information, I was instead clicking on competitors and led away from the business I was investigating. I share Kandis's experience to demonstrate the way that both the interface and the algorithmic design is taking on new dimensions of control and influence over her representation and access to information about her business. She has so little ability to impact the algorithm, and when she tries, the company subverts her ability to be racially and gender recognized—a type of recognition that is essential to her success as a business owner. The attempts at implementing a colorblind algorithm in lieu of human decision making has tremendous consequences. In the case of Kandis, what the algorithm says and refuses to say about her identity and the identity of her customers has real social and economic impact.

Imagining Alternatives: Toward Public Noncommercial Search

Neoliberal impulses in the United States to support market-driven information portals such as Google Search have consequences for finding high-quality information on the Internet about people and communities, since this is the primary pathway to navigating the web. This is one of the many contradictions of the current for-profit search and cloud-computing industry. Future research efforts might address questions that can help us understand the role of the design of platforms, interfaces, software, and experiences as practices that are culturally and gender situated and often determined by economic imperatives, power, and values. Such an agenda could forward a commitment to ensuring that pornographic or exploitive websites do not stand as the default identification for women on the web. Despite a climate wherein everything driven by market interests is considered the most expedient and innovative way of generating solutions, we see the current failings. Calling attention to these practices, however unpopular it might be, is necessary to foster a climate where information can be trusted and found to be reliable. What is needed is a decoupling of advertising and commercial interests from the ability to access high-quality information on the Internet, especially given its increasing prominence as the common medium in the United States.

When using a digital media platform, be it Google Search or Yelp or some other ranking algorithmic decision's default settings, it is possible to believe that it is normal to see a list of only a handful of possible results on the first page of a search, but this "normal" is a direct result of the way that human beings have consciously designed both software and hardware to function this way and no other.

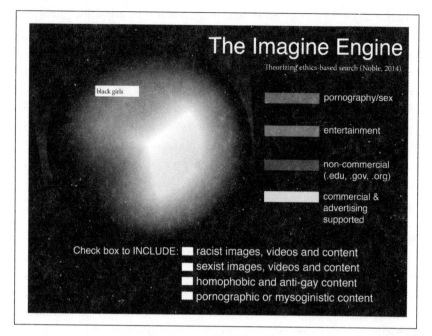

Figure C.1. S. U. Noble's interface of transparency: the imagine engine.

Imagine instead that all of our results were delivered in a visual rainbow of color that symbolized a controlled set of categories such that everything on the screen that was red was pornographic, everything that was green was business or commerce related, everything orange was entertainment, and so forth. In this kind of scenario, we could see the entire indexable web and click on the colors we are interested in and go deeply into the shades we want to see. Indeed, we can and should imagine search with a variety of other possibilities. In my own imagination and in a project I am attempting to build, access to information on the web could be designed akin to the color-picker tool or some other highly transparent interface, so that users could find nuanced shades of information and easily identify the borderlands between news and entertainment, or entertainment and pornography, or journalism and academic scholarship. In this scenario, I might also be able to quickly identify the blogosphere and personal websites.

Such imaginings are helpful in an effort to denaturalize and reconceptualize how information could be provided to the public vis-à-vis the search engine. In essence, we need greater transparency and public pressure to slow down the automation of our worst impulses. We have automated human decision making and then disavowed our responsibility for it. Without public funding and adequate information policy that protects the rights to fair representation online, an escalation in the erosion of quality information to inform the public will continue.

Where Are Black Girls Now?

Since I began the pilot study in 2010 and collected data through 2016, some things have changed. In 2012, I wrote an article for *Bitch Magazine*, which covers popular culture from a feminist perspective, after some convincing from my students that this topic is important to all people—not just Black women and girls. I argued that we all want access to credible information that does not foster racist or sexist views of one another. I cannot say that the article had any influence on Google in any definitive way, but I have continued to search for Black girls on a regular basis, at least once a month. Within about six weeks of the article hitting newsstands, I did another search for "black girls," and I can report that Google had changed its algorithm to some degree about five months after that article was published. After years of featuring pornography as the primary representation of Black girls, Google made modifications to its algorithm, and the results as of the conclusion of this research can be seen if figure C.2.

No doubt, as I speak around the world on this subject, audiences are often furiously doing searches from their smart phones, trying to reconcile these issues with the momentary results. Some days they are horrified, and other times, they are less concerned, because some popular and positive issue or organization has broken through the clutter and moved to a top position on the first page. Indeed, as this book was going into production, news exploded of biased information about the U.S. presidential election flourishing through Google and Facebook, which had significant consequences in the political arena.

I encourage us all to take notice and to reconsider the affordances and the consequences of our hyperreliance on these technologies as they shift and take on more import over time. What we need now, more than ever, is public policy that advocates protections from the effects of unregulated and unethical artificial intelligence.

Google   black girls   Sign in

All   Images   Videos   Shopping   News   More ▾   Search tools

About 301,000,000 results (0.42 seconds)

Black Girls Code
www.**blackgirlscode**.com/ ▾ Black Girls Code ▾
Black Girls Code, BlackGirlsCode, STEM education San Francisco, Technology training for girls, diversity learning, Social Entrepreneurship in San Francisco, ...

Black Girls Rock
www.**blackgirls**rockinc.com/ ▾
2016 **Black Girls** Rock! HONOREES. Rihanna ... TUNE IN TO CELEBRATE A NIGHT OF **BLACK GIRL** MAGIC WITH. **Black Girls** Rock!

Read More - Black Girls Rock
www.**blackgirls**rockinc.com/home/ ▾
Amandla Stenberg is an actress, fashionista and social activist. She has been featured in many TV shows such as Hunger Games and Sleep Hollow. She also ...

In the news

7-Year-Old Writes Book To Show Black Girls They Are Princesses
Huffington Post - 2 days ago
Morgan Taylor wants to make sure every little black and brown girl feels like royalty. Which is ...

Black Girls Code relaunching Saturday with gaming workshop
Miami Herald - 51 mins ago

More news for black girls

Black Girls Rock! Homepage - BET.com
www.bet.com/shows/**black-girls**-rock.html ▾ BET ▾
Check out all things **Black Girls** Rock! here. ... Rihanna Owns Her Role as a Rock Star · **Black Girls** Rock!, 2016, Highlights, Hillary Clinton, Beverly Bond ...

9 Types of Black Girls - YouTube
https://www.youtube.com/watch?v=HELQYU6nSiA ▾
Aug 12, 2015 - 30 LIKES FOR 9 TYPES OF BLACK FRIENDS!!!!!!!! These are 9 Types of **Black Girls** you are bound to come across in your lifetime. Most likely ...

(@darkskin.blackgirls) • Instagram photos and videos
https://www.instagram.com/darkskin.**blackgirls**/ ▾
Dedicated to Darkskin Women #BlackLivesMatter   Business Inquiries: darkskin .**blackgirls**@yahoo.com DM For a Feature Tag them if you know their ...

Black Girls RUN!
blackgirlsrun.com/ ▾
Welcome to the MOVEment | **Black Girls** RUN!**Black Girls** RUN!

Black Girls Are Easy |
blackgirlsareeasy.com/ ▾
Black Girls Are Easy has been voted the top dating and relationship advice website of the year!

Why Are Black Girls Disproportionally Pushed Out of Schools? - The ...
www.theatlantic.com/education/archive/2016/03/the...of-**black-girls**-in.../473718/
The "good girl" and "bad girl" dichotomy, as chronicled by Monique W. Morris in Pushout: The Criminalization of **Black Girls** in Schools, is a ...

Study: Black Girls Are Being Pushed Out of School : Code Switch : NPR
www.npr.org/sections/codeswitch/.../study-**black-girls**-are-being-pushed-out-of-school
News surrounding a confrontation in a Baltimore school is raising new questions about the role race plays in discipline for black girls. Baltimore ...

I Have a Problem With #BlackGirlMagic - Black Girls Aren't Magical ...
www.elle.com/life-love/a33180/why-i-dont-love-**blackgirl**magic/

See results about

Black Girls Code (Not-for-p..
Founder: Kimberly Bryant
Headquarters: San Francis...

Figure C.2. My last Google search on "black girls," June 23, 2016.

Between the time I wrote this book and the day it went into production, the landscape of U.S. politics was radically altered with the presidential defeat on November 8, 2016, of former secretary of state Hillary Clinton by Donald Trump. Within days, media pundits and pollsters were trying to make sense of the upset, the surprise win by Trump, particularly since Clinton won the popular vote by close to three million votes.

Immediately, there were claims that "fake news" circulating online was responsible for the outcome. Indeed, as I gave talks about this book in the weeks after the election, I could only note in my many public talks that "as I've argued for years about the harm toward women and girls through commercial information bias circulating through platforms like Google, no one has seemed to care until it threw a presidential election." Notably, one remarkable story about disinformation (patently false information intended to deceive) made headlines about the election results.

This new political landscape has dramatically altered the way we might think about public institutions being a major force in leveling the playing field of information that is curated in the public interest. And it will likely be the source of a future book that recontextualizes what information means in the new policy regime that ensues under the leadership of avowed White supremacists and disinformation experts who have entered the highest levels of public governance.

Agencies that could have played a meaningful role in supporting research about the role of information and research in society, including the Institute for Museum and Library Services, the National Endowment for the Humanities, and the National Endowment for the Arts, are all under the threat of being permanently defunded and dismantled as of the moment this book goes into production. In fact, public research universities are also facing serious threats in cuts to federal funding because of their lack of compliance with the new administration's policies. This has

Figure E.1. Google search for "final election results" leads to fake news. Source: *Washington Post*, November 14, 2016.

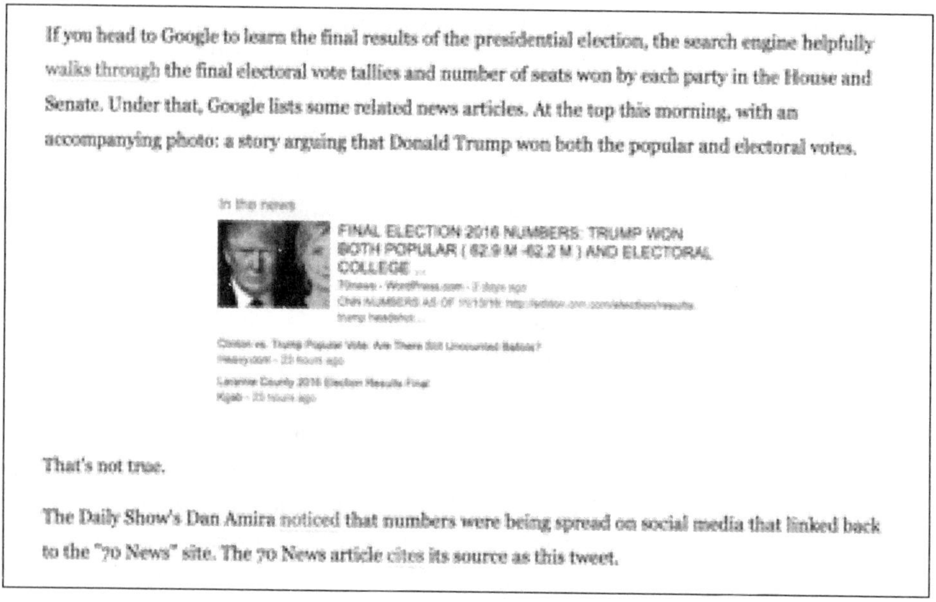

If you head to Google to learn the final results of the presidential election, the search engine helpfully walks through the final electoral vote tallies and number of seats won by each party in the House and Senate. Under that, Google lists some related news articles. At the top this morning, with an accompanying photo: a story arguing that Donald Trump won both the popular and electoral votes.

> In the news
>
> FINAL ELECTION 2016 NUMBERS: TRUMP WON
> BOTH POPULAR (62.9 M -62.2 M) AND ELECTORAL
> COLLEGE ...
> 70news - WordPress.com - 2 days ago
> CNN NUMBERS AS OF 11/13/16: http://edition.cnn.com/election/results
> trump headshot ...
>
> Clinton vs. Trump Popular Vote: Are There Still Uncounted Ballots?
> Heavy.com - 23 hours ago
> Laramie County 2016 Election Results Final
> Kjab - 23 hours ago

That's not true.

The Daily Show's Dan Amira noticed that numbers were being spread on social media that linked back to the "70 News" site. The 70 News article cites its source as this tweet.

Figure E.2. Google results on final election results incorrectly show Trump as the winner of the popular vote. Source: *Washington Post*, November 14, 2016.

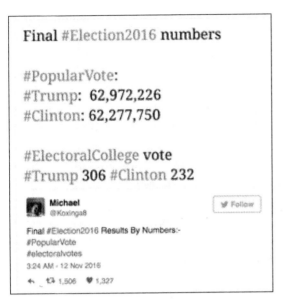

Figure E.3. Circulation of false information on Twitter shows Trump as the winner of the popular vote, November 14, 2016.

so radically altered the research landscape to the political right that scientists and researchers marched on Washington, D.C., on April 22, 2017, in response to orders that government-funded scientists and researchers stop conducting and disseminating research to the public. The potential for such a precedent may extend to public research universities, or at least many faculty members are working under the premise that this may not be out of the realm of possibility over the next four to eight years.

In this book, I have argued that the neoliberal political and economic environment has profited tremendously from misinformation and mischaracterization of communities, with a range of consequences for the most disenfranchised and marginalized among us. I have also argued for increased nonprofit and public research funding to explore alternatives to commercial information platforms, which would have included support of noncommercial search engines that could serve the public and pay closer attention to the circulation of patently false or harmful information. In the current environment, I would be remiss if I did not acknowledge, on the eve of the publication of this book, that this may not be viable at all given the current policy environment that is unfolding.

My hope is that the public will reclaim its institutions and direct our resources in service of a multiracial democracy. Now, more than ever, we need libraries, universities, schools, and information resources that will help bolster and further expand democracy for all, rather than shrink the landscape of participation along racial, religious, and gendered lines. Information circulates in cultural contexts of acceptability. It is not enough to simply want the most accurate and credible information to rise to the top of a search engine, but it is certainly an important step toward impacting the broader culture of information use that helps us make decisions about the distribution of resources among the most powerful and the most disenfranchised members of our society.

In short, we must fight to suspend the circulation of racist and sexist material that is used to erode our civil and human rights. I hope this book provides some steps toward doing so.

NOTES

INTRODUCTION

1. Matsakis, 2017.
2. See Peterson, 2014.
3. This term was coined by Eli Pariser in his book *The Filter Bubble* (2011).
4. See Dewey, 2015.
5. I use phrases such as "the N-word" or "n*gger" rather than explicitly using the spelling of a racial epithet in my scholarship. As a regular practice, I also do not cite or promote non–African American scholars or research that flagrantly uses the racial epithet in lieu of alternative phrasings.
6. See Sweney, 2009.
7. See Boyer, 2015; Craven, 2015.
8. See Noble, 2014.
9. The term "digital footprint," often attributed to Nicholas Negroponte, refers to the online identity traces that are used by digital media platforms to understand the profile of a user. The online interactions are often tracked across a variety of hardware (e.g., mobile phones, computers, internet services) and platforms (e.g., Google's Gmail, Facebook, and various social media) that are on the World Wide Web. Digital traces are often used in the data-mining process to profile users. A digital footprint can often include time, geographic location, and past search results and clicks that have been tracked through websites and advertisements, including cookies that are stored on a device or other hardware.
10. "Kandis" is a pseudonym.
11. See H. Schiller, 1996.

CHAPTER 1. A SOCIETY, SEARCHING

1. See UN Women 2013.
2. See Diaz, 2008; Segev, 2010; Nissenbaum and Introna, 2004
3. See Olson, 1998; Berman, 1971; Wilson, 1968; and Furner, 2007.
4. See Daniels, 2009, 2013; Davis and Gandy, 1999.
5. See Halavais, 2009, 1–2.
6. See Angwin et al., 2016.
7. See O'Neil, 2016, 8.
8. See Levin, 2016.
9. See Kleinman, 2015.

10. The debates over Google as a monopoly were part of a congressional Antitrust Subcommittee hearing on September 21, 2011, and the discussion centered around whether Google is causing harm to consumers through its alleged monopolistic practices. Google has responded to these assertions. See Kohl and Lee, 2011.

11. See Ascher, 2017.

12. See Leonard, 2009.

13. See Daniels, 2009, 2013; Brock, 2009.

14. See Kendall, 2002.

15. See Brock, 2009.

16. See S. Harding, 1987, 7.

17. See chapter 2 for a detailed discussion of the "Jewish" disclaimer by Google.

18. See hooks, 1992; Harris-Perry, 2011; Ladson-Billings, 2009; Miller-Young, 2007; Sharpley-Whiting, 1999; C. M. West, 1995; Harris, 1995; Collins, 1991; Hull, Bell-Scott, and Smith, 1982.

19. See Collins, 1991; hooks, 1992; Harris, 1995; Crenshaw, 1991.

20. See Brock, 2007.

21. The "digital divide" is a narrative about the lack of connectivity of underserved or marginalized groups in the United States that stems from the National Telecommunications and Information Administration report on July 8, 1999, *Falling through the Net: Defining the Digital Divide.*

22. See Inside Google 2010.

23. See Fallows, 2005; Purcell, Brenner, and Rainie, 2012.

24. A detailed discussion of this subject can be found in a Google disclaimer about the results that surface when a user searches on the word "Jew." The URL for this disclaimer (now defunct) was www.google.com/explanation.html.

25. Senate Judiciary Committee, Subcommittee on Antitrust, Competition Policy and Consumer Rights, 2011.

26. See Elad Segev's work on Google and global inequality (2010).

27. A good discussion of the ways that Google uses crowdsourcing as an unpaid labor pool for projects such as Google Image Labeler can be found in the blog *Labortainment* at http://labortainment.blogspot.com (last accessed June 20, 2012).

28. See the work of Cameron McCarthy, professor of education at the University of Illinois at Urbana-Champaign (1994).

29. See Nissenbaum and Introna, 2004; Vaidhyanathan, 2011; Segev, 2010; Diaz, 2008; and Noble, 2014.

30. This process has been carefully detailed by Levene, 2006.

31. Blogger, Wordpress, Drupal, and other digital media platforms make the process of building and linking to other sites as simple as the press of a button, rather than having to know code to implement.

32. See Spink et al., 2001; Jansen and Pooch, 2001; Wolfram, 2008.

33. See Markey, 2007.

34. See Ferguson, Kreshel, and Tinkham, 1990.

35. See Wasson, 1973; Courtney and Whipple, 1983.

36. See Smith, 1981.

37. See Bar-Ilan, 2007.

38. Google's official statement on how often it crawls is as follow: "Google's spiders regularly crawl the Web to rebuild our index. Crawls are based on many factors such as PageRank™, links to a page, and crawling constraints such as the number of parameters in a URL. Any number of factors can affect the crawl frequency of individual sites. Our crawl process is algorithmic; computer programs determine which sites to crawl, how often, and how many pages to fetch from each site. We don't accept payment to crawl a site more frequently." See Google, "About Google's Regular Crawling of the Web," accessed July 6, 2012, http://support.google.com/webmasters/bin/answer.py?hl=en&answer=34439.

39. Brin and Page, 1998a: 110.

40. Ibid.

41. Brin and Page, 1998b, 18, citing Bagdikian, 1983.

42. On June 27, 2012, the online news outlets *The Local* and *The Raw Story* reported on Google's settlement of the claim based on concerns over linking the word "Jew" with popular personalities. See AFP, 2012.

43. Anti-Defamation League, 2004.

44. Ibid.

45. See Zittrain and Edelman, 2002.

46. See SEMPO, 2010.

47. A website dedicated to the history of web memes attributes the precursor to the term "Google bombing" to Archimedes Plutonium, a Usenet celebrity, who created the term "searchenginebombing" in 1997. For more information, see "Google Bombing," Know Your Meme, accessed June 20, 2012, http://knowyourmeme.com/memes/google-bombing. Others still argue that the first Google bomb was created by Black Sheep, who associated the terms "French Military Victory" to a redirect to a mock page that looked like Google and listed all of the French military defeats, with the exception of the French Revolution, in which the French were allegedly successful in killing their own French citizens. The first, most infamous instance of Google bombing was the case of *Hugedisk* magazine linking the text "dumb motherfucker" to a site that supported George W. Bush. For more information, see Calore and Gilbertson, 2001.

48. Brin and Page note that in the Google prototype, a search on "cellular phone" results in PageRank making the first result a study about the risks of talking on a cell phone while driving.

49. See SEMPO, 2004, 4.

50. In 2003, the radio host and columnist Dan Savage encouraged his listeners to go to a website he created, www.santorum.com, and post definitions of the word "santorum" after the Republican senator made a series of antigay remarks that outraged the public.

51. See Hindman, 2009; Zittrain, 2008; Vaidhyanathan, 2011.

52. Steele and Iliinsky, 2010, 143.

53. See Hindman, 2009.

54. Ibid.

55. See Gulli and Signorini, 2005.

56. Federal Communications Commission, 2010.

57. Associated Press v. United States, 326 U.S. 1, 20 (1945). Diaz (2008) carefully traces the fundamental notion of deliberative democracy and its critical role in keeping the public informed, in the tradition of John Stuart Mill's treatise "On Liberty," which contends that democracy cannot flourish without public debate and discourse from the widest range of possible points of view.

58. See Van Couvering, 2004, 2008; Diaz, 2008; Noble, 2014; and Zimmer, 2009.

59. See Lev-On, 2008.

60. See Andrejevic, 2007.

61. See Goldsmith and Wu, 2006.

62. H. Schiller, 1996, 48.

63. See Fallows, 2005; Purcell, Brenner, and Rainie, 2012.

64. President Eisenhower forewarned of these projects in his farewell speech on January 17, 1961, when he said, "In the councils of government, we must guard against the acquisition of unwarranted influence, whether sought or unsought, by the military-industrial complex. The potential for the disastrous rise of misplaced power exists and will persist." Eisenhower, 1961.

65. Niesen, 2012.

66. The full report can be accessed at www.pewinternet.org.

67. See Epstein and Robertson, 2015.

68. Purcell, Brenner, and Rainie, 2012, 2. Pew reports these findings from a survey conducted from January 20 to February 19, 2012, among 2,253 adults, age eighteen and over, including 901 cellphone interviews. Interviews were conducted in English and Spanish. The margin of error for the full sample is plus or minus two percentage points.

69. Feuz, Fuller, and Stalder, 2011.

70. Google Web History is designed to track signed-in users' searches in order to better track their interests. Considerable controversy followed Google's announcement, and many online articles were published with step-by-step instructions on how to protect privacy by ensuring that Google Web History was disabled. For more information on the controversy, see Tsukayama, 2012. Google has posted official information about its project at http://support.google.com/accounts/bin/answer.py?hl=en&answer=54068&topic=14149&ctx=topic (accessed June 22, 2012).

71. Leigh Estabrook and Ed Lakner (2000) have conducted a national study on Internet control mechanisms used by libraries, which primarily consist of policies and user education rather than filtering. These policies and mechanisms are meant to deter users from accessing objectionable content, including pornography, but also other material that might be considered offensive.

72. See Corea, 1993; Dates, 1990; Mastro and Tropp, 2004; Stroman, Merrit, and Matabane, 1989.

73. The Chicago Urban League has developed a Digital Media Strategy that is specifically concerned with the content and images of Black people on the Internet. See the organization's website: www.thechicagourbanleague.org.

74. The NAACP Image Awards recognize positive images of Blacks in the media. See the organization's website: www.naacp.org.

75. See Hunt, Ramón, and Tran, 2016.

76. FreePress.org has a page dedicated to the issues of civil rights and media justice. See www.freepress.net/media_issues/civil_rights (accessed April 15, 2012).

77. The Federal Trade Commission is looking into the privacy issues facing Americans over Google's targeted and behavior-based advertising programs. It has also settled out of court over the Google book-digitization project, which was reported in the media as a "monopolistic online land grab" over public domain orphan works. See Yang and Easton, 2009.

78. See Roberts, 2016; Stone, 2010.

79. For more information, see Roberts, 2012.

80. Roberts, 2016.

81. See Heider and Harp, 2002; Gunkel and Gunkel, 1997; Pavlik, 1996; Kellner, 1995; Barlow, 1996.

82. See Heider and Harp, 2002.

83. Ibid., 289.

84. Berger, 1972, 64.

85. See Mayall and Russell, 1993, 295.

86. Gardner, 1980, 105–106.

87. Gunkel and Gunkel, 1997, 131.

88. Lipsitz, 1998, 370.

89. Ibid., 381.

90. See Mills, 2014.

91. See Winner, 1986; Pacey, 1983.

92. See Chouliaraki and Fairclough, 1999.

93. See Barlow, 1996.

94. See Segev, 2010.

95. Stepan, 1998, 28.

96. #Gamergate was an incident involving a group of anonymous harassers of women in the video-gaming industry, including Zoë Quinn and Brianna Wu, as well as the writer and critic Anita Sarkeesian, who faced death threats and threats of rape, among others. In response to challenges of white male supremacy, sexism, racism, and misogyny in video-game culture, many women video-game developers, feminists, and men supporting women in gaming were attacked online as well as stalked and harassed.

CHAPTER 2. SEARCHING FOR BLACK GIRLS

1. See Guynn, 2016.

2. See Hiles, 2015.

3. See Sinclair, 2004; Everett, 2009; Nelson, Tu, and Hines, 2001; Daniels, 2015; Weheliye, 2003; Eglash, 2002; Noble, 2012.

4. See chapter 2 for a detailed explanation of Google AdWords.

5. To protect the identity of subjects in the websites and advertisements, I intentionally erased faces and body parts using Adobe Photoshop while still leaving enough visual elements for a reader to make sense of the content and discourse of the text and images.

6. See Omi and Winant, 1994.

7. See Daniels, 2009.

8. Ibid., 56.

9. Treitler, 1998, 966.

10. See Golash-Boza, 2016.

11. Omi and Winant, 1994, 67.

12. See Daniels, 2013.

13. See Hall, 1989; Davis and Gandy, 1999.

14. See Fraser, 1996.

15. Jansen and Spink, 2006.

16. McCarthy, 1994, 91.

17. Davis and Gandy, 1999, 368.

18. Barzilai-Nahon, 2006.

19. See Segev, 2010.

20. Ibid.

21. See Williamson, 2014.

22. XMCP, 2008.

23. Morville, 2005, 4.

24. See C. M. West, 1995; hooks, 1992.

25. See Ladson-Billings, 2009.

26. See Yarbrough and Bennett, 2000.

27. See Treitler, 2013; Bell, 1992; Delgado and Stefancic, 1999.

28. See Davis and Gandy, 1999; Gray, 1989; Matabane, 1988; Wilson, Gutierrez, and Chao, 2003.

29. See Dates, 1990.

30. Punyanunt-Carter, 2008.

31. Ford, 1997.

32. Fujioka, 1999.

33. Pacey, 1983; Winner, 1986; Warf and Grimes, 1997.

34. See Pacey, 1983.

35. Winner, 1986.

36. Warf and Grimes, 1997, 260.

37. Brock, 2011, 1088.

38. Harvey, 2005; Fairclough, 1995.

39. See Boyle, 2003; D. Schiller, 2007.

40. See Davis, 1972.

41. See Dorsey, 2003.
42. See hooks, 1992, 62.
43. Ibid.
44. Dorsey, 2003.
45. Ibid.
46. U.S. Census Bureau, 2008.
47. According to the U.S. Census Bureau (2007). 5.4% of White married people live in poverty, compared to 9.7% of Blacks and 14.9% of Hispanics. Among single people, 22.5% of Whites live in poverty, compared to 44% of Blacks and 33.4% of Hispanics.
48. Ibid.
49. See the "Panel Study of Income Dynamics," reportedly the longest running longitudinal household survey in the world, conducted by the University of Michigan: http://psidonline.isr.umich.edu.
50. Lerner, 1986, 223.
51. Ibid.
52. See Sharpley-Whiting, 1999; Hobson, 2008.
53. See Braun et al., 2007.
54. Ibid., e271 (original notes omitted).
55. Ibid.
56. See Stepan, 1998.
57. See L. Harding, 2012.
58. See White, [1985] 1999.
59. See the museum's website: www.ferris.edu/jimcrow.
60. See Miller-Young, 2005; Harris-Perry, 2011.
61. See White, 1985/1999, 29. White's book is an excellent historical examination of the Jezebel portrayal, especially chapter 1, "Jezebel and Mammy" (27–61).
62. See C. M. West, 1995.
63. See Kilbourne, 2000; Cortese, 2008; O'Barr, 1994.
64. See Everett, 2009; Brock, 2009; Brock, Kvasny, and Hales, 2010.
65. See Kappeler, 1986.
66. Ibid., 3.
67. See Paasonen, 2011.
68. See ibid.; Bennett, 2001; Filippo, 2000; O'Toole, 1998; Perdue, 2002.
69. See Estabrook and Lakner, 2000.
70. Nash, 2008, 53.
71. Miller-Young, 2014.
72. Paasonen, 2010, 418.
73. Ibid.
74. Dines, 2010, 48.
75. Ibid., 47, 48.
76. Miller-Young, 2007, 267.
77. See hooks, 1992, 65.

78. Miller-Young, 2007, 262.
79. See Greer, 2003; France, 1999; Tucher, 1997.
80. See Markowitz, 1999.
81. See Burbules, 2001.
82. See Barth, 1966; Jenkins, 1994.
83. See Herring, Jankowski, and Brown, 1999, 363.
84. See Vaidhyanathan, 2011; Gandy, 2011.
85. See Jenkins, 1994.
86. See Harris, 1995.
87. See Jenkins, 1994.
88. Davis and Gandy, 1999, 367.
89. See Jenkins, 1994; Davis and Gandy, 1999.
90. See Ferguson, Kreshel, and Tinkham, 1990; Pease, 1985; Potter, 1954.
91. See Ferguson, Kreshel, and Tinkham, 1990; Tuchman, 1979.
92. See Rudman and Borgida, 1995; Kenrick, Gutierres, and Goldberg, 1989; Jennings, Geis, and Brown, 1980.
93. Kilbourne, 2000, 27.
94. Kuhn 1985, 10; quoted in hooks, 1992, 77.
95. See Paasonen, 2011; Gillis, 2004; Sollfrank, 2002; Haraway, 1991.
96. See Wajcman, 2010.
97. See Wajcman, 1991, 5.
98. Wajcman, 2010, 150.
99. See Everett, 2009, 149.
100. See Daniels, 2015.
101. See Everett, 2009.
102. Fouché, 2006, 640.

CHAPTER 3. SEARCHING FOR PEOPLE AND COMMUNITIES

1. Dylann Roof was indicted on federal hate crimes charges on July 22, 2015. Apuzzo, 2015.
2. The website of Dylann Roof's photos and writings, www.lastrhodesian.com, has been taken down but can be accessed in the Internet Archive at http://web.archive.org/web/20150620135047/http://lastrhodesian.com/data/documents/rtf88.txt.
3. See description of the CCC by the SPLC at www.splcenter.org/get-informed/intelligence-files/groups/council-of-conservative-citizens.
4. Gabriella Coleman, the Wolfe Chair in Scientific and Technological Literacy at McGill University, has written extensively about the activism and disruptions of the hackers known as Anonymous and the cultural and political nature of their work of whistleblowing and hacktivism. See Coleman, 2015.
5. FBI statistics from 2010 show that the majority of crime happens within race. They also note that "White individuals were arrested more often for violent

crimes than individuals of any other race, accounting for 59.3 percent of those arrests." See U.S. Department of Justice, 2010.

6. See Daniels, 2009, 8.

CHAPTER 4. SEARCHING FOR PROTECTIONS FROM SEARCH ENGINES

1. See Associated Press, 2013.
2. See Gold, 2011.
3. Ibid. The original post can be found at http://you-aremyanchor.tumblr.com/post/7530939623.
4. See Cyber Civil Rights Initiative, "Revenge Porn Laws," accessed August 9, 2017, www.cybercivilrights.org.
5. Rocha, 2014.
6. Ohlheiser, 2015.
7. See Judgment of the Court (Grand Chamber), 13 May 2014, Google Spain SL, Google Inc. v. Agencia Español de Protección de Datos (AEPD), Mario Costeja González, http://curia.europa.eu.
8. See Xanthoulis, 2013.
9. See Charte du droit à l'oubli dans les sites collaboratifs et les moteurs de recherche, September 30, 2010.
10. See Xanthoulis, 2013; Kuschewsky, 2012.
11. See Jones, 2016.
12. See Purcell, Brenner, and Rainie, 2012.
13. See UnpublishArrest.com, "Unpublish, Permanently Publish or Edit Content," accessed August 9, 2017, www.unpublisharrest.com/unpublish-mugshot/.
14. See Sweeney, 2013.
15. Blanchette and Johnson, 2002.
16. Ibid., 34.
17. Gandy, 1993, 285.
18. See Caswell, 2014.
19. See "Explore a Google Data Center with Street View," YouTube, linked from Google, "Inside Our Data Centers," accessed August 17, 2017, www.google.com/about/datacenters/inside/.
20. Google, "Inside Look: Data and Security," accessed August 17, 2017, www.google.com/about/datacenters/inside/data-security/.
21. "Security Whitepaper: Google Apps Messaging and Collaboration Products," 2011, linked from Google, "Data and Security," accessed August 16, 2016, www.google.com/about/datacenters/inside/data-security/.
22. See Storm, 2014.
23. Blanchette and Johnson, 2002, 36.
24. See Xanthoulis, 2012, 85, citing Fleischer, 2011.
25. Ibid.
26. See Google, 2012.

27. A comprehensive timeline of Edward Snowden's whistleblowing on the U.S. government's comprehensive surveillance program is detailed by the *Guardian* newspaper in MacAskill and Dance, 2013.

28. Tippman, 2015.

29. Kiss, 2015.

30. Goode, 2015.

31. See Robertson, 2016.

32. Ibid.

CHAPTER 5. THE FUTURE OF KNOWLEDGE IN THE PUBLIC

1. See the plan at "The Plan for Dartmouth's Freedom Budget: Items for Transformative Justice at Dartmouth," *Dartblog*, accessed August 9, 2017, www.dartblog.com/Dartmouth_Freedom_Budget_Plan.pdf.

2. Peet, 2016.

3. Ibid.

4. Ibid.

5. Qin, 2016.

6. Sanford Berman documents the sordid history of racist classification in the Library of Congress in his canonical work *Prejudices and Antipathies* (1971). A follow-up to his findings was written thirty years later by Steven A. Knowlton in the article "Three Decades since *Prejudices and Antipathies*: A Study of Changes in the Library of Congress Subject Headings" (2005).

7. Peet, 2016.

8. Furner, 2007, 148.

9. Ibid., 147.

10. Ibid., 169.

11. See Olson, 1998.

12. See Anderson, 1991, 37–46.

13. Hudson, 1996, 256; Anderson, 1991.

14. The first documented evidence of print culture is attributed to Chinese woodblock printing. See Hyatt Mayor, 1971, 1–4.

15. See Saracevic, 2009.

16. See Berman, 1971; Olson, 1998.

17. Berman, 1971, 15.

18. Ibid., 5.

19. See ibid.; Palmer and Malone, 2001.

20. See Berman, 1971, 5.

21. Ibid.

22. Olson, 1998, 233.

23. Ibid., 234

24. Ibid., 234–235.

25. Ibid., 235.

26. Ibid.

27. See Cornell, 1992; Olson, 1998.
28. See Olson, 1998, 237.
29. See C. West, 1996, 84.
30. See Berman, 1971, 18.
31. Ibid., citing Mosse, 1966.
32. See Wilson, 1968, 6.
33. Berman, 1971, 19, citing Marshall, personal communication, June 23, 1970.
34. Ibid., 20.
35. Reidsma, 2016.
36. See Galloway, 2008.
37. See Galloway, Lovink, and Thacker, 2008.
38. See Galloway, 2008.
39. Battelle, 2005, 6.
40. See Brin and Page, 1998a.
41. Saracevic, 1999, 1054.
42. Ibid.
43. Saracevic, 2009, 2570.
44. See Bowker and Star, 1999.
45. See Saracevic, 2009.
46. See Brock, 2011.
47. Ibid., 1101.
48. See Fuchs, 2008.

CHAPTER 6. THE FUTURE OF INFORMATION CULTURE

1. See Federal Communications Commission, 2010
2. Ibid.
3. H. Schiller, 1996, 44.
4. Cohen, 2016.
5. See McChesney and Nichols, 2009; H. Schiller, 1996.
6. See Harris-Perry, 2011; hooks, 1992.
7. Arreola, 2010.
8. See the website of the Society of Professional Journalists Code of Ethics, www.spj.org.
9. See Darnton, 2009; Jeanneney, 2007.
10. See Jeanneney, 2007.
11. See *Authors Guild v. Google*, Case 1:05-cv-08136-DC, Document 1088, November 14, 2013.
12. Darnton, 2009, 2.
13. See Search King v. Google, 2003.
14. See Dickinson, 2010.
15. Ibid., 866.
16. Ibid.
17. Ingram, 2011.

18. See Wilhelm, 2006.

19. See Sinclair, 2004.

20. See Luyt, 2004.

21. See van Dijk and Hacker, 2003; and Pinkett, 2000.

22. See Rifkin, 2000.

23. See Segev, 2010.

24. See Rifkin, 1995.

25. The term "prosumer" is a portmanteau of "producer" and "consumer" that is often used to indicate a higher degree of digital literacy, economic participation, and personal control over the means of technology production. The term is mostly attributed, in this context, to Alvin Toffler, a futurist who thought that the line between traditional economic consumer and producer would eventually blur through engagements with technology and that this participation would generally lead to greater mass customization of products and services by corporations. See Toffler, 1970, 1980; Tapscott, 1996; Ritzer and Jurgenson, 2010.

26. Ritzer and Jurgenson, 2010, 14.

27. See Smythe, 1981/2006.

28. See Fuchs, 2011.

29. Ibid.

30. Ibid., 43.

31. Ibid.

32. A list of Google's global assets and subsidiaries can be found in its SEC filings: www.sec.gov/Archives/edgar/data/1288776/000119312507044494/dex2101.htm.

33. See recent news coverage discussing U.S. Department of Labor data and the significant decline of Blacks, Latinos, and women in the Silicon Valley technology industries: Swift, 2010.

34. See Meyer, 2016.

35. See Glusac, 2016.

36. See Eddie and Prigg, 2015.

37. See Mosher, 2016.

38. See Fuchs, 2011.

39. See Noble and Roberts, 2015.

40. See Department of Labor, Office of the Secretary, "Notice of Final Determination Revising the List of Products Requiring Federal Contractor Certification as to Forced or Indentured Child Labor Pursuant to Executive Order 13126," which prohibits coltan that has been produced by child labor from entering the United States.

41. Kristi Esseck covered this issue in her article "Guns, Money and Cell Phones" (2011). The United Nations also issued a report, submitted by Secretary General Kofi Annan, about the status of companies involved in coltan trafficking and the impact of investigations by the UN into the conflicts arising from such practices in the Democratic Republic of the Congo. The report can be accessed at www.un.org/Docs/journal/asp/ws.asp?m=S/2003/1027 (accessed July 3, 2012).

42. Coltan mining is significantly understudied by Western scholars but has been documented in many nongovernmental organizations' reports about the near-slavery economy in the Congo that is the result of Western dependence on "conflict minerals" such as coltan that have been the basis of ongoing wars and smuggling regimes that have extended as far as Rwanda, Uganda, and Burundi. See reviews in the *New York Times* as well as a detailed overview of the conditions in the Congo due to mining by Anup Shah, at www.globalissues.org, which asserts that an elite network of multinational companies, politicians, and military leaders have essentially kept the issues from the view of the public. See Hardenaug, 2001; Shah, 2010.

43. While less formal scholarship has been dedicated to this issue, considerable media attention in 2011 and 2012 has been focused on the labor conditions in parts of China where Apple manufactures its products. While some of the details of the journalistic reporting have been prone to factual error in location and dates, there is considerable evidence that labor conditions by Apple's supplier Foxconn are precarious and rife with human-rights abuses. See Duhigg and Barboza, 2012.

44. See Fields, 2004.

45. Wallace, 1990, 98.

46. See Hobson, 2008.

47. See Harvey, 2005.

48. See Jensen, 2005; Brown, 2003; Burdman, 2008.

49. See Harvey, 2005.

50. The Children's Internet Protection Act (CIPA) was adopted by the FCC in 2001 and is designed to address filtering of pornographic content from any computers in federally funded agencies such as schools and libraries. The act is designed to incentivize such organizations with Universal E-Rate discounts for using filters and providing Internet safety policies. See FCC, "Children's Internet Protection Act," accessed August 9, 2017, www.fcc.gov/guides/childrens-internet-protection-act.

51. The Child Safe Viewing Act of 2007 is designed to regulate objectionable adult-themed material so that children cannot see it on mobile devices. The FCC is investigating the use of blocking software or devices for use on television and mobile devices through the use of a V-Chip that can allow adults to block content. See FCC, "Protecting Children from Objectionable Content on Wireless Devices," accessed August 9, 2017, www.fcc.gov/guides/protecting-children-objectionable-content-wireless-devices.

52. The National Urban League reported in 2010 startling statistics about the economic crisis, specific to African Americans: (1) less than half of black and Hispanic families own a home (47.4% and 49.1%, respectively), compared to three-quarters of White families; and (2) Blacks and Hispanics are more than three times as likely as whites to live below the poverty line. See National Urban League, 2010.

53. See McGreal, 2010.

54. See Jensen, 2005; McGreal, 2010.
55. See Neville et al., 2012.
56. See Pawley, 2006.
57. See Tettegah, 2016.
58. See Brown, 2003; Crenshaw, 1991.
59. See Lipsitz, 1998; Brown, 2003; Burdman, 2008.
60. See Tynes and Markoe, 2010.
61. See Brown, 2003.
62. Ibid.
63. See Lipsitz, 1998; Jensen, 2005.

CONCLUSION

1. See Tate, 2003.
2. See Daniels, 2008.

3. This suppression of Kandis's business, according to her, is not based on her lack of popularity but, rather, on her unwillingness to pay more to Yelp to have her competitors taken off her page.
4. Kandis described an experience of having two of her clients who are not regular reviewers on Yelp post positive reviews about her, only to have them sequestered from her page. She described her conversations with Yelp customer service agents, from which she deduced that these reviews were seen as "fraudulent" or inauthentic reviews that she must have solicited.

REFERENCES

AFP. (2012, May 23). Google's "Jew" Suggestion Leads to Judge Order. *The Local France.* Retrieved from thelocal.fr.

Anderson, B. (1991). *Imagined Communities: Reflections on the Origin and Spread of Nationalism* (2nd ed.). London and New York: Verso.

Andrejevic, M. (2007). Surveillance in the Digital Enclosure. *Communication Review, 10*(4), 295–317.

Angwin, J., Larson, J., Mattu, S., and Kirchner, L. (2016). Software Used to Predict Criminality Is Biased against Black People. *TruthOut.* Retrieved from www.truth-out.org.

Anti-Defamation League. (2004). ADL Praises Google for Responding to Concerns about Rankings of Hate Sites. Retrieved from www.adl.org.

Apuzzo, M. (2015, July 22). Dylann Roof, Charleston Shooting Suspect, Is Indicted on Federal Hate Crimes. *New York Times.* Retrieved from www.nytimes.com.

Arreola, V. (2010, October 13). Latinas: We're So Hot We Broke Google. *Ms. Magazine Blog.* Retrieved from www.msmagazine.com.

Ascher, D. (2017). The New Yellow Journalism. Ph.D. diss., University of California, Los Angeles.

Associated Press. (2013, January 16). Calif. Teacher with Past in Porn Loses Appeal. *USA Today.* Retrieved from www.usatoday.com.

Associated Press v. United States. (1945). 326 U.S. 1, US Supreme Court.

Bagdikian, B. (1983). *The Media Monopoly.* Boston: Beacon.

Bar-Ilan, J. (2007). Google Bombing from a Time Perspective. *Journal of Computer-Mediated Communication, 12*(3), article 8. Retrieved from http://jcmc.indiana.edu.

Barlow, J. P. (1996). A Declaration of the Independence of Cyberspace. Electronic Frontier Foundation. Retrieved from http://projects.eff.org/barlow/Declaration-Final.html.

Barth, F. (1966). *Models of Social Organization.* London: Royal Anthropological Institute.

Barzilai-Nahon, K. (2006). Gatekeepers, Virtual Communities and the Gated: Multidimensional Tensions in Cyberspace. *International Journal of Communications, Law and Policy, 11,* 1–28.

Battelle, J. (2005). *The Search: How Google and Its Rivals Rewrote the Rules of Business and Transformed Our Culture.* New York: Portfolio.

Bell, D. (1992). *Faces at the Bottom of the Well.* New York: Basic Books.

Bennett, D. (2001). Pornography-dot-com: Eroticising Privacy on the Internet. *Review of Education, Pedagogy, and Cultural Studies, 23*(4), 381–391.

Berger, J. (1972). *Ways of Seeing*. London: British Broadcasting Corporation and Penguin Books.

Berman, S. (1971). *Prejudices and Antipathies: A Tract on the LC Subject Heads Concerning People*. Metuchen, NJ: Scarecrow.

Blanchette J. F., and Johnson, D. G. (2002). Data Retention and the Panoptic Society: The Social Benefits of Forgetfulness. *Information Society, 18*, 33–45.

Bowker, G. C., and Star, S. L. (1999). *Sorting Things Out: Classification and Its Consequences*. Cambridge, MA: MIT Press.

Boyer, L. (2015, May 19). If You Type a Racist Phrase in Google Maps, the White House Comes Up. *U.S. News*. Retrieved from www.usnews.com.

Boyle, J. (2003). The Second Enclosure Movement and the Construction of the Public Domain. *Law and Contemporary Problems, 66*(33), 33–74.

Braun, L., Fausto-Sterling, A., Fullwiley, D., Hammonds, E. M., Nelson, A., et al. (2007). Racial Categories in Medical Practice: How Useful Are They? *PLoS Medicine 4*(9): e271. doi:10.1371/journal.pmed.0040271.

Brin, S., and Page, L. (1998a). The Anatomy of a Large-Scale Hypertextual Web Search Engine. *Computer Networks and ISDN Systems, 30*(1–7), 107–117.

Brin, S., and Page, L. (1998b). The Anatomy of a Large-Scale Hypertextual Web Search Engine. Stanford, CA: Computer Science Department, Stanford University. Retrieved from http://infolab.stanford.edu/backrub/google.html.

Brock, A. (2007). *Race, the Internet, and the Hurricane: A Critical Discourse Analysis of Black Identity Online during the Aftermath of Hurricane Katrina*. Doctoral dissertation. University of Illinois at Urbana-Champaign.

Brock, A. (2009). Life on the Wire. *Information, Communication and Society, 12*(3), 344–363.

Brock, A. (2011). Beyond the Pale: The Blackbird Web Browser's Critical Reception. *New Media and Society 13*(7), 1085–1103.

Brock, A., Kvasny, L., and Hales, K. (2010). Cultural Appropriations of Technical Capital. *Information, Communication and Society, 13*(7), 1040–1059.

Brown, M. (2003). *Whitewashing Race: The Myth of a Color-Blind Society*. Berkeley: University of California Press.

Burbules, N. C. (2001). Paradoxes of the Web: The Ethical Dimensions of Credibility. *Library Trends, 49*, 441–453.

Burdman, P. (2008). Race-Blind Admissions. Retrieved from www.alumni.berkeley.edu.

Calore, M., and Gilbertson, S. (2001, January 26). Remembering the First Google Bomb. *Wired*. Retrieved from www.wired.com.

Castells, M. (2004). Informationalism, Networks, and the Network Society: A Theoretical Blueprinting. In M. Castells (Ed.), *The Network Society: A Cross-Cultural Perspective*, 3–48. Northampton, MA: Edward Elgar.

Caswell, M. (2014). *Archiving the Unspeakable: Silence, Memory, and the Photographic Record in Cambodia*. Madison: University of Wisconsin Press.

Chouliaraki, L., and Fairclough, N. (1999). *Discourse in Late Modernity*. Vol. 2. Edinburgh: Edinburgh University Press.

Cohen, N. (2016). *Writers' Rights: Freelance Journalists in a Digital Age*. Montreal: McGill-Queen's University Press.

Coleman, E. G. (2015). *Hacker, Hoaxer, Whistleblower, Spy: The Many Faces of Anonymous*. London: Verso.

Collins, P. H. (1991). *Black Feminist Thought: Knowledge, Consciousness, and the Politics of Empowerment*. New York: Routledge.

Corea, A. (1993). Racism and the American Way of Media. In A. Alexander and J. Hanson (Eds.), *Taking Sides: Clashing Views on Controversial Issues in Mass Media and Society*, 24–31. Guilford, CT: Dushkin.

Cornell, D. (1992). *The Philosophy of the Limit*. New York: Routledge.

Cortese, A. (2008). *Provocateur: Images of Women and Minorities in Advertising*. Lanham, MD: Rowman and Littlefield.

Courtney, A., and Whipple, T. (1983). *Sex Stereotyping in Advertising*. Lexington, MA: D. C. Heath.

Cowie, E. (1977). Women, Representation and the Image. *Screen Education, 23,* 15–23.

Craven, J. (2015, May 20). If You Type 'N——House' into Google Maps, It Will Take You to the White House. *Huffington Post*. Retrieved from www.huffingtonpost.com.

Crenshaw, K. W. (1991). Mapping the Margins: Intersectionality, Identity Politics, and Violence against Women of Color. *Stanford Law Review, 43*(6), 1241–1299.

Daniels, J. (2008). Race, Civil Rights, and Hate Speech in the Digital Era. In Anna Everett (Ed.), *Learning Race and Ethnicity: Youth and Digital Media*, 129–154. Cambridge, MA: MIT Press.

Daniels, J. (2009). *Cyber Racism: White Supremacy Online and the New Attack on Civil Rights*. Lanham, MD: Rowman and Littlefield.

Daniels, J. (2013). Race and Racism in Internet Studies: A Review and Critique. *New Media & Society, 15*(5), 695–719. doi:10.1177/1461444812462849.

Daniels, J. (2015). "My Brain Database Doesn't See Skin Color": Color-Blind Racism in the Technology Industry and in Theorizing the Web. *American Behavioral Scientist, 59,* 1377–1393.

Darnton, R. (2009, December 17). Google and the New Digital Future. *New York Review of Books*. Retrieved from www.nybooks.com.

Dates, J. (1990). A War of Images. In J. Dates and W. Barlow (Eds.), *Split Images: African Americans in the Mass Media*, 1–25. Washington, DC: Howard University Press.

Davis, A. (1972). Reflections on the Black Woman's Role in the Community of Slaves. *Massachusetts Review, 13*(1–2), 81–100.

Davis, J. L., and Gandy, O. H. (1999). Racial Identity and Media Orientation: Exploring the Nature of Constraint. *Journal of Black Studies, 29*(3), 367–397.

Delgado, R., and Stefancic, J. (1999). *Critical Race Theory: The Cutting Edge*. Philadelphia: Temple University Press.

Dewey, C. (2015, May 20). Google Maps' White House Glitch, Flickr Auto-tag, and the Case of the Racist Algorithm. *Washington Post*. Retrieved from www.washingtonpost.com.

Diaz, A. (2008). Through the Google Goggles: Sociopolitical Bias in Search Engine Design. In A. Spink and M. Zimmer (Eds.), *Web Searching: Multidisciplinary Perspectives*, 11–34. Dordrecht, The Netherlands: Springer.

Dicken-Garcia, H. (1998). The Internet and Continuing Historical Discourse. *Journalism and Mass Communication Quarterly, 75*, 19–27.

Dickinson, G. M. (2010). An Interpretive Framework for Narrower Immunity under Section 230 of the Communications Decency Act. *Harvard Journal of Law and Public Policy, 33*(2), 863–883.

DiMaggio, P., Hargittai, E., Neuman, W. R., and Robinson, J. P. (2001). Social Implications of the Internet. *Annual Review of Sociology, 27*, 307–336.

Dines, G. (2010). *Pornland: How Porn Has Hijacked Our Sexuality*. Boston: Beacon.

Dorsey, J. C. (2003). "It Hurt Very Much at the Time": Patriarchy, Rape Culture, and the Slave Body-Semiotic. In L. Lewis (Ed.), *The Culture of Gender and Sexuality in the Caribbean*, 294–322. Gainesville: University Press of Florida.

Duhigg, C., and Barboza, D. (2012, January 25). In China, Human Costs Are Built into an iPad. *New York Times*. Retrieved from www.nytimes.com.

Dunbar, A. (2006). Introducing Critical Race Theory to Archival Discourse: Getting the Conversation Started. *Archival Science, 6*, 109–129.

Dyer, R. (1997). *White*. London: Routledge.

Eddie, R., and Prigg, M. (2015, November 13). "This Does Not Represent Our Values": Tim Cook Addresses Racism Claims after Seven Black Students Are Ejected from an Apple Store and Told They "Might Steal Something." *Daily Mail*. Retrieved from www.dailymail.co.uk.

Eglash, R. (2002). Race, Sex, and Nerds: From Black Geeks to Asian American Hipsters. *Social Text, 20*(2), 49–64.

Eglash, R. (2007). Ethnocomputing with Native American Design. In L. E. Dyson, M. A. N. Hendriks, and S. Grant (Eds.), *Information Technology and Indigenous People*, 210–219. Hershey, PA: Idea Group.

Eisenhower, D. (1961). President's Farewell Address, January 17. Retrieved July 25, 2012, from www.ourdocuments.gov.

Epstein, R., and Robertson, R. (2015). The Search Engine Manipulation Effect (SEME) and Its Possible Impact on the Outcomes of Elections. *PNAS, 112*(33), E4512–E4521.

Esseck, K. (2011, June). Guns, Money and Cell Phones. *Industry Standard Magazine*. Retrieved from www.globalissues.org.

Estabrook, L., and Lakner, E. (2000). Managing Internet Access: Results of a National Survey. *American Libraries, 31*(8), 60–62.

Evans, J., McKemmish, S., Daniels, E., and McCarthy, G. (2015). Self-Determination and Archival Autonomy: Advocating Activism. *Archival Science, 15*(4), 337–368.

Everett, A. (2009). *Digital Diaspora: A Race for Cyberspace.* Albany: SUNY Press.

Fairclough, N. (1995). *Critical Discourse Analysis.* London: Longman.

Fairclough, N. (2003). *Analysing Discourse: Textual Analysis for Social Research.* London: Routledge.

Fairclough, N. (2006). *Language and Globalization.* London: Routledge.

Fairclough, N. (2007). *Analysing Discourse.* New York: Taylor and Francis.

Fallows, D. (2005, January 23). Search Engine Users. Pew Research Center. Retrieved from www.pewinternet.org.

Federal Communications Commission. (2010). *National Broadband Plan: Connecting America.* Retrieved from www.broadband.gov/download-plan/.

Ferguson, J. H., Kreshel, P., and Tinkham, S. F. (1990). In the Pages of *Ms.*: Sex Role Portrayals of Women in Advertising. *Journal of Advertising, 19*(1), 40–51.

Feuz, M., Fuller, M., and Stalder, F. (2011). Personal Web Searching in the Age of Semantic Capitalism: Diagnosing the Mechanisms of Personalization. *First Monday, 16*(2–7). Retrieved from www.firstmonday.org.

Fields, G. (2004). *Territories of Profit.* Stanford, CA: Stanford Business Books.

Filippo, J. (2000). Pornography on the Web. In D. Gauntlett (Ed.), *Web.Studies: Rewiring Media Studies for the Digital Age,* 122–129. London: Arnold.

Fleischer, P. (2011, March 9). Foggy Thinking about the Right to Oblivion, *Peter Fleischer: Privacy . . . ?* (blog). Retrieved from http://peterfleischer.blogspot.com/2011/03/foggy-thinking-about-right-tooblivion.html.

Forbes, J. D. (1990). The Manipulation of Race, Caste and Identity: Classifying Afro-Americans, Native Americans and Red-Black People. *Journal of Ethnic Studies, 17*(4), 1–51.

Ford, T. E. (1997). Effects of Stereotypical Television Portrayals of African Americans on Person Perception. *Social Psychology Quarterly, 60,* 266–278.

Foucault, M. (1972). *The Archaeology of Knowledge.* Trans. R. Swyer. London: Tavistock.

Fouché, R. (2006). Say It Loud, I'm Black and I'm Proud: African Americans, American Artifactual Culture, and Black Vernacular Technological Creativity. *American Quarterly, 58*(3), 639–661.

France, M. (1999). Journalism's Online Credibility Gap. *Business Week, 3650,* 122–124.

Fraser, N. (1996). *Social Justice in the Age of Identity Politics: Redistribution, Recognition, and Participation. The Tanner Lectures on Human Values.* Stanford, CA: Stanford University Press.

Fuchs. C. (2008). *Internet and Society: Social Theory in the Information Age.* New York: Routledge.

Fuchs, C. (2011). Google Capitalism. *Triple C: Cognition, Communication, Cooperation, 10*(1), 42–48.

Fuchs, C. (2014). *Digital Labour and Karl Marx.* New York: Routledge.

Fujioka, Y. (1999). Television Portrayals and African-American Stereotypes: Examination of Television Effects When Direct Contact Is Lacking. *Journalism and Mass Communication Quarterly, 76,* 52–75.

Furner, J. (2007). Dewey Deracialized: A Critical Race-Theoretic Perspective. *Knowledge Organization, 34*, 144–168.

Galloway, A. R. (2008). The Unworkable Interface. *New Literary History, 39*(4), 931–956.

Galloway, A. R., Lovink, G., and Thacker, E. (2008). Dialogues Carried Out in Silence: An Email Exchange. *Grey Room, 33*, 96–112.

Gandy, O. H., Jr. (1993). *The Panoptic Sort: A Political Economy of Personal Information.* Boulder, CO: Westview.

Gandy, O. H., Jr. (1998). *Communication and Race: A Structural Perspective.* London: Arnold.

Gandy, O. H., Jr. (2011). Consumer Protection in Cyberspace. *Triple C: Cognition, Communication, Co-operation, 9*(2), 175–189. Retrieved from www.triple-c.at.

Gardner, T. A. (1980). Racism in Pornography and the Women's Movement. In L. Lederer (Ed.), *Take Back The Night: Women on Pornography*, 105–114. New York: William Morrow.

Gillis, S. (2004). Neither Cyborg nor Goddess: The (Im)possibilities of Cyberfeminism. In S. Gillis, G. Howie, and R. Munford (Eds.), *Third Wave Feminism: A Critical Exploration*, 185–196. London: Palgrave.

Glusac, E. (2016, June 21). As Airbnb Grows, So Do Claims of Discrimination. *New York Times*. Retrieved from www.nytimes.com.

Golash-Boza, T. (2016). A Critical and Comprehensive Sociological Theory of Race and Racism. *Sociology of Race and Ethnicity, 2*(2), 129–141. doi:2332649216632242.

Gold, D. (2011, November 10). The Man Who Makes Money Publishing Your Nude Pics. *The Awl*. Retrieved from www.theawl.com.

Goldsmith, J. L., and Wu, T. (2006). *Who Controls the Internet? Illusions of a Borderless World.* New York: Oxford University Press.

Goode, E. (2015, May 14). Open Letter to Google from 80 Internet Scholars: Release RTBF Compliance Data. *Medium*. Retrieved from www.medium.com/@ellgood.

Google. (2012, August 10). An Update to Our Search Algorithms. *Inside Search*. Retrieved from http://search.googleblog.com.

Gramsci, A. (1992). *Prison Notebooks*. Ed. J. A. Buttigieg. New York: Columbia University Press.

Gray, H. (1989). Television, Black Americans, and the American Dream. *Critical Studies in Mass Communication, 6*(4), 376–386.

Greer, J. D. (2003). Evaluating the Credibility of Online Information: A Test of Source and Advertising Influence. *Mass Communication and Society, 6*(1), 11–28.

Gulli, A., and Signorini, A. (2005). The Indexable Web Is More than 11.5 Billion Pages. In *Proceedings of the WWW2005*. Retrieved from http://www2005.org.

Gunkel, D. J., and Gunkel. A. H. (1997). Virtual Geographies: The New Worlds of Cyberspace. *Critical Studies in Mass Communication, 14*, 123–137.

Guynn, J. (2016, July 15). Facebook Takes Heat for Diversity "Pipeline" Remarks. *USA Today*. Retrieved from www.usatoday.com.

Hacker, A. (1992). *Two Nations: Black and White, Separate, Hostile, Unequal.* New York: Scribner's.

Halavais, A. (2009). *Search Engine Society*. Cambridge, MA: Polity.

Hall, S. (1989). Ideology. In E. Barnouw, G. Gerbner, W. Schramm, et al. (Eds.), *International Encyclopedia of Communications*, 307–311. New York: Oxford University Press and the Annenberg School for Communication.

Haraway, D. J. (1991). *Simians, Cyborgs, and Women: The Reinvention of Nature*. London: Free Association Books.

Hardenaug, B. (2001, August 12). The Dirt in the New Machine. *New York Times*. Retrieved from www.nytimes.com.

Harding, L. (2012, April 17). Swedish Minister Denies Claims of Racism over Black Woman Cake Stunt. *Guardian*. Retrieved from www.theguardian.com.

Harding, S. (1987). *Feminism and Methodology*. Buckingham, UK: Open University Press.

Hargittai, E. (2000). Open Portals or Closed Gates? Channeling Content on the World Wide Web. *Poetics, 27*, 233–253.

Hargittai, E. (2003). The Digital Divide and What to Do about It. In D. C. Jones (Ed.), *New Economy Handbook*, 822–839. San Diego, CA: Academic Press.

Harris, C. (1995). Whiteness as Property. In K. Crenshaw, B. Gotanda, G. Peller, and K. Thomas (Eds.), *Critical Race Theory: The Key Writings That Informed the Movement*. New York: New Press.

Harris-Perry, M. V. (2011). *Sister Citizen: Shame, Stereotypes, and Black Women in America*. New Haven, CT: Yale University Press.

Harvey, D. (2005). *A Brief History of Neoliberalism*. Oxford: Oxford University Press.

Heider, D., and Harp, D. (2002). New Hope or Old Power: Democracy, Pornography and the Internet. *Howard Journal of Communications, 13*(4), 285–299.

Herring, M., Jankowski, T. B., and Brown, R. E. (1999). Pro-Black Doesn't Mean Anti-White: The Structure of African-American Group Identity. *Journal of Politics, 61*(2), 363–386.

Hiles, H. (2015, March 18). Silicon Valley Venture Capital Has a Diversity Problem. *Recode*. Retrieved from www.recode.net.

Hindman, M. S. (2009). *The Myth of Digital Democracy*. Princeton, NJ: Princeton University Press.

Hirst, P. Q., and Thompson, G. F. (1999). *Globalization in Question: The International Economy and the Possibilities of Governance* (2nd ed.). Cambridge, MA: Polity.

Hobson, J. (2008). Digital Whiteness, Primitive Blackness. *Feminist Media Studies, 8*, 111–126. doi:10.1080/00220380801980467.

hooks, b. (1992). *Black Looks: Race and Representation*. Boston: South End.

Hudson, N. (1996). Nation to Race: The Origin of Racial Classification in Eighteenth-Century Thought. *Eighteenth-Century Studies, 29*(3), 247–264.

Hull, G. T., Bell-Scott, P., and Smith, B. (1982). *All the Women Are White, All the Blacks Are Men, but Some of Us Are Brave: Black Women's Studies*. Old Westbury, NY: Feminist Press.

Hunt, D., Ramón, A., and Tran, M. (2016). *2016 Hollywood Diversity Report: Busine$$ as Usual?* Ralph J. Bunche Center for African American Studies at UCLA. Retrieved from www.bunchecenter.ucla.edu.

Hyatt Mayor, A. (1971). *Prints and People*. Princeton, NJ: Metropolitan Museum of Art.

Ingram, M. (2011, September 22). A Google Monopoly Isn't the Point. *GigaOM*. Retrieved from www.gigaom.com..

Inside Google. (2010, June 2). *Traffic Report: How Google Is Squeezing Out Competitors and Muscling into New Markets*. Consumer Watchdog. Retrieved from www.consumerwatchdog.org.

Jansen, B., and Pooch, U. (2001). A Review of Web Searching Studies and a Framework for Future Research. *Journal of the American Society for Information Science and Technology, 52*(3), 235–246.

Jansen, B., and Spink, A. (2006). How Are We Searching the World Wide Web? A Comparison of Nine Search Engine Transaction Logs. *Information Processing and Management, 42*(1), 248–263.

Jeanneney, J. N. (2007). *Google and the Myth of Universal Knowledge: A View from Europe*. Chicago: University of Chicago Press.

Jenkins, R. (1994). Rethinking Ethnicity: Identity, Categorization and Power. *Ethnic and Racial Studies, 17*(2), 197–223.

Jennings, J., Geis, F. L., and Brown, V. (1980). Influence of Television Commercials on Women's Self-Confidence and Independent Judgment. *Journal of Personality and Social Psychology, 38*(2), 203–210. doi:10.1037/0022-3514.38.2.203.

Jensen, R. (2005). *The Heart of Whiteness: Confronting Race, Racism, and White Privilege*. San Francisco: City Lights.

Jones, M. L. (2016). *Ctrl+Z: The Right to Be Forgotten*. New York: NYU Press.

Kang, J. (2000). Cyber-race. *Harvard Law Review, 113*, 1130–1208.

Kappeler, S. (1986). *The Pornography of Representation*. Minneapolis: University of Minnesota Press.

Kellner, D. (1995). Intellectuals and New Technologies. *Media, Culture and Society, 17*, 427–448.

Kendall, L. (2002). *Hanging Out in the Virtual Pub: Masculinities and Relationships Online*. Berkeley: University of California Press.

Kenrick, D. T., Gutierres, S. E., and Goldberg, L. L. (1989). Influence of Popular Erotica on Judgments of Strangers and Mates. *Journal of Experimental Social Psychology, 25*, 159–167.

Kilbourne, J. (2000). *Can't Buy My Love: How Advertising Changes the Way We Think and Feel*. New York: Simon and Schuster.

Kilker, E. (1993). Black and White in America: The Culture and Politics of Racial Classification. *International Journal of Politics, Culture and Society, 7*(2), 229–258.

Kiss, J. (2015, May 14). Dear Google: Open Letter from 80 Academics on "Right to Be Forgotten." *Guardian*. Retrieved from www.theguardian.com.

Kleinman, Z. (2015, August 11). What Else Does Google's Alphabet Do? BBC News. Retrieved from www.bbc.com.

Knowlton, S. (2005). Three Decades since *Prejudices and Antipathies*: A Study of Changes in the Library of Congress Subject Headings. *Cataloging and Classification Quarterly, 40*(2), 123–145.

Kohl, P., and Lee, M. (2011, December 19). Letter to Honorable Jonathan D. Leibowitz, Chairman, Federal Trade Commission. Retrieved from www.kohl.senate.gov.

Kopytoff, V. (2007, May 18). Google Surpasses Microsoft as World's Most-Visited Site. *The Technology Chronicles* (blog), *San Francisco Chronicle*. Retrieved from http://blog.sfgate.com/techchron/author/vkopytoff.

Krippendorff, K. (2004). *Content Analysis: An Introduction to Its Methodology*. Thousand Oaks, CA: Sage.

Kuhn, A. (1985). *The Power of the Image: Essays on Representation and Sexuality*. New York: Routledge.

Kuschewsky, M. (Ed.). (2012). *Data Protection and Privacy: Jurisdictional Comparisons*. European Lawyer Reference. New York: Thomson Reuters.

Ladson-Billings, G. (2009). "Who You Callin' Nappy-Headed?" A Critical Race Theory Look at the Construction of Black Women. *Race, Ethnicity and Education, 12*(1), 87–99.

Leonard, D. (2009). Young, Black (or Brown), and Don't Give a Fuck: Virtual Gangstas in the Era of State Violence. *Cultural Studies Critical Methodologies, 9*(2), 248–272.

Lerner, G. (1986). *The Creation of Patriarchy*. New York: Oxford University Press.

Levene, M. (2006). *An Introduction to Search Engines and Navigation*. Harlow, UK: Addison Wesley.

Levin, A. (2016, August 2). Alphabet's Project Wing Delivery Drones to Be Tested in U.S. Bloomberg Politics. Retrieved from www.bloomberg.com.

Lev-On, A. (2008). The Democratizing Effects of Search Engine Use: On Chance Exposures and Organizational Hubs. In A. Spink and M. Zimmer (Eds.), *Web Searching: Multidisciplinary Perspectives*, 135–149. Dordrecht, The Netherlands: Springer.

Lipsitz, G. (1998). *The Possessive Investment in Whiteness: How White People Profit from Identity Politics*. Philadelphia: Temple University Press.

Luyt, B. (2004). Who Benefits from the Digital Divide? *First Monday, 8*(9). Retrieved from www.firstmonday.org.

MacAskill, E., and Dance, G. (2013, November 1). NAS Files: Decoded. *Guardian*. Retrieved from www.theguardian.com.

Markey, K. (2007). Twenty-Five Years of End-User Searching, Part 1: Research Findings. *Journal of the American Society for Information Science and Technology, 58*(8), 1071–1081.

Markowitz, M. (1999). How Much Are Integrity and Credibility Worth? *EDN, 44*, 31.

Mastro, D. E., and Tropp, L. R. (2004). The Effects of Interracial Contact, Attitudes, and Stereotypical Portrayals on Evaluations of Black Television Sitcom Characters. *Communication Research Reports, 21*, 119–129.

Matabane, P. W. (1988). Cultivating Moderate Perceptions on Racial Integration. *Journal of Communication, 38*(4), 21–31.

Matsakis, L. (2017, August 5). Google Employee's Anti-Diversity Manifesto Goes "Internally Viral." Motherboard. Retrieved from https://motherboard.vice.com.

Mayall, A., and Russell, D. E. H. (1993). Racism in Pornography. *Feminism and Psychology. 3*(2), 275–281. doi:10.1177/0959353593032023.

McCarthy, C. (1994). Multicultural Discourses and Curriculum Reform: A Critical Perspective. *Educational Theory, 44*(1), 81–98.

McChesney, R. W., and Nichols, J. (2009). *The Death and Life of American Journalism: The Media Revolution That Will Begin the World Again*. New York: Nation Books.

McGreal, C. (2010, May 17). A $95,000 Question: Why Are Whites Five Times Richer than Blacks in the US? *Guardian*. Retrieved from www.guardian.co.uk.

Meyer, R. (2016, July 21). Twitter's Famous Racist Problem. *Atlantic*. Retrieved from www.theatlantic.com.

Miller, P., and Kemp, H. (2005). *What's Black about It? Insights to Increase Your Share of a Changing African-American Market*. Ithaca, NY: Paramount.

Miller-Young, M. (2005). Sexy and Smart: Black Women and the Politics of Self-Authorship in Netporn. In K. Jacobs, M. Janssen, and M. Pasquinelli (Eds.), *C'lick Me: A Netporn Studies Reader*, 205–216. Amsterdam: Institute of Network Cultures.

Miller-Young, M. (2007). Hip-Hop Honeys and Da Hustlaz: Black Sexualities in the New Hip-Hop Pornography. *Meridians: Feminism, Race, Transnationalism, 8*(1), 261–292.

Miller-Young, M. (2014). *A Taste for Brown Sugar: Black Women in Pornography*. Durham, NC: Duke University Press.

Mills, C. W. (2014). *The Racial Contract*. Ithaca, NY: Cornell University Press.

Morville, P. (2005). *Ambient Findability*. Sebastopol, CA: O'Reilly.

Mosco, V. (1988). *The Political Economy of Information*. Madison: University of Wisconsin Press.

Mosco, V. (1996). *The Political Economy of Communication: Rethinking and Renewal*. London: Sage.

Mosher, A. (2016, August 10). Snapchat under Fire for "Yellowface" Filter. *USA Today*. Retrieved from www.usatoday.com.

Mosse, G. L. (1966). *Nazi Culture: Intellectual, Cultural, and Social Life in the Third Reich*. New York: Grosset and Dunlap.

Nakayama, T., and Krizek, R. (1995). Whiteness: A Strategic Rhetoric. *Quarterly Journal of Speech, 81*(3), 291–309.

Nash, J. C. (2008). Strange Bedfellows: Black Feminism and Antipornography Feminism. *Social Text, 26*(4 97), 51–76. doi:10.1215/01642472–2008–010.

National Telecommunications and Information Administration. (1999, July 8). *Falling through the Net: Defining the Digital Divide*. Retrieved from www.ntia.doc.gov/report/1999/falling-through-net-defining-digital-divide.

National Urban League. (2010). *State of Black America Report*. Retrieved from www.nul.org.

Nelson, A., Tu, T. L. N., and Hines, A. H. (2001). *Technicolor: Race, Technology, and Everyday Life*. New York: NYU Press.

Neville, H., Coleman, N., Falconer, J. W., and Holmes, D. (2005). Color-Blind Racial Ideology and Psychological False Consciousness among African Americans. *Journal of Black Psychology, 31*(1), 27–45. doi:10.1177/0095798404268287.

Newport, F. (2007, September 28). Black or African American? Gallup. Retrieved from www.gallup.com.

Niesen, M. (2012). The Little Old Lady Has Teeth: The U.S. Federal Trade Commission and the Advertising Industry, 1970–1973. *Advertising & Society Review*, 12(4). http://doi.org/10.1353/asr.2012.0000.

Nissenbaum, H., and Introna, L. (2004). Shaping the Web: Why the Politics of Search Engines Matters. In V. V. Gehring (Ed.), *The Internet in Public Life*, 7–27. Lanham, MD: Rowman and Littlefield.

Noble, S. U. (2012). Missed Connections: What Search Engines Say about Women. *Bitch* 12(54), 37–41.

Noble, S. U. (2013, October). Google Search: Hyper-visibility as a Means of Rendering Black Women and Girls Invisible. *InVisible Culture*, 19. Retrieved from http://ivc.lib.rochester.edu.

Noble, S. U. (2014). Teaching Trayvon: Race, Media, and the Politics of Spectacle. *Black Scholar*, 44(1), 12–29.

Noble, S. U., and Roberts, S. T. (2015). Through Google Colored Glass(es): Emotion, Class, and Wearables as Commodity and Control. In S. U. Noble and S. Y. Tettegah (Eds.), *Emotions, Technology, and Design*, 187–212. London: Academic Press.

Norris, P. 2001. *Digital Divide: Civic Engagement, Information Poverty, and the Internet Worldwide*. New York: Cambridge University Press.

O'Barr, W. M. (1994). *Culture and the Ad: Exploring Otherness in the World of Advertising*. Boulder, CO: Westview.

Ohlheiser, A. (2015, December 3). Revenge Porn Purveyor Hunter Moore Is Sentenced to Prison. *Washington Post*. Retrieved from www.washingtonpost.com.

Olson, H. A. (1998). Mapping beyond Dewey's Boundaries: Constructing Classificatory Space for Marginalized Knowledge Domains. In G. C. Bowker and S. L. Star (Eds.), *How Classifications Work: Problems and Challenges in an Electronic Age*, special issue, *Library Trends*, 47(2), 233–254.

Omi, M., and Winant, H. (1994). *Racial Formation in the United States: From the 1960s to the 1990s*. New York: Routledge.

O'Neil, C. (2016). *Weapons of Math Destruction: How Big Data Increases Inequality and Threatens Democracy*. London: Crown.

O'Toole, L. (1998). *Pornocopia: Porn, Sex, Technology and Desire*. London: Serpent's Tail.

Paasonen, S. (2010). Trouble with the Commercial: Internets Theorised and Used. In J. Hunsinger, L. Klastrup, and M. Allen (Eds.), *The International Handbook of Internet Research*, 411–422. Dordrecht, The Netherlands: Springer.

Paasonen, S. (2011). Revisiting Cyberfeminism. *Communications: European Journal of Communication Research*, 36(3), 335–352.

Pacey, A. (1983). *The Culture of Technology*. Cambridge, MA: MIT Press.

Palmer, C. L., and Malone, C. K. (2001). Elaborate Isolation: Metastructures of Knowledge about Women. *Information Society*, 17(3), 179–194.

Pariser, E. (2011). *The Filter Bubble: What the Internet Is Hiding from You.* New York: Penguin.

Pasquale, F. (2015). *The Black Box Society: The Secret Algorithms That Control Money and Information.* Cambridge, MA: Harvard University Press.

Pavlik, J. V. (1996). *New Media Technology: Cultural and Commercial Perspectives.* Boston: Allyn and Bacon.

Pawley, C. (2006). Unequal Legacies: Race and Multiculturalism in the LIS Curriculum. *Library Quarterly, 76*(2), 149–169.

Pease, O. (1985). *The Responsibilities of American Advertising.* New Haven, CT: Yale University Press.

Peet, L. (2016, June 13). Library of Congress Drops Illegal Alien Subject Heading, Provokes Backlash Legislation. *Library Journal.* Retrieved from www.libraryjournal.com.

Perdue, L. (2002). *EroticaBiz: How Sex Shaped the Internet.* New York: Writers Club Press.

Peterson, Latoya. (2014, January 25). Post on *Racialicious* (blog). Retrieved from http://racialicious.tumblr.com/post/72346551446/kingjaffejoffer-holliebunni-this-was-seen.

Pinkett, R. (2000, April 24–28). Constructionism and an Asset-Based Approach to Community Technology and Community Building. Paper presented at the eighty-first annual meeting of the American Educational Research Association (AERA), New Orleans, LA.

Postmes, T., Spears, R., and Lea, M. (1998). Breaching or Building Social Boundaries? SIDE-Effects of Computer-Mediated Communication. *Communication Research, 25,* 689–715.

Potter, D. M. (1954). *People of Plenty.* Chicago: University of Chicago Press.

Punyanunt-Carter, N. M. (2008). The Perceived Realism of African-American Portrayals on Television. *Howard Journal of Communications, 19,* 241–257.

Purcell, K., Brenner, J., and Rainie, L. (2012, March 9). Search Engine Use 2012. Pew Research Center. Retrieved from www.pewinternet.org.

Qin, S. (2016, March 28). Library of Congress to Replace Term 'Illegal Aliens.' *Dartmouth.* Retrieved from www.thedartmouth.com.

Rainie, L., and Madden, M. (2015, March). Americans' Privacy Strategies Post-Snowden. Pew Research Center. Retrieved from www.pewinternet.org.

Rajagopal, I., and Bojin, N. (2002). Digital Representation: Racism on the World Wide Web. *First Monday, 7*(10). Retrieved from www.firstmonday.org.

Reidsma, M. (2016, March 11). Algorithmic Bias in Library Discovery Systems. Matthew Reidsma's blog. Retrieved from http://matthew.reidsrow.com/articles/173.

Rifkin, J. (1995). *The End of Work: The Decline of the Global Labor Force and the Dawn of the Post-Market Era.* New York: Putnam.

Rifkin, J. (2000). *The Age of Access: The New Culture of Hypercapitalism, Where All of Life Is a Paid-For Experience.* New York: J. P. Tarcher/Putnam.

Ritzer, G., and Jurgenson. N. (2010). Production, Consumption, Prosumption. *Journal of Consumer Culture, 10*(1), 13–36. doi:10.1177/1469540509354673.

Roberts, S. T. (2012). Behind the Screen: Commercial Content Moderation (CCM). *The Illusion of Volition* (blog). Retrieved from www.illusionofvolition.com.

Roberts, S. T. (2016). Commercial Content Moderation: Digital Laborers' Dirty Work. In S. U. Noble and B. Tynes (Eds.), *The Intersectional Internet*, 147–160. New York: Peter Lang.

Robertson, T. (2016, March 20). Digitization: Just Because You Can, Doesn't Mean You Should. Tara Robertson's blog. Retrieved from www.tararobertson.ca.

Rocha, V. (2014, December 4). "Revenge Porn" Conviction Is a First under California Law. *Los Angeles Times*. Retrieved from www.latimes.com.

Rogers, R. (2004). *Information Politics on the Web*. Cambridge, MA: MIT Press.

Rudman, L. A., and Borgida, E. (1995). The Afterglow of Construct Accessibility: The Behavioral Consequences of Priming Men to View Women as Sexual Objects. *Journal of Experimental Social Psychology, 31*, 493–517.

Saracevic, T. (1999). Information Science. *Journal of the American Society for Information Science, 50*(12), 1051–1063.

Saracevic, T. (2009). Information Science. In M. J. Bates and M. N. Maack (Eds.), *Encyclopedia of Library and Information Science*, 2570–2586. New York: Taylor and Francis.

Schiller, D. (2007). *How to Think about Information*. Urbana: University of Illinois Press.

Schiller, H. (1996). *Information Inequality: The Deepening Social Crisis in America*. New York: Routledge.

Search King, Inc., v. Google Technology, Inc. (2003). Case No. Civ-02–1457-M. W.D. Okla. Jan. 13). Retrieved from www.searchking.com.

Sedgwick, E. K. (1990). *Epistemology of the Closet*. Berkeley: University of California Press.

Segev, E. (2010). *Google and the Digital Divide: The Bias of Online Knowledge*. Oxford, UK: Chandos.

Senate Judiciary Committee, Subcommittee on Antitrust, Competition Policy, and Consumer Rights. (2011, September 21). *The Power of Google: Serving Consumers or Threatening Competition?* Retrieved from www.judiciary.senate.gov/hearings.

Senft, T., and Noble, S. U. (2014). Race and Social Media. In J. Hunsinger and T. Senft (Eds.), *The Routledge Handbook of Social Media*, 107–125. New York: Routledge.

Shah, A. (2010, August 21). Hidden Cost of Mobile Phones, Computers, Stereos and VCRs? Global Issues. Retrieved from www.globalissues.org.

Sharpley-Whiting, T. D. (1999). *Black Venus: Sexualized Savages, Primal Fears, and Primitive Narratives in French*. Durham, NC: Duke University Press.

Sinclair, B. (2004). Integrating the Histories of Race and Technology. In B. Sinclair (Ed.), *Technology and the African American Experience: Needs and Opportunities for Study*, 1–17. Cambridge, MA: MIT Press.

Smith, L. C. (1981). Citation Analysis. *Library Trends, 30*(1), 83–106.

Smythe, D. W. (1981/2006). On the Audience Commodity and Its Work. In M. G. Durham and D. Kellner (Eds.), *Media and Cultural Studies*, 230–256. Malden, MA: Blackwell.

Sollfrank, C. (2002). The Final Truth about Cyberfeminism. In H. von Oldenburg and C. Reiche (Eds.), *Very Cyberfeminist International*, 108–113. Hamburg: OBN.

Spink, A., Wolfram, D., Jansen, B. J., and Saracevic, T. (2001). Searching the Web: The Public and Their Queries. *Journal of the American Society for Information Science and Technology, 52*(3), 226–234.

Steele, J., and Iliinsky, N. (2010). *Beautiful Visualization*. Sebastopol, CA: O'Reilly.

Stepan, N. (1998). Race, Gender, Science and Citizenship. *Gender and History, 10*(1), 26–52.

Stone, B. (2010, July 18). Concern for Those Who Screen the Web for Barbarity. *New York Times*. Retrieved from www.nytimes.com.

Storm, D. (2014, July 9). Think You Deleted Your Dirty Little Secrets? Before You Sell Your Android Smartphone . . . *ComputerWorld*. Retrieved from www.computer-world.com.

Stratton, J. (2000). Cyberspace and the Globalization of Culture. In D. Bell and B. Kennedy (Eds.), *The Cybercultures Reader*, 721–731. New York: Routledge.

Stratton Oakmont, Inc. v. Prodigy Services Co. (1995). No. 31063/94. 1995 WL 323710. N.Y. Sup. Ct.

Stroman, C. A., Merrit, B. D., and Matabane, P. W. (1989). Twenty Years after Kerner: The Portrayal of African Americans on Prime-Time Television. *Howard Journal of Communication, 2*, 44–56.

Sweeney, L. (2013). Discrimination in Online Ad Delivery. *Communications of the ACM, 56*(5), 44–54.

Sweney, M. (2009, November 25). Michelle Obama "Racist" Picture That Is Topping Google Images Removed. *Guardian*. Retrieved from www.theguardian.com.

Swift, M. (2010, February 11). Blacks, Latinos and Women Lose Ground at Silicon Valley Tech Companies. *San Jose Mercury News*. Retrieved from www.mercurynews.com.

Tapscott, D. (1996). *The Digital Economy: Promise and Peril in the Age of Networked Intelligence*. New York: McGraw-Hill.

Tate, G. (Ed.). (2003). *Everything but the Burden: What White People Are Taking from Black Culture*. New York: Broadway Books.

Tettegah, S. Y. (2016). The Good, the Bad, and the Ugly: Color-Blind Racial Ideology. In H. A. Neville, M. E. Gallardo, and D. W. Sue (Eds.), *The Myth of Racial Color Blindness: Manifestations, Dynamics, and Impact*, 175–190. Washington, DC: American Psychological Association.

Tippman, S. (2015, July 14). Google Accidentally Reveals Data on "Right to Be Forgotten" Requests. *Guardian*. Retrieved from www.theguardian.com.

Toffler, A. (1970). *Future Shock*. New York: Random House.

Toffler, A. (1980). *The Third Wave*. New York: Morrow.

Treitler, V. (1998). Racial Categories Matter Because Racial Hierarchies Matter: A Commentary. *Ethnic and Racial Studies, 21*(5), 959–968.

Treitler, V. (2013). *The Ethnic Project: Transforming Racial Fiction into Ethnic Factions*. Stanford, CA: Stanford University Press.

Tsukayama, H. (2012, February 29). How to Clear Your Google Search History, Account Info. *Washington Post*. Retrieved from www.washingtonpost.com.

Tucher, A. (1997). Why Web Warriors Might Worry. *Columbia Journalism Review, 36*, 35–36.

Tuchman, G. (1979). Women's Depiction by the Mass Media: Review Essay. *Signs: Journal of Women in Culture and Society, 4*(3), 528–542.

Tynes, B. M., and Markoe, S. L. (2010). The Role of Color-Blind Racial Attitudes in Reactions to Racial Discrimination on Social Network Sites. *Journal of Diversity in Higher Education, 3*(1), 1–13.

UN Women. (2013). UN Women Ad Series Reveals Widespread Sexism. Retrieved from www.unwomen.org.

U.S. Census Bureau. (2007). Current Population Survey: People in Families by Family Structure, Age, and Sex, Iterated by Income-to-Poverty Ratio and Race.

U.S. Census Bureau. (2008). Table B-2: Poverty Status of People by Age, Race, and Hispanic Origin: 1959–2008. In *Income, Poverty, and Health Insurance Coverage in the United States: 2008*, Report P60–236, 50–55. Washington, DC: U.S. Census Bureau.

U.S. Department of Justice, Federal Bureau of Investigation. (2010). Table 43: Arrests, by Race, 2010. In *Crime in the United States: 2010*. Retrieved from http://ucr.fbi.gov/crime-in-the-u.s/2010/crime-in-the-u.s.-2010/tables/table-43.

Vaidhyanathan, S. (2006). Critical Information Studies: A Bibliographic Manifesto. *Cultural Studies, 20*(2–3), 292–315.

Vaidhyanathan, S. (2011). *The Googlization of Everything (and Why We Should Worry)*. Berkeley: University of California Press.

Van Couvering, E. (2004). New Media? The Political Economy of Internet Search Engines. Paper presented at the annual conference of the International Association of Media and Communications Researchers, Porto Alegre, Brazil.

Van Couvering, E. (2008). The History of the Internet Search Engine: Navigational Media and the Traffic Commodity. In A. Spink and M. Zimmer (Eds.), *Web Searching: Multidisciplinary Perspectives*, 177–206. Dordrecht, The Netherlands: Springer.

van Dijk, J., and Hacker, K. (2003). The Digital Divide as a Complex and Dynamic Phenomenon. *Information Society, 19*(4), 315–326.

van Dijk, T. A. (1991). *Racism and the Press*. London: Routledge.

Wajcman, J. (1991). *Feminism Confronts Technology*. University Park: Pennsylvania State University Press.

Wajcman, J. (2010). Feminist Theories of Technology. *Cambridge Journal of Economics,* *34,* 143–152.

Wallace, M. (1990). *Invisibility Blues: From Pop to Theory.* London: Verso.

Warf, B., and Grimes, J. (1997). Counterhegemonic Discourses and the Internet. *Geographical Review, 87*(2), 259–274.

Wasson, H. (1973). The Ms. in Magazine Advertising. In R. King (Ed.), *Proceedings: Southern Marketing Association 1973 Conference,* 240–243. Blacksburg: Virginia Polytechnic Institute and State University.

Weheliye, A. G. (2003). "I Am I Be": The Subject of Sonic Afro-Modernity. *Boundary 2, 30*(2), 97–114.

West, C. (1996). Black Strivings in a Twilight Civilization. In H. L. Gates Jr. and C. West, *The Future of the Race,* 53–114. New York: Knopf.

West, C. M. (1995). Mammy, Sapphire, and Jezebel: Historical Images of Black Women and Their Implications for Psychotherapy. *Psychotherapy, 32*(3), 458–466.

White, D. G. (1985/1999). *Ar'n't I a Woman? Female Slaves in the Plantation South.* New York: Norton.

Wilhelm, A. G. (2006). *Digital Nation: Towards an Inclusive Information Society.* Cambridge, MA: MIT Press.

Williamson, Z. (2014, July 19). Porn SEO. Zack Williamson's blog. Retrieved from www.zackwilliamson.com.

Wilson, C. C., Gutierrez, F., and Chao, L. M. (2003). *Racism, Sexism, and the Media: The Rise of Class Communication in Multicultural America.* Thousand Oaks, CA: Sage.

Wilson, P. (1968). *Two Kinds of Power: An Essay on Bibliographical Control.* Berkeley: University of California Press.

Winner, L. (1986). *The Whale and the Reactor: A Search for Limits in an Age of High Technology.* Chicago: University of Chicago Press.

Wolfram, D. (2008). Search Characteristics in Different Types of Web-Based IR Environments: Are They the Same? *Information Processing and Management, 44*(3), 1279–1292.

Xanthoulis, N. (2012, May 22). Conceptualising a Right to Oblivion in the Digital World: A Human Rights-Based Approach. SSRN. Retrieved from http://dx.doi.org/10.2139/ssrn.2064503.

XMCP. (2008, January 21). Yes Dear, There Is Porn SEO, and We Can Learn a Lot from It. *YouMoz* (blog). Retrieved from www.moz.com.

Yang, J. L., and Easton, N. (2009, July 26). Obama & Google (a Love Story). *Fortune.* Retrieved from http://money.cnn.com.

Yarbrough, M., and Bennett, C. (2000). Cassandra and the "Sistahs": The Peculiar Treatment of African American Women in the Myth of Women as Liars. *Journal of Gender, Race, and Justice, 3*(2), 626–657.

Zeran v. America Online, Inc. (1997). 129 F.3d 327 (4th Cir.).

Zimmer, M. (2008). Preface: Critical Perspectives on Web 2.0. *First Monday, 13*(3). Retrieved from www.firstmonday.org.

Zimmer, M. (2009). Web Search Studies: Multidisciplinary Perspectives on Web Search Engines. In J. Hunsinger, L. Klastrup, and M. Allen (Eds.), *International Handbook of Internet Research*, 507–521. Dordrecht, The Netherlands: Springer.

Zittrain, J. (2008). *The Future of the Internet and How to Stop It.* New Haven, CT: Yale University Press.

Zittrain, J., and Edelman, B. (2002). Localized Google Search Result Exclusions: Statement of Issues and Call for Data. Retrieved from http://cyber.harvard.edu/filtering/google/.

INDEX

Figures are indicated by italics.

Adelsohn Liljeroth, Lena, 95, *97*
advertising: impact on society, 105–6; before the internet, 173–75; role in search results, 11, 16, 24, 36, 38, 54. *See also* commercial interests; search engine optimization
advertising companies, 5, 50, 123; bias, 89, 105–6, 116; profit motive, 36, 124; role in search results, 24, 38, 40–41, 56. *See also* Google Search
affirmative action, 12, 174
African-American community, hair salon, 173–74
African sexuality, 94–95
Airbnb rental discrimination, 163
algorithmic oppression, 1–2, 4, 10, 80, 84, 173
algorithms: big data bias, 29, 31, 36; conceptualizations, 24; democratic practices online debunked, 49; discriminatory effect, 6, 13, 28, 85, 173, 175–76; perception of neutrality, 37, 44, 56, 171; "racist algorithms," 9; reflection of programmers, 1, 26. *See also* Google PageRank; Kandis
Ali, Kabir, 80
Alphabet, 34–35; cultural imperialism, 86; expansion into surveillance technologies, 28
Anderson, Benedict, 136
Angwin, Julia, 27
Anonymous (hacker group), 112, 194n4
Anti-Defamation League, 42, 44, 157, 160
"antidiversity" manifesto, 2

Apple: labor condition in China, 164, 199n43; profiling in store, 163
Arreola, Veronica, 155
artificial intelligence, 1–2, 148; financial and housing crisis of 2008 role, 27; future criminality predictions, 27
ArtStor, bias in metadata management, 145–47
Ascher, Diana, 29
Associated Press v. United States, 190n57

Baartman, Sara, 94–96, 100
Bagdikian, Ben, 41
Bar-Ilan, Judit, 47
Barlow, John Perry, 61
Baron, Jill, 134
Battelle, John, 148
Berger, John, 58
Berman, Sanford, 139, 143–44
bias. *See* advertising companies; algorithms; search engines; Twitter
Bitch, 4, 181
Black, Diane, 135
Black feminism, 29–33, 92–93; antipornography rhetoric and scholarship, 100
black feminist technology studies (BFTS), 171–72
Black Girls (rock band), 69
Black Girls Code, 26, 64–65
'black girls' search results, 17–21, 31, 49, 64, 66–68, *103*, 160, 192n5; Chicago Urban League, 191n73; first search results, 3–4, 5; improvements, 10, 181–82; pornification, 11, 86

ABOUT THE AUTHOR

Safiya Umoja Noble is Assistant Professor in the Department of Information Studies in the Graduate School of Education and Information Studies at the University of California, Los Angeles. She also holds appointments in the Departments of African American Studies, Gender Studies, and Education. Noble is the co-editor of two books, *The Intersectional Internet: Race, Sex, Culture and Class Online* and *Emotions, Technology & Design.*